Technology Transfer, Dependence, and Self-Reliant Development in the Third World

Technology Transfer, Dependence, and Self-Reliant Development in the Third World

The Pharmaceutical and Machine Tool Industries in India

Sunil K. Sahu

Westport, Connecticut
London

Library of Congress Cataloging-in-Publication Data

Sahu, Sunil K., 1948–
    Technology transfer, dependence, and self-reliant development in
the third world : the pharmaceutical and machine tool industries in
India / Sunil K. Sahu.
      p.   cm.
    Includes bibliographical references and index.
    ISBN 0–275–95961–9 (alk. paper)
    1. Pharmaceutical industry—India. 2. Machine tool industry—
India. 3. Technology transfer—India. I. Title.
HD9672.I52S24 1998
338.4'76151'0954—dc21   98–16899

British Library Cataloguing in Publication Data is available.

Library of Congress Catalog Card Number: 98–16899
ISBN: 0–275–95961–9

First published in 1998

Praeger Publishers, 88 Post Road West, Westport, CT 06881
An imprint of Greenwood Publishing Group, Inc.

Printed in the United States of America

The paper used in this book complies with the
Permanent Paper Standard issued by the National
Information Standards Organization (Z39.48–1984).

10 9 8 7 6 5 4 3 2 1

Copyright Acknowledgments

The author and publisher gratefully acknowledge permission to use quotes from Louis T. Wells, Jr.,
editor, *The Product Life Cycle and International Trade*. Boston: Division of Research, Harvard Business School, 1972, p. 15. Copyright © 1972 by the President and Fellows of Harvard College. Reprinted by permission of Harvard Business School Press.

Every reasonable effort has been made to trace the owners of copyright materials in this book, but in
some instances this has proven impossible. The author and publisher will be glad to receive information leading to more complete acknowledgments in subsequent printings of the book and in the
meantime extend their apologies for any omissions.

In memory of my father. For my mother and for

Indu, Munjot, and Punita.

Contents

Illustrations

FIGURES

Acknowledgments

This book spans many years, during which I have collected numerous debts. During my field study in India, originally in the summer and fall of 1986 and on two subsequent occasions—in 1992 and 1996—I received help from many officials associated with various ministries of the Government of India (Ministry of Chemical and Fertilizers, Ministry of Health, Ministry of Industry), the Planning Commission, the Department of Science and Technology, and the India Investment Center. While collecting data from the various research institutes and laboratories in Delhi, Lucknow, and Bangalore (the National Institute of Science Technology and Development, Council on Scientific and Industrial Research; Corporate Study Group, the Indian Institute of Public Administration; the National Council of Applied Economic Research; the Federation of Indian Chamber of Commerce and Industry; the Center for Drug Research Institute; and the Central Machine-Tool Institute) I was assisted by numerous people.

The managers of various pharmaceutical companies, especially Hindustan Antibiotic Limited (HAL) and Indian Drug and Pharmaceutical Limited (IDPL), the two large public sector companies; Ranbaxy and CIPLA, the two fast-growing Indian companies in the private sector; and Bayer, Pfizer, Roche, Hoechst, Merind, and Glindia, the leading foreign companies in the private sector were generous with their time and information. The officials of the Indian Machine Tool Manufacturers Association in Bombay and the Association of Indian Engineering Industry (in 1986 renamed Confederation of Engineering Industry), New Delhi, gave me full access to the data on the machine tool industry. I am thankful to the Hindustan Machine Tools (HMT) senior managers—including the managing director, general manager, company manager, projects managers, and research and development (R&D) manager—for granting me personal interviews and for acquainting me with the details regarding different aspects in the transfer of machine tool technology to their company.

Thanks go to Dr. S. M. Patil, the former chairman and managing director of HMT, who granted me three lengthy interviews at his home, which gave me insights into the efforts made by HMT to absorb and assimilate imported technology, especially during the years Dr. Patil was the managing director. I would also like to thank Dr. Nitya Anand, former director, Central Drug Research Institute; B. K. Keayla, former manager, corporate planning, IDPL; Dr. Y. K. Hameid, managing director, CIPLA; K. Jayaraman, consultant, Pfizer Ltd.; Arvind Nayar, the then director of the Organization of Pharmaceutical Producers in India (OPPI), Bombay; and Dr. Mira Shiva, director of the Voluntary Health Association of India for generously giving their time during personal interviews and for helping me gain access to important data on the pharmaceutical industry. These interviews broadened my understanding of the dynamics of technological dependence in the machine tool and pharmaceutical industries in the Third World and provided empirical evidence for a clear understanding of what makes India different from most developing nations.

I owe special gratitude to Professors Susanne and Lloyd Rudolph, University of Chicago, who have been involved in this project from the beginning. Without their support this book would not have been possible. They have commented on its earlier drafts and have contributed to this project in more ways than I can acknowledge here. I have also benefited from the comments made by members of the South Asian Political Economy Workshop, University of Chicago, where I presented the case of the pharmaceutical industry.

The research for this study, including my travels to India for data collection on two occasions, and its publication has been supported by the Faculty Development Committee, the John and Janice Fisher Fund for Faculty Development, and the Presidential Discretionary Fund at DePauw University. I am thankful to my colleagues Marthe Chandler and Ted Jelen, Tom Hall, William Harman, Nafhat Nasr, Shanker Shetty, and Paul Watt for their support, and to David Guinee, Robert Newton, Keith Opdahl, and Bruce Stinebrickner for making comments and suggestions on parts of the manuscript. Bob Newton was also generous with his time in helping me with computer-related problems I encountered in preparing the camera-ready copy of the manuscript. Kenneth Kirkpatrick helped me with the figures and my student Thomas Mentzer with the tables and formatting. Their help has definitely improved the quality of the book, but they bear no responsibility for the facts, analyses, and interpretations presented in this book.

This book is dedicated to my late father, who witnessed my research effort but did not live long enough to see the final product; to my mother, who taught me the right values; and to my wife, Indu Vohra, and our two daughters, Munjot and Punita. My deepest appreciation and gratitude go to Indu, who has been a source of constant support and encouragement. She made it possible for me to go to India twice for extended periods of field research while she took care of our children and pursued her career. She made critical comments on this book at a stage when my research needed a clear direction. Indu has, in fact, lived with this book from beginning to end more than anyone else. I cannot thank her enough. Munjot and Punita showed great understanding, especially during the summer and Christmas breaks, when I spent countless hours away from them in my quiet study working on this book. Without their understanding, it would not have been completed.

1

Introduction

In the last two decades, the transfer of technology from the developed to the developing nations has emerged as an important issue in Third World development and international political economy; indeed, technology transfer is likely to remain a major North-South issue for some time to come.[1] The scholarly debate on the issues involved in the transfer of technology has mainly been at a high level of generalization and therefore theoretical. A survey of the literature would reveal that there is a limited base of empirical research testing various propositions of the existing theories on technology transfer. There is a need for more intensive case studies in order to comprehend the dynamics of the transfer process between the technology-supplying firms and the recipient firm or country, especially what happens to the technology after it has been imported. Does the process of absorption, adaptation, and further innovation increase the recipient country's international technological capability? Does it reduce external technological dependence?

This study addresses these questions. It incorporates both the macro features of technological dependence and the micro features at the level of the individual industry/firm. It seeks to evaluate empirically the main propositions of the two contending theoretical approaches—dependency theory and the bargaining school—regarding the effect of technology transfer on the development of technological capability and self-reliant development in the Third World. It attempts to do this through the study of the pharmaceutical and machine tool industries in India from the 1950s, when India launched its five year plans, to 1991, when India adopted the policy of economic liberalization.

Machine tools and pharmaceuticals, seemingly two unrelated industries, have been selected for many reasons. First, the two industries are vital to the economy of India and other developing nations. In industrial development, a crucial role is assigned to the machine tool industry because it is this industry that provides heterogeneous parts and components and final products, which can transform basic metals, wood, and plastic into finished products. The pharmaceutical industry, on the other hand, is significant in maintaining the health of the nation and therefore valuable for the economy, since pharmaceuticals contribute toward the avoidance of the loss of working days.

Second, in both industries, a large-scale transfer of industrial technology has taken place in the last three decades. The pharmaceutical industry, known for its high technological component, is dominated by the multinationals and is among the most profitable industries in the world. India had to acquire the technological know-how of drug production from the industrially advanced countries—both Western and Socialist—in the post-independence period. It acquired its machine tool technology mainly from the Western multinationals. The high proportion of foreign technology acquired by the two industries can be observed in the following statistics: Of the total 6,959 foreign collaboration agreements approved by the government between 1957 and 1982, industrial machinery and machine tools accounted for 40 percent (2,754) and chemical and pharmaceuticals 15 percent (1,056). Machine tools and pharmaceuticals ranked, therefore, first and third, respectively, in industrial distribution.[2] Third, the two industries have acquired technology from abroad through almost all the available modes: from turnkey to licensing agreements and from direct foreign investment and financial participation to joint ventures and production-sharing arrangements. I will compare and evaluate the pros and cons of different modes of acquiring technology and make broad generalizations. My study suggests that a firm's decision to select a particular mode of technology transfer depends as much on the technology market as on the level of its technological capability.

Finally, there are both public and private sector firms in the two industries. Whereas the machine tool industry is dominated by a public sector firm Hindustan Machine Tools (HMT) and there are a number of private sector companies (more than 112 in the organized sector) following the technological lead of HMT, the pharmaceutical industry is divided into three sectors: public, private foreign, and private national. In the case of the latter, the government policy in the last decade has sought to encourage the growth, expansion, and technological self-reliance of the Indian private sector. Government regulation of the foreign sector, my study will suggest, has "dislodged the multinationals,"[3] as Dennis Encarnation puts it, from their position of technological hegemony to one of playing a secondary although important role in the industry. The role of the public sector companies in the development of in-house research and development (R&D) will also be examined. Furthermore, I will test the hypothesis of whether public sector firms, compared with private sector companies, pursue policies that lead to an increase in the technological capability of the firm and hence greater technological self-reliance.

The objectives of this book are thus multifold. First, the different modes utilized by the two industries for acquiring foreign technology in the last four decades are examined. Most developing countries are believed to have little knowledge of the alternative sources of technology. Due to their lack of technical information, they are considered incapable of selecting appropriate technology and of bargaining effectively with technology suppliers. I will empirically verify these propositions of dependency theory by analyzing the different modes through which technology has been acquired by the machine tool and pharmaceutical industry in India. A cost-benefit analysis of technology transfer at the firm/industry level will be made, which will explain more precisely the kind of changes that have taken place in India's technological dependence in the last three decades. Second, what happens to technology at the firm/industry level once it has been transferred by the foreign firm (an important question for the understanding of technological self-reliance) will be addressed in this study. In particular, I will analyze the process of assimilation, adaptation, innovation, and indigenous development of pharmaceutical and machine tool technology through in-house research at the firm level.

Third, I will examine the role of the state in enhancing a country's technological capability and tehnological self-reliance. Do state interventionist policies stifle or promote technological self-reliance in the Third World? I will answer this question by analyzing the effect of the Indian government's stringent rules regarding royalties, lump-sum payments, the length of technical collaboration agreements, the Patent Law, the strict regulation of the foreign multinationals (Foreign Exchange Regulation Act), the policy of reservation for the national sector in the pharmaceutical industry (under the New Drug Policy of 1978), and the liberalization of technology import policy in the late 1980s. I will also verify empirically the proposition that the government regulatory policies of the late 1960s and 1970s, which were aimed at promoting technological self-reliance, actually created technological obsolescence in many industries in India.

Fourth, the relationship between India's growing indigenous technological capability and technological self-reliance will be explored by analyzing the promotion of research and development (R&D) at the firm level, the in-house transfer of technology in a unitary industrial setup, the transfer of technology from laboratory to industry, and the horizontal transfer of technology (the ability of an enterprise to transfer its own technology to other enterprises) in the two industries under study.

The study will suggest that there has been a significant increase in in-house R & D activities in the two industries in both the public and private sector. But the pattern varies. In the pharmaceutical industry, the national sector has contributed more to technological self-reliance than the foreign sector: the public sector companies, by entering into the production of bulk drugs, and the private sector firms, by manufacturing the patented drugs either through the in-house developed processes or by taking advantage of the compulsory licensing provisions of the 1970 Patent Law. The drug multinationals have shown reluctance to undertake R&D activities for the manufacture of bulk drugs from the basic stages. The success rate of up-scaling of technology from the lab to the industry has, however, been very small and the country is lagging behind in the manufacture of modern synthetic drugs. The government policy of uneconomic plant capacities, which are mandated by antimonopoly laws, and the inefficiencies that result from what the Rudolphs have called "organizational involution"[4] have contributed to technological obsolescence in the industry.

In the machine tool industry, Hindustan Machine Tools (HMT), a public sector company that enjoys 40 percent market share, has been the leader in acquiring technology through foreign collaborations—designing its own machines, carrying out in-house R&D activities, and working closely with the machine tool institute (CMTI) for the production of high-technology machines. The private sector companies, such as Bharat Fritz Werner, have followed the lead of HMT in all these areas. HMT is among the most profitable public sector enterprises in India and has made a significant contribution toward India's industrialization in the last three decades. In the 1980s, however, the company found itself lagging behind the international machine tool manufacturers in the Numerical Control and Computer Numerical Control (NC/CNC) technology. The reasons for this technological lag are found mainly at the firm level and not in the behavior of technology-supplying multinationals. (Dependency theory has minimized the role of domestic factors.) This study will suggest that a developing country can move from a situation of technological dependence to self-reliance if the government formulates a policy of self-reliance that is supplemented at the firm level by, among other things, a prudent decision on the import of technology, a dedication to improving the capability for managing and mastering[5] the imported technology, and a commitment to the development of in-house R&D.

Finally, the study will examine the role of the public sector firms—IDPL in the pharmaceutical industry and HMT in the machine tool industry—in promoting South-South technology transfer. In this era of globalization and economic interdependence among nations, attention has increasingly been focused on the possibility of greater economic cooperation related to technology, trade, and finance among developing nations. At the June 1990 Kuala Lumpur summit of G-15 and the recent Nonaligned Movement (NAM) Summit meetings, for example, the developing nations expressed the need to further economic cooperation among themselves, as their interests are being ignored by the industrialized countries. In their view, the existing international institutions serve the interests of the industrialized countries more than those of the developing nations; therefore the Kuala Lumpur conference proposed to set up a South Investment, Trade and Technology Data Exchange Center to promote and disseminate information on investment and trade opportunities available among these countries.

This study will thus contribute to the current debate on the possibility of South-South technology transfer and economic cooperation. My analysis will show that HMT in the machine tool industry and IDPL in the pharmaceutical industry are among the leading Third World firms exporting technology and offering many technical services to other developing nations. The newly industrializing countries, such as India, can therefore make a significant contribution to South-South economic and technical cooperation.

NOTES

1. Ross Singleton, "Knowledge and Technology: The Basis of Wealth and Power," in David N. Balaam and Michael Veseth (eds.), *Introduction to International Political Economy* (Upper Saddle River, N.J.: Prentice Hall, 1996), p. 200.

2. Sanjaya Lall, "Trade in Technology by a Slowly Industrializing Country: India," in Nathan Rosenberg and Claudio Frischtak (eds.), *International Technology Transfer: Concepts, Measures, and Comparisons* (New York: Praeger, 1985), p. 50.

3. See Dennis J. Encarnation, *Dislodging Multinationals: India's Strategy in Comparative Perspective* (Ithaca: Cornell University Press, 1989).

4. See Lloyd I. Rudolph and Susanne H. Rudolph, *In Pursuit of Laxmi: The Political Economy of the Indian State* (Chicago: University of Chicago Press, 1987), Ch. 1.

5. Technological mastery has been defined as "operational command over technological knowledge, manifested in the ability to use this knowledge effectively and achieved by the application of technological effect." See Carl J. Dahlman and Larry E. Westphal, "The Meaning of Technological Mastery in Relation to Transfer of Technology," *Annals, American Academy of Political and Social Sciences*, No. 458 (Nov. 1981): 12-25.

2

Theoretical Approaches to Technology Transfer

Development debates in recent years have increasingly focused on the relationship between technology and industrialization in the developing countries and the issues related to the transfer of technology from the industrialized West to the developing nations.[1] In the 1950s and 1960s, technology was identified as one of the prime motivating forces of development because it seemed to offer the best hope of improving the quality of life in the developing countries.[2] It was thought that poverty in the Third World, generally associated with technological backwardness, could be alleviated by bringing about technological progress, which was recognized as the major determinant of growth. In the last two decades, technology emerged as the key resource for industrial growth and development. Technology stimulates both the supply and demand for output: By reducing costs, it expands the inevitable surplus, and by permitting a fall in prices, it increases the real demand for goods and services. It generates new wealth faster than other productive assets—natural resources, capital, labor, or favorable location. Thus, although technology is but one element in overall development strategies, its influence is considered to be massive. "If new wealth is the golden egg," as Goulart puts it, "technology is the hen that lays it."[3]

It is not surprising therefore that there has been a shift in emphasis in most developing countries toward the role of technology in development efforts. The ability to industrialize through the mere transfer of already existing technology from the industrialized to the developing nations, rather than independent invention, was considered to be the basic advantage of being a "late-comer."

Technology, however, is not a free but an economic good, which is bought and sold internationally in a predominantly sellers' market. In recent years, international trade in technology has been growing at a rate comparable to or faster than that for commodities. The transnational corporations (TNCs) of the industrialized countries have a virtual monopoly over the transfer, sale, or "commercialization" of technology, as they are responsible for about 80 to 90 percent of such transfers to the Third World.[4] In fact, the technology issue has been dominated by the role of the United States since it performs more research and development (R&D) than all other Organization for Economic Cooperation and Development (OECD) countries combined. The direct investment activities of American TNCs constitute "by far the most important channel by which industrial technology created in the North is transferred to developing nations."[5] Since the institutional vehicle of technology transfer has largely been TNCs, it has given rise to many problems.

The debate on North-South technology transfer, which has inspired a large literature in the last two decades, has focused mainly on the questions of sources, ownership, appropriateness, and costs and benefits to developing nations. These issues have been increasingly politicized, especially after the adoption of the Declaration and Program of Action on the Establishment of a New International Economic Order (NIEO) by the sixth special session of the United Nations General Assembly in May 1974. In recent years, developing nations have often accused the advanced countries and their TNCs of narrow selfishness, charging exorbitant fees or royalties, enforcing a multitude of restrictive provisions, and completely neglecting the recipients' interests. Partly in response to the demands of the growing number of Third World countries in international organizations, various UN bodies and agencies, such as the UNIDO, UNCTAD, and Center for Transnational Corporations, have sponsored research on various aspects of technology transfer from the developed to the developing countries. The question of ever-increasing technological dependence of the developing nations has figured prominently in these debates. The technological dependence has been identified to stem from the developing countries' incapacity to invent new processes and products and also from the fact that they are lacking in areas such as engineering design, choice of techniques, management and marketing.[6]

Recognizing the salience of technology in development and the dependence of the Third World on the industrialized countries for technology, in the 1970s and early 1980s, many countries—notably Argentina, Brazil, India, and Mexico—passed legislation and imposed new regulations for improved control over the technology transfer process. At the regional level, the Latin American nations in 1967 articulated the concept of technology, and "science and technology were incorporated in the political language and decisions of the Inter-American system."[7] At the international level, efforts have been made to draft a worldwide code governing technology transfer.

The actual experience in technology transfer has, however, belied the expectations of most developing nations. Although there has been much discussion about the development of an international code of behavior and rules of law to regulate the behavior of transnational enterprise, the international code on technology transfer remains incomplete. There are serious differences among the parties involved as divergent approaches to the subject have been advanced.[8] Regional initiatives such as the OAS and CACM (Central American Common

Market) have languished, primarily because of the "disagreement over the primacy of national over international law in the settlement of disputes and because Latin (and Central) American opposition to restrictive business practices is limited to the behavior of North American firms."[9] National regulatory efforts, however, appear to have been largely successful, especially in those developing countries that have sought to find new ways of making technology autonomous from the influence of investors and proprietors in advanced countries.

Therefore, technological self-reliance (TSR) emerged as a major theme in national development policies and international negotiations in the 1980s. It is conceived to be the key to ending or reducing technological dependence. Although there is no precise definition of TSR, it includes "the ability to make autonomous national decisions on technology—to choose, implement, manage and operate technology and to innovate."[10] Technological self-determination means, as Hass puts it, making "autonomous decisions about the critical elements of knowledge needed to select the desired products and processes" and assessing and limiting "foreign influences in shaping one's cultural and economic future."[11]

THEORIES AND APPROACHES TO TECHNOLOGY TRANSFER

Two contending theories on and approaches to technology transfer—dependency theory and the bargaining school—have been advanced.

Dependency Theory and Technological Dependence

Dependency theory isolates technology as a key to development and focuses on TNCs as the primary technology suppliers. It perceives technology transfer as providing a short cut to Third World development. Some theorists even take the extreme view that superior capital-intensive technology is necessary for this short cut as "underdeveloped technology in an underdeveloped country simply accelerates the problem of underdevelopment, rather than eliminating it."[12] However, most dependency theorists identify technology as one of the prime motive forces of development. It is the acquisition of technology from the TNCs that has been blamed by them for weakening local productive capabilities and technological infrastructures.

Dependency theorists reject the neo-classical economic theory that the bargaining for technology occurs in a situation of "bilateral monopoly." They believe that the technological and industrial dependence of the Third World evolved after the Second World War, mainly because of the "technological monopoly exercised by imperialist centers" in the form of the direct investments made by TNCs.[13] Dependency theorists such as Osvaldo Sunkel, Celso Furtado, and Stephen Hymer believe that the TNCs are motivated by business considerations (profit maximization) rather than development considerations (social welfare) of the client countries. They argue therefore that the TNC has the negative effect of inhibiting the development of technological infrastructure in the developing countries, especially if the mode of such transfer is direct foreign investment, which most transnationals seem to prefer.[14] Since much of the technology transfer to the developing countries has been effected through the medium of direct investment by TNCs, the transfer of technology from the parent company to the foreign subsidiaries in such cases takes place as a purely "internal" process, which provides "opportunities to manipulate the prices of goods and services supplied by one part of the enterprise to another."[15]   It has often been claimed that transfer price manipulation is more widespread in less developed countries than in more developed countries,[16] so that the prices that TNCs set for intra-firm exports and imports across national boundaries have been the subject of continued controversy.

Dependency theory views the international market for technology as even more imperfect than for other commodities because of (1) incomplete information for buyers, (2) lack of competition among sellers, and (3) restrictive business practices routinely included in contractual arrangements. This affects not only the "price" (terms and conditions) but also the quality of the technology supplied. It is alleged that most of the technology supplied to the Third World is second- or third-rate. Dependency theorists also make a distinction between the transfer of technology between developed countries and transfer from the developed to the developing countries. In the case of the former, the transfer of technology does not amount to dependence because most of these developed countries are engaged in both import and export of technology, and the two-way flow generally tends to correct some of the deficiencies of the market mechanism. Even countries that import most of their technology and export very little—for example, New Zealand and Canada—are not considered technologically dependent.[17] There exists in those countries an adequate infrastructure (scientific institutions; R&D facilities; vocational, technical, and management-training institutions; and skilled personnel of different specializations) and a suitable cultural environment that allows them to absorb the imported technology easily. The interdependence among the developed countries has, in fact, been accelerated by a remarkable boom in foreign direct investment. As the OECD data indicate,[18] most direct investment from advanced industrial economies ends up in other developed countries.

Developing countries, on the other hand, not only import more than developed countries, but they also rely on a small number of industrialized states as the major source of technological development.[19] In such a situation, "the limitations of the market are compounded against them, rather than cancelled out in their favor."[20] Moreover, most developing countries are faced with serious shortages of foreign exchange. These factors often lead to an unequal bargaining position of developing countries in technology transactions. Hart explains the situation in the following way:

Suppose that A trades with a large number of nations but receives only a small proportion of its imports from and sends only a small proportion of its exports to any particular nation (including B) while B's trade is highly concentrated in a few trading partners (including A). Suppose also that A imports and exports a wide variety of commodities while B tends to import manufactured or technological goods while exporting a limited variety of goods, most of which are unprocessed. Finally, suppose that A's trade makes up only a small proportion of its national product while B's trade makes a large proportion of its national product. Then doesn't it seem likely that A can get its way with B if it chooses to threaten the disruption of trade?[21]

Technological dependence is thus defined, mainly, in terms of the balance of trade between the developed and developing countries. The advocates of the theory view the relationship between the supplier and the recipient of technology to be inherently unequal and therefore exploitative.

The transnationals are also accused of neglecting R&D activities by subsidiaries and affiliates, which make the affiliates dependent on the parent company for the flow of technological improvements. Even with joint ventures, technology ownership remains a major element of control. This has resulted in widening rather than narrowing the technological gap between the industrialized and nonindustrialized countries—only 4 percent of worldwide R&D takes place in the developing world.[22] The direct and indirect costs of this dependence has been estimated to be between $30 and $50 billion a year.[23]

There are other not easily perceived real costs, or benefits foregone, for the Third World countries, resulting from (1) limitations imposed in transfer agreements; (2) the transfer of wrong or inappropriate technology; (3) inadequate or delayed transfer; (4) the non-transfer of technology; and (5) the long-term influence of imported technology on deflecting national policies away from a sound development of local technological capabilities.[24] It should, however, be noted that the more sophisticated dependency theorists, especially Cardoso[25] and Evans,[26] recognize that the transfer of technology does facilitate the expansion of industrial output in the developing countries, as exemplified by the industrial developments that have taken place in countries such as Brazil, Argentina, and Mexico. But they posit that the acquisition of industrial technology has, by and large, inhibited the ability of these countries to adapt, modify, and assimilate their existing technology and to develop new technologies.

Technological dependence is both the cause and effect of general dependency relationships, and the existing international system of stratified power relations reinforces rather than reduces technological dependence.[27] Inter alia, technological dependence leads to foreign investment, loss of control, and the introduction of "alien patterns" of consumption and production in the recipient country. The dependence on the advanced countries for imports, markets, management, finance, and technology results in the emergence of an enclave economy, which in turn creates a society "in the image of the advanced countries requiring further imports of technology to satisfy new demands, and to enable the industries to survive and expand."[28] A vicious circle is thus created, whereby a weak technology system reinforces dependence, and dependence perpetuates weakness (see Figure 2.1).

Figure 2.1
The "Vicious Circle" of Technological Dependence

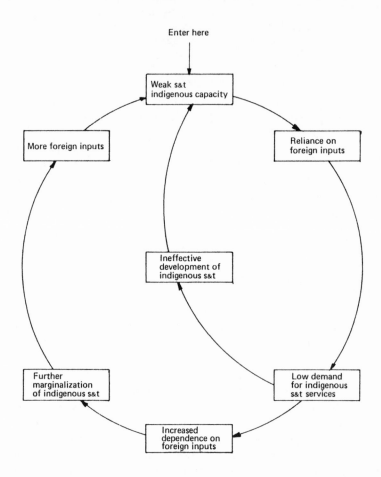

Source: UNIDO, *Technological Self-Reliance of the Developing Countries: Towards Operational Strategies* (Vienna: United Nations, 1981), p. 9. S&t= science and technology

The Bargaining Model

The contending approach to technology transfer is the predominant nonneoclassical framework provided by liberal economists who have dealt with the issue of the transfer of technology only as a subcomponent of the general debate about multinational firms and the possibility of antitrust action.[29] The bargaining model, associated mainly with the works of Charles Kindleberger and with Raymond Vernon and his colleagues at the Harvard Business School's Multinational Enterprise Project, agrees with the dependency theorists that the TNCs have been the most effective carriers of industrial technology to the developing countries.[30] However, contrary to the dependency argument, the advocates of the bargaining school recognize the potential benefits that TNCs can offer their host countries and believe that direct foreign investment does not contribute to the net outflow of capital from the developing countries; there is no quantitative evidence that the transfer of Western technology has had an adverse effect on the industrialization of the Third World. In fact, it has been argued that the economic consequences of a particular technology transfer depend on a set of interrelated factors:

a. the motivations, strategies, and capabilities of technology suppliers—conditioned, in part, by government policies and economic conditions;

b. the astuteness, bargaining powers, and absorptive capabilities of recipient enterprises—as reinforced or conditioned by government action and economic policies; and

c. the nature, quantum, and complexities of technology transferred.[31]

Technology transfer is thus viewed to be a dynamic and complex process, rather than a static and simple one, because the situation of the buyer is considered to be variable, not an equal partner a priori and not necessarily a passive player in the negotiating process that takes place between the supplier and the recipient. The theory posits that the nature of the relationship between the technology supplier and the technology recipient is an empirical question, to be investigated rather than presumed a priori from the structural relationship. In particular, as the number of potential suppliers increases over time and the national absorptive capacity improves, it is expected that the terms of transfer would be more favorable for technology importers. A careful examination of the conditions under which technology transactions actually take place would reveal that they result in a variety of outcomes, dependency being but one of them. For instance, the technology-importing country may feel constrained or dependent if the options open to it are narrow at a given time (which may be the case if the importing country totally lacks technological capability). Hence, a meaningful discussion of technology transfer must include a careful examination of the variables related to both the supplier and the recipient of technology (the strengths and weaknesses of the two; the nature of the international technology market; the laws and regulations that control the flow of technology; and the level of scientific, technological, and managerial development in the recipient country). It is therefore likely that the competitive conditions under which technology can be obtained through various mechanisms would "vary greatly with the branch of industry and the change over time with the shifting world structure of the industry and the competitive position of its component firms."[32]

The dependency hypothesis that the initial weakness of the Third World in scientific and technological capacity would perpetuate technological dependence has been challenged on empirical grounds. In recent years, East Asian and other newly industrialized countries (NICs) have not only been producing a wide range of sophisticated industrial goods, but they have also acquired over the years technological capability that enables them to seek technology from alternative sources and to drive hard bargains with the supplier firms. Moreover, development strategies and regulation of technology imports by a number of developing countries have improved their terms of technology trade.[33]

Bargaining theory also provides a more sophisticated explanation of the reasons why the technology supplied by TNCs tends to be more capital-intensive. It is partly a result of the desire of the oligopolists to reduce risk and uncertainty and partly a response to the objectives of what Wells calls the "engineering man." By examining the complex factors that influence managers in their choice of technologies, Wells concludes that the business manager in the Third World does not behave solely as an "economic man," whose objective is to minimize costs through labor-intensive production process, but also as an "engineering man," whose objective is to lead toward more sophisticated, automated technology.[34]

The relationship between the host country (HC) and the TNC has been studied using the balance of bargaining power framework (Moran, Vernon, Mikesell), which is considered "the currently accepted paradigm of HC-TNC relations in international political economy."[35] This paradigm grew out of the seminal formulation of Kindleberger and Herrick,[36] who conceptualized the relationship between the TNC and a Third World government as one of "bilateral monopoly." Using concepts derived from game theory (mostly assuming a two-person non-zero-sum game), the bargaining model suggests that in the event of a conflict between the host government and the TNC over the distribution of surplus (or rent) from a project, the interest of the host country lies in some kind of negotiated settlement.[37] Vernon, by introducing the concept of "obsolescing bargaining," provides a dynamic framework for an understanding of the evolution of bargaining relations between a host country and a foreign company over the life of a project.

The HC-TNC relationship is viewed as a dialectical process: The TNC's presence in an economy, which may be brought about by concessions from the host country to the TNC, "itself generates forces which cause its ultimate obsolescence."[38] The obsolescing bargaining model predicts that the initially favorable investment agreement for the foreigner is likely to be subsequently renegotiated in favor of the host country. Once the foreign investment is "sunken," it is argued, the host country is in a much stronger position to control and extract greater rents, and the foreign company cannot credibly threaten to withdraw.[39] The process accelerates by the oligopolistic rivalry among TNCs. As competition among rivals accentuates product life-cycle, host governments learn to play one oligopolist off another. The product life-cycle theory, as formulated by Vernon[40] and Wells[41] posits that most products pass through a relatively rapid cycle of "life-stages" from birth to senescence through rapid growth, spread, and maturation. The product life-cycle theory deviates from the assumptions of perfect competition and identical production functions among nations, which are essential for the neoclassical theory of international trade. It also recognizes the real-world imperfections and the multiplicity of other institutional rigidities. It is therefore argued that the monopoly power of the innovating corporation during the early stages of the product's life begins to fall as the product and its technologies become widely known. In the later stages, most product markets tend to pass through a transition from "monopoly to oligopoly to workable competition."[42] The product life-cycle theory thus claims to predict sequentially which group of countries—industrialized, NICs or least industrialized—is likely to enjoy a comparative advantage at a particular stage of the life cycle of a product. The sequence of the movement of competitive advantage is presented in Figure 2.2.

Analyzing the comparative advantages that the United States enjoys in international trade for products that are relatively new—that is, having a high technology content—Wells argues that the monopoly condition arises from the "availability" factor, namely, being first in the market.[43] The monopoly of the innovator, however, is not considered to be permanent; the length of the "imitation lag" determines how long the monopoly position lasts. As Mazumdar explains:

With the passage of time and in response to consumer feed-back, the product becomes standardized, characterized by most sought-after features. At this mature stage, its intensive factor inputs changes from skilled labor to capital, as specialized equipment is designed for its manufacture in assembly lines, thereby exploiting economies of scale. Also, the demand for the product abroad becomes significant, and the foreign production, either by a local imitator or by an American (innovating country) multinational firm, to reduce cost. Other U.S.-based producers, whose competitive positions are threatened, follow suit with their own direct foreign investment ventures. The immediate effect of this change in production location is the loss of exports by the innovating country. In the long run, the country can altogether lose its competitive advantage and turn into a net importer.[44]

The product life-cycle theory thus takes into consideration the real-world imperfections in international trade. Recognizing these imperfections, the bargaining model predicts that the transfer of production technology through TNCs will bring several benefits to the developing countries. According to a recent review, they are three-fold:

First, they will transmit rapidly the latest technologies to the host country. Second, their international rivalry will propel many into profitable markets in developing countries,

Figure 2.2
A Schematic Presentation of the U.S. Trade
Position in the Product Life Cycle

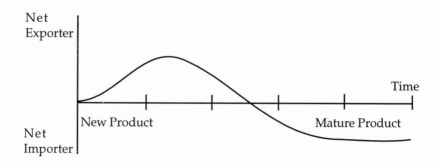

Phase I	Phase II	Phase III	Phase IV	Phase V
All production in U. S.	Production started in Europe	Europe exports to LDC's	Europe exports to U. S.	LDC's export to U. S.
U. S. exports to many countries	U. S. exports mostly to LDC's	U. S. exports to LDC's displaced		

Source: Louis T. Wells, Jr. (Ed.), *The Product Life Cycle and International Trade* (Boston: Division of Research, Harvard Business School, 1972), p. 15. Copyright 1972 by the President and Fellows of Harvard College. Reprinted by permission of Harvard Business School Press.

reducing market concentration and speeding the deterioration of entry barriers—ultimately resulting in more price-competitive markets. Third, as markets expand, local entrepreneurs will be stimulated and domestic firms will soon capture a substantial share of the market, making complete the transfer of technology, capital and income gains to the developing countries.[45]

The bargaining position of the host country is further enhanced over time because of the cumulative effects of the TNC's own operation. "The technology transferred and the experience accumulated," Agmon and Hirsch explain, "have at least in part the characteristics of public goods; they become the property of the host country in the sense that the relevant information and knowledge is acquired by citizens of the host country. These assets become part of the country's human capital and they cannot be withdrawn even if the MNC subsequently departs."[46]

Moreover, it is argued that the developing countries could effectively bargain with the technology suppliers by formulating national policies on technology transfer. Since the parties involved in the negotiating process are usually TNCs and Third World governments, and not individuals or firms from the developing countries, it gives the latter the decisive advantages as "they make the laws, i.e., they establish the 'rules of the game' and they can *change* the rules."[47] In sum, the bargaining school holds that the prolonged contact of the developing countries with TNCs gives the former the experience needed to manage these relations more effectively and ultimately cause the balance of bargaining power to shift in their favor.

The bargaining framework is thus a "model of economic nationalism based on rational self-interest" and it also provides, as Moran writes, "a hopeful perspective about the eventual strengthening of the hand of Third World authorities in renegotiating the initial agreement to capture more and more of the benefits from foreign investment."[48]

Recent changes in the international technology market provide empirical evidence in support of several bargaining hypotheses. There are indications that the international technology market has become increasingly competitive. The competitive position of the United States, in particular, is seen to be eroding relative to that of the importing countries,[49] mainly because of the emergence of Western Europe and Japan as alternative sources for technology.[50] In the changed environment, the transfer of industrial technology to the Third World is no longer limited to the "mature" products, but it also includes some of the latest technology, especially in industries related to aircraft, automobiles, computers, consumer electronics, and chemical engineering.[51] With the development of local technological capability, the "technological distance" between suppliers and recipients is also becoming smaller and the bargaining strength of the recipient is most likely to increase.[52]

These findings, however, may be too optimistic. The bargaining power model of HC-TNC interaction has been used extensively in the empirical study of natural resources industries such as petroleum and copper.[53] Where, however, this framework has been extended to the study of manufacturing industries, it has led to more cautious conclusions. The bargaining framework has recently been used by Douglas Bennett and Kenneth Sharpe[54] in their study of the automobile industry in Mexico, by Gary Gereffi[55] in his study of the pharmaceutical industry in Mexico, by Joseph Grieco[56] in his study of the computer industry in India, and by Stephen Kobrin[57] in a cross-national study. The conclusions of these studies do not show an unambiguous shift in the bargaining power to host countries.

The pattern of bargaining power may vary depending on the nature of the industry. Whereas in the extractive industry the bargaining power of the host country may be lower at the time of the entry of foreign capital (because of the uncertainties about the amount, quality, and cost of extraction), in manufacturing industries the "power of the [host] state is likely to be greatest in the beginning (because the host country can set the conditions for TNC access to the local market)."[58] Kobrin's study also finds that "manufacturing is not characterized by the inherent, structurally based, and secular obsolescence that is found in the natural resource-based industries."[59] However, Grieco demonstrated in case of the Indian computer industry that technological change, over time, increased rather than diminished the host country's bargaining power vis-a-vis the international computer industry.[60] The findings of statistical tests by N. Fagre and Louis Wells[61] and Donald Lecraw[62] are nonetheless consistent with the hypothesis of the bargaining model. However, there is a limited base of empirical research testing various propositions of the bargaining model. The findings of these studies are not conclusive, merely tentative.

DEFINITION OF TECHNOLOGICAL SELF-RELIANCE

Since technology is available in both embodied form (capital goods, blue prints, etc.) and disembodied form (information, know-how, etc.), it is difficult to define self-reliance in technology as a measurable concept. Unlike material self-reliance—food grains, for example, which may be defined in terms of some degree of "self-sufficiency,"[63]—self-reliance in technology does not mean self-sufficiency or autarky, as there is hardly any country in the world capable of self-sufficiency in technology. The dependency argument that structural disengagement would have a stimulating effect on the development of local technological capabilities has been quite popular with a number of Third World leaders and left intellectuals, especially in the 1970s and early 1980s. However, it appears to be an option open only to large developing countries such as India, China, and Brazil, and even there the costs of disengagement of technological development have been found to be fairly high as witnessed in China's disastrous Great Leap Forward experiment under the leadership of Mao in the late 1950s. In order to overcome its technological weaknesses, China in the 1980s and 1990s has carefully strengthened its links with the market economies, especially the United States, in order to acquire new technology from the West. India, on the other hand, has not only been importing technology from both socialist (former Soviet bloc countries) and market-economy countries, although on a selective basis, but it has also entered the world market through nationally owned companies, and it is a supplier of technology to a number of developing nations. There is a need, therefore, to take a fresh look at a definition of technological dependence that will help us understand the conditions that perpetuate dependency and how developing countries could overcome them.

Dependence should not be measured by a developing country's reliance on outside suppliers of technology but rather by the "inability to control the direction, speed and social effects of technological evolution."[64] Technological self-reliance or autonomy must be conceived in terms of the capacity to identify national technological needs and to select and apply both foreign and domestic technology under conditions that enhance the growth of national technological capability. A concrete measure of technological self-reliance is the "marginal propensity to R&D investment relative to technology import." Thus, a country can be said to be more self-reliant "if over time its expenditure on technology import reduces relative to its expenditure on R&D and vice versa."[65] The pattern of technological development in Japan suggests that government policies can reduce technological dependence. Although Japan relied heavily on licensing agreements for acquiring technology, especially between 1950 and 1975, and had virtually excluded direct foreign investment, its private industry had committed a larger share of total R&D compared to the private sector in industrial countries. Therefore, even though the Japanese spent a considerable amount on the import of technology, they spent more than four times on local R&D, which resulted in a rapid development of the country's technological capability and self-reliance.[66] The example of East Asian NICs has also shown that judicious import and adaptation of relevant technology can be a speedy way to economic growth by enhancing indigenous technological capability.

The growth of technological capacity, which is the key to a country's technological self-reliance, has been totally overlooked by the dependency theorists because of their reliance on a structural mode of analysis. However, the dependency assumption about extremely weak technological capabilities in the Third World has been challenged on empirical grounds in the last decade. Scholars who examined technological processes and change in the Third World found that empirical evidence did not support the dependency hypothesis and started questioning the dependency explanation. Because of changes in the ability to master and adapt imported technology in the last two decades, especially in the newly industrializing Asian and Latin American countries, some scholars have suggested that the concept of a "dependence/self-reliance continuum" could best explain the growing technological capacity of these countries. As Subrahmanian points out:

At first [the developing country] may have only mere capacity to import technology for imitating domestic manufacture of foreign goods, which puts it in a state of technological dependence. If the [country] follows up the import with domestic investment on R&D it raises its capacity to adopt imported technology to local conditions, and further to make incremental improvements, and still further to innovate and generate together new process-es/products and even to become an exporter of technology. The country thus moves along the technology dependence-independence continuum and becomes self-reliant.[67]

The growth of technological capability depends on a country's policy concerning science and technology. Such a policy provides linkages between the three segments of the "Sabato triangle"—namely, research (scientific/technological infrastructure by way of universities, R&D centers), production (industry), and development policy (government's fiscal, budgetary, and economic planning activities). As Goulart explains,

[I]f an institutional triangle functions vigorously, technology will contribute directly to development. But if the triangle is absent or weak—that is, if the apexes are not connected or if instruments are deficient—any technology locally produced or imported will make but a slight contribution to development. The policy conclusion Sabato reaches is that triangles must be deliberately set up for each major sector within domestic economies, as well as for absorbing and disseminating technology acquired from without.[68]

Although the Sabato triangle has been widely accepted in Latin America and other developing nations, the role of the state in creating indigenous technological capability[69] through the emphasis on education in science and technology has been underscored by the policymakers in the Third World. While in the 1950s and 1960s the role of science in the developing world was viewed from a modernizing standpoint, in the last two decades the question of science policy has become closely related to "how LDC governments should respond in particular instances."[70] Two distinct approaches to education in science and technology have been followed by the developing countries. While most African countries have emphasized the need to extend and improve science and technology teaching at all levels,[71] many NICs, notably India, have invested heavily in sustained "elite" scientific and technological education for almost four decades.

While the emphasis on primary education has resulted in higher literacy rates in many countries—Tanzania, for example, has an 85 percent literacy rate—it has not significantly enhanced the technological capability of these countries, nor has it reduced their technological dependence. By contrast, India—through its emphasis on selective education in science, engineering, and technology[72]—has created over the years a substantial cadre of highly trained, skilled people who have contributed to the country's capability to adapt, assimilate, and generate technology in accordance with its development needs in both the industrial and agricultural sectors. The policy of selective higher education in India had created by the late 1960s a scientific and technological infrastructure that allowed it to become more self-reliant by taking steps to weaken the links between Indian firms and their technology suppliers abroad and to strengthen the links between the firms and public laboratories within the country. It is not surprising therefore that India is among the leaders within the NICs that have exported their technologies in the international markets.[73]

NOTES

1. The scope of this study is confined to industrial manufacturing technology.

2. In those days, there was a belief in a purely technological solution to the problems of poverty and economic backwardness in the underdeveloped world. President Truman, for example, emphasized in Point Four of his 1949 Inaugural Address, "We must embark on a bold new program for making the benefits of our scientific advances and industrial progress available for the improvement and growth of underdeveloped areas." Quoted in Nathan Rosenberg, *Perspectives on Technology* (London: Cambridge University Press, 1976), p. 151; also, see John Montgomery, *Technology and Civil Life: Making and Implementing Development Decisions* (Cambridge, Mass.: MIT Press, 1974), p. 52.

3. Dennis Goulart, *The Uncertain Promise: Value Conflicts in Technology Transfer* (Washington, D.C.: Overseas Development Council, 1977), p. 34.

4. UNIDO, *Technological Self-Reliance of the Developing Countries: Towards Operational Strategies*, Development and Transfer of Technology Series No. 15 (Vienna: United Nations, 1981), p. 5.

5. Rachel McCulloch, "Technology Transfer of Developing Countries: Implications of International Regulation," *Annals, American Academy of Political and Social Sciences*, 458 (Nov. 1981): 111-112.

6. Charles Cooper, "The Transfer of Industrial Technology to the Underdeveloped Countries," *Bulletin of the Institute of Development Studies*, 3, No. 3 (Oct. 1970): 3.

7. Earl Ingerson and Wayne C. Braggs (eds.), *Science, Government and Industry for Development* (Austin: University of Texas Press, 1976).

8. Tharp identifies at least four approaches to the subject. They are the Free Market model, the European Community model, the Multinational Consortium approach, and the Development Community approach. See Paul A. Tharp, Jr., "Transnational Enterprises and International Regulation: A Survey of Various Approaches in International Organization," *International Organization*, 30, No. 1 (Winter 1976): 47-73.

9. Ernst B. Hass, "Technological Self-Reliance for Latin America: The OAS Contribution," *International Organization,* 34, No. 4 (Autumn 1980): 542; Devora Grynspan, "Technology Transfer Patterns and Industrialization in LDCs: A Study of Licensing in Costa Rica," *International Organization*, 36, No. 4 (Autumn 1982): 541-570.

10. Jairam Ramesh and Charles Weiss (eds.), *Mobilizing Technology for World Development* (New York: Praeger, 1979).

11. Hass, "Technological Self-Reliance for Latin America," p. 543.

12. Arghiri Emmanuel, *Appropriate or Underdeveloped Technology?* (New York: John Wiley & Sons, 1982).

13. Theotoni Dos Santos, "The Structure of Dependence," in K. T. Fann and Donald C. Hodges (eds.), *Readings in U.S. Imperialism* (Boston: Peter Sargent Publisher, 1971), p. 226.

14. See Osvaldo Sunkel, "National Development Policy and External Dependence in Latin America," *Journal of Development Studies*, 6, No. 1 (1969): 23-48; Celso Furtado, "The Concept of External Dependence in the Study of Underdevelopment," in Charles K. Wilber (ed.), *The Political Economy of Development and Underdevelopment* (New York: Random House, 1970); and Stephen Hymer, *The International Operation of National Firms: A Study of Direct Foreign Investment* (Cambridge: MIT Press, 1976).

15. UNIDO, "Technological Self-Reliance of the Developing Countries: Towards Operational Strategies," p. 7.

16. Sylvain Plasscheert, "Transfer Pricing Problem in Developing Countries," in Alan M. Rugman and Lorraine Eden (eds.), *Multinationals and Transfer Pricing* (New York: St. Martin's Press, 1985), p. 247; Constantine V. Vaitsos, "Transfer of Resources and Preservation of Monopoly Rents," Harvard Center for International Affairs Economic Development Report No. 168, 1970.

17. Foreign-owned companies account for more than 20 percent of industrial production in West Germany and more than 50 percent in Canada. However, neither Canada nor West Germany has experienced the slightest loss of sovereignty. Brazil, on the other hand, with $30 billion of foreign investment, which is largely responsible for that country's growing industrialization (especially in automotive, office equipment, farm machinery, and pharmaceutical industries), would be considered dependent.

18. OECD; cited in *Fortune*, March 14, 1988, p. 46.

19. Frances Stewart, *Technology and Underdevelopment* (Boulder, Colo.: Westview Press, 1977), p. 118.

20. Surendra J. Patel, "The Technological Dependence of Developing Countries," *Journal of Modern African Studies*, 12, No. 1 (March 1974): 1-18.

21. Jeffrey Hart, "Three Approaches to the Measurement of Power in International Relations," *International Organization*, 30, No. 2 (Spring 1976): 293.

22. Ramesh and Weiss, *Mobilizing Technology for World Development*, p. 29.

23. Surendra J. Patel, Editorial to the Special Issue on "Integrated Technology Transfer," *Impact of Science on Society*, 28, No. 4 (Oct.-Dec. 1978): 307; and "Plugging into the System," *Development Forum*, (Oct. 1978): 12-13.

24. Patel, "The Technological Dependence of Developing Countries," p. 12.

25. Fernando Henrique Cardoso and Enzo Faletto, *Dependency and Development in Latin America* (Berkeley: University of California Press, 1979).

26. Peter B. Evans, *Dependent Development: The Alliance of Multinational, State, and Local Capital in Brazil* (Princeton, N.J.: Princeton University Press, 1979).

27. Stewart, p. 138.

28. UNIDO, "Technological Self-Reliance of the Developing Countries," p. 10.

29. G. K. Helleiner, "International Technology Issues: Southern Needs and Northern Responses," in Jagdish N. Bhagwati (ed.), *The New International Economic Order: The North-South Debate* (Cambridge, Mass.: MIT Press, 1977), p. 297.

30. Raymond Vernon, *Sovereignty at Bay: The Multinational Spread of U.S. Enterprise* (New York: Basic Books, 1971).

31. Jack Baranson, "Technology Export Can Hurt Us," *Foreign Policy*, No. 25 (Winter 1976-77): 187.

32. United Nations. *The Acquisition of Technology from Multinational Corporations by Developing Countries* (New York: United Nations, 1974), p. 47.

33. Stephan Haggard, "The Newly Industrializing Countries in the International System," *World Politics*, 38 (Jan. 1986): 345.

34. Louis T. Wells, Jr., "Economic Man and the Engineering Man," in Robert Stobaugh and Louis Wells (eds.), *Technology Crossing Borders: The Choice, Transfer, and Management of International Technology Flows* (Boston, Mass.: Harvard Business School Press, 1984).

35. Stephen J. Kobrin, "Testing the Bargaining Hypothesis in the Manufacturing Sector in Developing Countries," *International Organization*, 41, No. 4 (Autumn 1987): 610.

36. Charles Kindleberger and Bruce Herrick, *Economic Development*, 3rd ed. (New York: McGraw Hill, 1977).

37. Charles P. Kindleberger, *American Business Abroad: Six Lectures on Direct Investment* (New Haven: Yale University Press, 1969); R. F. Mikesell, "Conflict in Foreign Investor-Host Country Relations: A Preliminary Analysis," in his (ed.), *Foreign Investment in the Petroleum and Mineral Industries* (Baltimore: Johns Hopkins University Press, 1971).

38. Tamir Agmon and Seev Hirsch, "Multinational Corporations and the Developing Economics: Potential Gains in a World of Imperfect Markets and Uncertainty," *Oxford Bulletin of Economics and Statistics*, 41, No. 4 (November 1979): 333.

39. Alfred Stepan, *The State and Society: Peru in Comparative Perspective* (Princeton, N.J.: Princeton University Press, 1978).

40. Raymond Vernon, *Storm Over the Multinationals: The Real Issue* (Cambridge, Mass.: Harvard University Press, 1977).

41. Louis T. Wells (ed.), *The Product Life Cycle and International Trade* (Cambridge, Mass.: Harvard University Press, 1972).

42. Vernon, *Storm Over the Multinationals*, p. 91.

43. See Wells, "Economic Men and the Engineering Men."

44. Badiul Alam Mazumdar, *Innovations, Product Developments, and Technology Transfers: An Empirical Study of Dynamic Competitive Advantage, the Case of Electronic Calculator* (Washington, D.C.: University Press of America, 1982), p. 18.

45. Richard Newfarmer (ed.), *Profits, Progress and Poverty: Case Studies of International Industries in Latin America* (Notre Dame, Ind.: University of Notre Dame Press, 1985), p. 22.

46. Agmon and Hirsch, "Multinational Corporations and the Developing Economies," p. 342.

47. Ibid., p. 341.

48. Theodore H. Moran, "Multinational Corporations and the Developing Countries: An Analytical View," in his (ed.), *Multinational Corporations: The Political Economy of Foreign Direct Investment* (Lexington, Mass.: Lexington, 1985), p. 5.

49. Robert Gilpin, *U.S. Power and the Multinational Corporation: The Political Economy of Foreign Direct Investment* (New York: Basic Books, 1975).

50. There has been a decline in the U.S. share from a little over 50 percent in 1971 to 46.3 percent in total OECD R&D in 1981. Despite this decline, the United States still leads the field in the dissemination of technology through the export of goods (Madeuf).

51. Baranson, "Technology Export Can Hurt Us," p. 184; Kobrin, "Testing the Bargaining Hypotheses in the Manufacturing Sector in Developing Countries," p. 610.

52. Mariluz Cortes and Peter Bocock, *North-South Technology Transfer: A Case Study of Petrochemicals in Latin America* (Baltimore: Johns Hopkins University Press, 1984), p. 93.

53. See, for example, Theodore H. Moran, *Multinational Corporations and the Politics of Dependence: Copper in Chile* (Princeton, N.J.: Princeton University Press, 1974); David N. Smith and Louis T. Wells, Jr., *Negotiating Third World Mineral Agreements* (Cambridge, Mass.: Bellinger, 1975); Franklin Tugwell, *The Politics of Oil in Venezuela* (Stanford, Calif.: Stanford University Press, 1975); Adalberto S. Pinelo, *The Multinational Corporation as a Force in Latin American Politics: A Case Study of the International Petroleum Corporation in Peru* (New York: Praeger, 1973); Richard S. Sklar, *Corporate Power in an African State: The Political Impact of Multinational Mining Companies in Zambia* (Berkeley: University of California Press, 1975); Rex Bosson and Bension Varon, *The Mining Industry and Developing Countries* (New York: Oxford University Press, for the World Bank, 1977); Raymond Mikesell, *Foreign Investment in Copper Mining: Case Studies in Mines in Peru and Papua New Guinea* (Washington D.C.: Resources for the

Future, 1975); S. K. B. Asante, "Restructuring Transnational Mineral Agreements," *American Journal of International Law*, 73 (1979): 335-371; S. Sideri and S. Johns (eds.), *Mining for Development in the Third World: Multinational Corporations, State Enterprise and the International Economy* (New York: Pergamon, 1980); and *Structure and Strategy in the International Copper Industry* (New York: U.N. Center on Transnational Corporations, 1981).

54. Douglas C. Bennett and Kenneth E. Sharpe, *Transnational Corporation Versus the State: The Political Economy of the Mexican Auto Industry* (Princeton, N.J.: Princeton University Press, 1985).

55. Gary Gereffi, *The Pharmaceutical Industry and Dependency in the Third World* (Princeton, N.J.: Princeton University Press, 1983).

56. Joseph Grieco, "Between Dependency and Autonomy: India's Experience with the International Computer Industry," *International Organization*, 36, No. 3 (Summer 1982): 609-632; and *Between Dependency and Autonomy: India's Experience with the International Computer Industry* (Berkeley: University of California Press, 1984).

57. Kobrin, "Testing the Bargaining Hypothesis."

58. Gereffi, *The Pharmaceutical Industry and Dependency in the Third World*, pp. 47-48.

59. Kobrin, "Testing the Bargaining Hypothesis," p. 635.

60. Grieco, "Between Dependency and Autonomy."

61. N. Fagre and Louis T. Wells, Jr., "Bargaining Power of Multinationals and Host Government," *Journal of International Business Studies*, 13 (Fall 1982): 9-21.

62. Donald J. Lecraw, "Bargaining Power, Ownership, and Profitability of Transnational Corporations in Developing Countries," *Journal of International Business Studies*, 15 (Spring/Summer 1984): 27-43.

63. K. K. Subrahmanian, "Towards Technological Self-Reliance: An Assessment of Indian Strategy and Achievement in Industry," in P. R. Brahmanand and V. R. Panchamukhi (eds.), *The Development Process of the Indian Economy* (Bombay: Himalaya, 1987), p. 422.

64. Goulart, *The Uncertain Promise*.

65. Subrahmanian, "Towards Technological Self-Reliance," pp. 423-424.

66. See Yoshihiro Tsurumi, "Technology Transfer and Foreign Trade: The Case of Japan, 1950-1966," unpublished DBA Thesis, Harvard Business School, 1968; and N. Rosenberg, "The International Transfer of Industrial Technology: Past and Present," in OECD, *North/South Technology Transfer: The Adjustment Ahead* (Paris: OECD, 1982).

67. Subrahmanian, "Towards Technological Self-Reliance," p. 424. Also see Homi Katrak, "Imported Technology, Enterprise Size and R&D in a Newly Industrializing Country: The Indian Experience," *Oxford Bulletin of Economics and Statistics*, 47, No. 3 (August 1985): 213-229.

68. Goulart, *The Uncertain Promise*, p. 82.

69. Indigenous technological development means the development of independent technological learning capacity and independent technology creating capacity. For a definition of the two concepts, see Ronald Dore, "Technological Self-Reliance: Sturdy Ideal or Self-Serving Rhetoric," in Martin Fransman and Kenneth King (eds.), *Technological Capability in the Third World* (New York: St. Martin's Press, 1984).

70. See Norman Clark, *The Political Economy of Science and Technology* (New York: Basil Blackwell, 1985), p. 182; Robin Clarke, *Science and Technology in World Development* (Oxford: Oxford University Press, 1985).

71. See UNESCO, "Preparatory Meeting of Experts for the Conference of Ministers of Education," Harare, June 21-25, 1982.

72. The number of universities in India has increased from 20 at the time of independence to 157 in 1987, which includes "nationally important" universities and five Indian Institutes of Technology (IITs), which have a restricted curriculum focused on science and engineering. In science and engineering alone, 3,040 Ph.D.s were awarded in 1983-84, which was 44 percent of the total doctoral awards. India's stock of science and technology personnel was 2.7 million in 1985, which was the third largest in the world. For details, see F. A. Long, "Science, Technology and Industrial Development in India," *Technology in Society*, 10 (1988): 395-416 and A. Rahman, *Science and Technology in India* (New Delhi: National Institute of Science, Technology and Development Studies, 1984).

73. The government of India started promoting, in the late 1970s, the export of capital and technology by Indian business as a way out of domestic industrial stagnation. See P. Mohanan Pillai, "Technology Transfer, Adaptation and Assimilation," *Economic and Political Weekly*, Nov. 24, 1979, pp. M121-M126. For a systematic study of India as an exporter of technology see Sanjaya Lall, "Exports of Technology by Newly-Industrializing Countries: An Overview," *World Development*, 12, Nos. 5/6 (1984): 471-480.

3

Technology Transfer and the Indian Experience

The 4½ decades of planned development in India have brought about a substantial diversification in its industrial base, with the consequence that it can now produce a wide range of industrial products. Over the years, India has achieved almost total self-reliance in basic and capital goods industries, which now account for about one-half of the total value added in manufacturing. In various sectors—such as mining, irrigation, power, transport and communication—indigenous capacities have already been established to the point of "virtual self-sufficiency so that further expansion can be based primarily on indigenous equipment."[1] India's growing technological capability has enabled it to be the leading exporter of technologies among the developing nations.[2] Yet, the government is concerned that "in large areas of economic activities, relatively obsolete, cost-ineffective technology continues to be applied, the pace of scientific and technological innovation remains unimpressive, and the adoption of the available scientific and technological knowledge is tardy."[3]

India's acquisition of a high degree of technological capability has been accompanied by technological obsolescence and inefficiencies in many of its industries. This paradoxical situation can be explained by examining the policy setting in which technology transfer takes place in India. This chapter briefly describes India's import of technology since the 1950s, the cost of technology transfer, the science and technology policy, the R&D activities, the import-export and industrial policy, and the export of technology.

TECHNOLOGY IMPORTS

It is generally true that India has achieved a greater degree of self-reliance in the manufacture of a wide range of consumer goods through a government policy that blocked foreign technology in many industries crucial to economic development, but its industrialization strategy of developing an integrated industrial structure in basic and heavy industry has resulted in importing technology since the beginning of the Second Five Year Plan in 1955-56. India's adoption of a strategy of import substitution—to protect the domestic industry, particularly in consumer goods—further led to its dependence on foreign technology. Its industrial strategy involved extensive collaboration for the import of technology in metallurgical industries, capital goods, transport, consumer durables, agricultural exports, and the engineering and pharmaceutical industries.

Even though the Indian government has followed a strict policy toward multinational corporations, especially from the late 1960s until the early 1980s, the number of foreign collaboration agreements approved by the government is quite large. As Table 3.1 indicates, between 1957 and 1977 the government approved 5,254 foreign agreements (both licensing and direct investments), of which the public sector accounted for approximately 5 percent and the private sector 95 percent. The number of foreign collaborations approved between 1974 and 1984 totaled 4,667. After the liberalization of India's import policy under Prime Minister Rajiv Gandhi, the rate of approval reached 740 in 1984 and 1,024 in 1985, with a moderate decline between 1986 and 1989. The average number of foreign collaborations approved per year thus went up from 270 in the 1970s to 660 in the early 1980s. The rate of approvals was particularly high during the Second and Third Five Year Plan periods—the years of the "big push" to industry—and in the 1980s when a new thrust was given to industry. But when industrial growth decelerated between 1966 and 1982,[4] there was a substantial drop in the number of technical collaborations approved. Between 1985 and 1990, the total number of new agreements approved was 5,203.[5] Therefore, the number of technical collaboration agreements entered into by India has been viewed by some analysts as a vital sign of growth and industrialization, "rather than being a depressor of economic growth."[6]

India's technical collaboration agreements are heavily concentrated in technologically intensive fields of manufacturing such as capital goods and advanced intermediates (chemicals). The data presented in Table 3.2 show that of all the agreements approved by the government between 1957 and 1970, more than 50 percent were related to electrical and nonelectrical machinery, machine tools, and transport equipment. If all the foreign collaboration agreements approved by the government between 1957 and 1982 are taken into account (6,959), the industrial distribution shows a similar pattern: Industrial machinery and machine tools accounted for 40 percent; electrical equipment and electronics, 19 percent; chemical and pharmaceuticals, 15 percent; transport and construction equipment, 9 percent; and technical consultancy, only 1 percent.[7] In the industry distribution, the Reserve Bank of India (RBI) survey for 1977-78 to 1980-81 also found that "machinery and machine tools alone accounted for 45 percent of the companies with purely technical collaboration agreements."[8]

Table 3.1
Foreign Collaboration Proposals Approved by Government

Year	Number of Approvals
1948-55	284
1956	82
1957	81
1958	103
1959	150
1960	380
1961	403
1962	298
1963	298
1964	471
1965	296
1966	202
1967	182
1968	131
1969	135
1970	183
1971	245
1972	257
1973	265
1974	359
1975	271
1976	277
1977	267
1978	307
1979	267
1980	526
1981	389
1982	591
1983	673
1984	740
1985	1,024
1986 (November)	600

Sources: Reserve Bank of India, (a) *Foreign Collaboration in Indian Industry: Survey Report* (Bombay,1968), (b) *Foreign Collaboration in India: Second Survey Report* (Bombay,1974), and (c) *Foreign Collaboration in Indian Industry: Fourth Survey Report* (Bombay,1985); *Business Environment*, 1986; *Hindu*, November 8, 1986.

Since the list of government approvals includes renewals, amendments, and agreements that have already expired, the total number of agreements approved by the government, while indicative of the trend in growth of foreign technical collaboration, may be misleading because it does not give a correct account of the number of agreements in force. Moreover, the list does not indicate the number of approved agreements that were never taken up. In a survey of 1,815 collaboration agreements approved by the government between 1975 and 1981, it was found that 63 percent of them were never implemented.[9] "If this could be generalized to the universe of agreements," according to Sanjaya Lall, "only some 2,600 agreements (including those with equity investment) materialized in 1957-82, and about 1,200 pure technical ones in 1969-82."[10] It is also important to distinguish between

Table 3.2
Technical Collaboration Agreements Classified by Industry, 1957-70

		1957	1958	1959	1960	1961	1962	1963	1964	1965	1966	1967	1968	1969 Dec. 1970	Jan. 1957- Dec. 1970	Total
1.	Electrical equipment, apparatus, components	4	6	9	46	69	63	52	35	22	21	24	16	16	21	404
2.	Industrial machinery (other than textile machinery)	6	3	8	34	47	29	40	68	40	44	19	25	32	43	433
3.	Machine tools and accessories	-	4	6	26	35	17	26	33	14	19	21	15	3	12	231
4.	Transport equipment	5	7	13	38	23	26	24	26	7	12	11	4	6	14	261
5.	Basic chemicals	7	8	18	25	37	4	4	26	14	10	11	7	4	4	179
6.	Chemical products	3	2	9	8	13	38	24	25	20	5	12	5	7	10	181
7.	Heavy electrical equipment	7	6	4	35	28	-	2	20	10	8	13	10	4	5	151
8.	Iron & steel products	2	5	11	25	17	12	13	21	9	12	2	7	2	6	124
9.	Instruments	-	-	1	19	9	12	21	20	17	7	8	-	7	1	124
10.	Textile machinery	1	1	4	15	15	4	5	15	18	10	1	7	3	6	105
11.	Materials handling & construction equipment	1	1	4	18	19	4	4	13	8	8	9	3	7	5	104
12.	Castings & forgings	1	-	1	9	10	5	12	27	5	6	1	1	1	-	79
13.	Drugs & pharmaceuticals	4	8	4	11	7	9	6	6	5	3	5	5	1	3	77
14.	Ceramic & glassware	2	3	2	10	11	10	5	8	3	4	-	2	3	2	65
15.	Paper & paper products	2	2	-	9	10	5	5	4	5	2	1	2	1	1	49
16.	Metal & metal products	2	1	1	3	6	6	8	5	1	1	5	2	2	4	47
17.	Technical consultantry	-	2	1	-	-	5	9	4	1	1	4	2	2	5	38
18.	Agricultural machinery & implements	1	-	3	4	2	3	3	2	2	3	2	4	9	4	42
19.	Fertilizers	-	-	-	-	2	1	1	-	3	3	-	1	-	1	12
20.	Pesticides	1	2	2	1	1	-	-	-	-	-	1	2	-	-	10
21.	Others	32	42	49	44	43	43	37	47	38	23	32	11	25	36	500
	Total	81	103	150	380	403	298	298	403	242	202	182	135	135	183	3,191

Source: V.N. Balasubramanyam, *The Economy of India* (London: Weidenfeld and Nicolson, 1984), p. 150.

different types of technology transfer agreements, especially direct foreign investment (DFI) versus pure technical collaboration agreements. The RBI surveys,
which attempt to study the agreements in force rather than those approved, suggest
that in the 1960s there was a higher proportion of agreements by foreign
subsidiaries and foreign minority companies than by the Indian companies.
Balasubramanyam's study confirmed that "the will to transfer technology on the
part of the foreign firms was much less in the case of technical collaboration
agreements than in the case of direct investment and joint ventures."[11]

While India encouraged technology transfer through DFI until the mid-
1960s (partly because of the foreign exchange crisis of the late 1950s), in the late
1960s it opted for technology import via licensing. Although the government
standardized the procedure of technology import in the early 1950s and gave
approval for technology imports, specific policies on technology transfer were
formulated between 1965 and 1968.The technology import policy included five
important features:

1. Royalty ceilings were prescribed for various industries;

2. The standard permitted duration of agreement was reduced from 10 to 5 years. Renewals
   were not allowed unless they involved more advanced or different technology;

3. The only export restrictions that were permitted were to countries where the technology
   exporter had had subsidiaries, affiliates or licensees;

4. The use of a technology supplier's trademark was not allowed in India;

5. No restrictions were allowed on the technology importer's right to sell or sublicense the
   technology.[12]

The government thus tried to regulate the transfer of the cost of technology import
down. India was the first developing nation that took restrictive measures to
discourage technology imports via private capital investment or minority foreign
capital participation. Enos has estimated that between 1969 and 1979, DFI and
joint ventures accounted for only 14.7 percent of India's technology acquisitions.[13]

The implementation of government policies brought significant results:
The duration of agreements registered a sharp decline, and the share of outright sale
of technology increased sharply. In his study of technological change in Indian
industry, Desai found that whereas 36 percent of the agreements between 1951 and
1967 were for ten years, between 1977 and 1980, ten-year agreements had come
down to 3 percent and the "share of outright sales of technology rose from 13 to 29
percent."[14]

The RBI data, presented in Table 3.3, reveal that in the 1970s there was
a substantial increase (more than 20 percent) over the previous decade in the
number of purely technical collaboration agreements signed between Indian public
and private firms and technology-supplying companies. In the wake of India's

Table 3.3
Foreign Technical Collaboration Agreement in Force,
1961 through 1980: Classification of Companies

	1961-1964		1964-1970		1977-1980	
	Number	Percent	Number	Percent	Number	Percent
1. Subsidiaries	144	13.4	167	15.2	49	7.2
2. Minority Foreign Capital Participation	445	42.3	489	44.5	300	44.6
3. Pure Technical Collaboration (Indian Companies, Private & Public)	462	44.0	442	40.3	424	63.2
Total	1,051	100.0	1,098	100.0	673	100.0

Note: While a subsidiary is a company incorporated in India but having a majority (more than 50 percent) holding in equity capital by a single foreign company, minority participation is where such holdings are 50 percent or less. Companies that have no foreign company equity capital participation but have technical collaboration agreements fall into the pure technical collaboration group.
Sources: RBI, (a) *Foreign Collaboration in Indian Industry: Survey Report* (Bombay, 1968), (b) *Foreign Collaboration in Indian Industry: Second Survey Report* (Bombay, 1974), and (c) *Foreign Collaboration in Indian Industry: Fourth Survey Report* (Bombay, 1985).

liberalization of the economy in the 1980s, foreign equity participation remained low. In 1985-86, for example, of the 133 companies that entered the capital market to set up various projects, only 16 (12.7 percent) had foreign equity participation.[15]

Between 1969 and 1982, India had, in fact, approved equity flows of only $80 million, half of which did not materialize. A total of $40 million direct foreign investment in 14 years compares favorably with the record of other newly industrializing countries in the 1970s: a net inflow of $14 billion in Brazil, $7 billion in Mexico, $648 million in South Korea, and $1.5 billion in Argentina.[16] Another measure of comparison is the stock of direct foreign investment as a percentage of the Gross National Product (GNP) and stock of the Gross Domestic Investment (GDI) in a country. In 1977-78 these stocks were comparatively low in India: 2.1 and 1.1, respectively—as against 4.8 and 2.6 percent in Argentina, 6.6 and 4.2 percent in Brazil, 5.6 and 3.3 percent in Mexico, and 3.1 and 2.4 percent in South Korea.[17] Thus compared to other NICs, India's imports of technology have indeed been small. However, the technology import situation underwent significant change in the wake of the policy of economic liberalization adopted by the Rao government in 1991.

Cost of Technology Imports

There is a vast body of theoretical and empirical literature on multinationals as exporters of technology to developing nations through DFI. Most studies suggest that multinationals prefer this mode of transfer. In the literature on technology transfer, a distinction is made between direct and indirect cost of technology import. The direct cost usually consists of royalties, technical know-how fees, profits, dividends, and interest payments—whether technology is transferred through DFI or through a purely technical collaboration agreement. Indirect cost refers to the phenomenon of import dependence and the implications of technology import on balance of payments, industrial structure, equity, and technological environment. Although it is possible to quantify the direct cost, the issue of indirect cost does not easily lend itself to quantitative verifications. A quantitative assessment of real costs is thus difficult to make, especially at the national level.

The data on private sector companies' remittances on account of profits, dividends, royalties, technical fees, and interest payments between 1956-57 and 1981-82 are presented in Table 3.4. The total remittances by the Indian companies show a steady, gradual increase from Rs. 29.7 crores in 1957-58 to Rs. 398.85 crores in 1981-82 (for recent years the figures are even higher). The drastic increase in technical fees from Rs. 43.97 crores in 1979-80 to Rs. 270.70 crores in 1981-82 is due mainly to the sophisticated technology acquired by Indian companies in recent years. Mature technologies are more costly to obtain. Since the royalty rate was low after the mid-1960s—1.8 to 3.0 percent after taxes—the technology suppliers started charging higher technical fees.[18]

However, an empirical study of 211 technology-importing firms, using the data collected by the National Council of Applied Economic Research (NCAER), has found that in a large majority of collaborations, there was very little increase in lump-sum payments between the late 1970s and early 1980s. Ghayur Alam has found that "while the average lump-sum payments made by 615 collaborations during 1977-79 was Rs. 16.3 lakhs, during 1980-83 it had increased to Rs. 17.46 lakhs."[19] His study reveals that out of 1,459 agreements, only 73 had involved payments of Rs. 1 crore each, which accounted for 40 percent of the total outgo. It can therefore be hypothesized that the large increase in lump-sum payments in the early 1980s (shown as fees in column 5, Table 3.3) was due to the import liberalization policies of the early 1980s. Import liberalization has resulted in a "few, but well publicized instances, where technology payments have been larger than those in the past."[20] Furthermore, the table suggests a significant decline in the remittance of profits by foreign firms in the late 1970s and early 1980s, due mainly to the dilution of equity by subsidiaries in response to the Foreign Exchange Regulation Act (FERA) of 1973.

India's direct cost of acquiring technology when compared to other NICs appears to be rather low. Lall has made a comparison of foreign licensed technology in India (based on the data collected from 433 largest private sector and

Table 3.4
Remittances Abroad by Indian Private Sector Companies
1956-57 to 1982-83

(Rs. Crore) Year	Profits	Dividends	Royalties	Technical Fees	Interest	Total Remittances
1956-57	19.4	7.1	1.2	-	2.7	30.4
1957-58	17.4	8.8	0.9	-	2.6	29.7
1958-59	20.0	8.3	1.3	-	5.2	34.8
1959-60	16.4	11.7	1.8	-	6.2	36.1
1960-61	18.9	12.6	2.5	-	7.6	41.6
1961-62	12.4	18.5	2.4	-	7.2	40.5
1962-63	19.4	21.5	3.6	-	4.5	49.0
1963-64	12.8	18.8	4.6	-	10.8	47.0
1964-65	15.6	22.0	4.4	3.6	6.2	51.8
1965-66	13.50	19.40	2.95	6.98	-	42.83
1966-67	14.47	28.77	5.13	10.43	-	58.80
1967-68	15.95	32.70	4.32	14.68	-	67.65
1968-69	12.96	30.25	4.78	17.97	12.73	78.69
1969-70	12.72	31.41	5.80	13.05	9.28	72.26
1970-71	13.12	43.48	5.23	20.63	12.80	95.26
1971-72	9.94	38.87	5.86	13.90	12.13	80.70
1972-73	15.54	39.08	7.33	11.33	15.60	88.88
1973-74	21.91	37.51	6.21	14.08	16.27	95.98
1974-75	7.19	18.46	8.46	12.56	36.70	83.37
1975-76	20.36	24.84	10.49	25.66	24.65	106.00
1976-77	19.39	48.47	15.88	37.80	25.11	146.65
1977-78	10.13	68.01	19.50	28.14	22.70	148.48
1978-79	10.24	54.35	12.65	36.31	26.63	118.50
1979-80	14.37	50.92	0.53	43.97	25.22	144.01
1980-81	12.10	55.92	8.88	104.93	22.32	204.15
1981-82	12.16	58.92	15.99	270.70	41.08	398.85

Sources: Economic Intelligence Service, *Basic Statistics Relating to the Indian Economy*, vol. 1: All India (Bombay: Center for Monitoring Indian Economy, 1985); K. V. Swaminathan and S. Varadarajan, "Cooperation in High Technology," unpublished paper, 1984, cited in Nagesh Kumar, "Technology Policy in India: An Overview of Its Evolution and an Assessment," in P. R. Brahmanand and V. R. Panchamukhi (eds.), *The Development Process of the Indian Economy* (Bombay: Himalaya Publishing House, 1987), pp. 469-470.

203 largest public sector companies) with that in Korea, Brazil, and Mexico (based on the data from the World Development Report, 1979). Lall has calculated, after deflating licensing payments by manufacturing value added, that in 1979 Mexico had the highest dependence on foreign licensed technology (2.7 percent), followed by Brazil (1.9 percent), South Korea (1.1 percent), and India (0.7 to 0.8 percent).

The contribution of imported technology to production value has been found to be fairly high in India.[21] According to a recent study, whereas India remits 0.32 percent of its GNP toward the import of foreign technologies, the contribution of foreign technologies to the production value is about 8.3 percent of the GNP.[22]

In the import of capital goods, India was also found to be least dependent among the NICs: While India's import was $1.6 billion in 1978-79, for Brazil it was

$4.4 billion (1980); for Mexico, $3.5 billion (1980); and for South Korea, $5.3 billion (1979).[23] How did India succeed in maintaining such a low level of technological dependence compared to other NICs? An answer to this question will entail an analysis of India's science and technology policy.

SCIENCE AND TECHNOLOGY POLICY

The importance of science and technology in national development was recognized by the nationalist leaders as early as 1939, when the Indian National Congress appointed a national planning committee chaired by Jawaharlal Nehru. After independence, the planning commission, formed in March 1950 and also chaired by Prime Minister Nehru, took the view that planned development in India had to concentrate on socioeconomic and technological change. India's First Five Year Plan (1951-56) devoted a whole chapter to science and technology, stressing the importance of scientific and industrial research in India's development. The plan maintained:

The pace of economic development depends on a variety of factors which constitute the psychological and sociological setting within which the economy operates. . . . Basically, development involves securing higher productivity all round and this is a function of the degree of technological advance the community is able to make. The problem is not one merely of adopting and applying the process and techniques developed elsewhere, but of developing new techniques suited to local conditions. Modern technology is changing rapidly and no country can hope to maintain a steady pace of advance unless it keeps abreast of current developments.[24]

The emphasis was on mastering the latest technology to increase productivity. For Nehru, the role of science in India's development was crucial. He talked of promoting a "scientific temper," that is, the popularization of scientific outlook among the people. A Ministry of Scientific Research and Natural Resources was created (Nehru kept the portfolio to himself, which added to the importance of the ministry), and the government gave priority to the establishment of an infrastructure for research and development. This infrastructure consisted of a chain of national laboratories formed by the Council of Scientific and Industrial Research (CSIR, formed in 1942); establishment of the Department of Atomic Energy, the Department of Science and Technology, and the Department of Scientific and Industrial Research, as well as expansion of the science and technology departments of the universities; the creation of institutes of technology (IITs); and the provision of adequate resources to meet the requirements of these organizations.[25]

Although the Second Five Year Plan (1956-61), which outlined the strategy of developing basic and heavy industry in the public sector, emphasized scientific research like the First Five Year Plan, the Scientific Policy Resolution (passed by the Parliament in 1958) recognized the need for creation of science and technology manpower and emphasized the training of scientific personnel. The institutions established in the ensuing years to train science and technology manpower have produced impressive results. In about 25 years, India has succeeded in creating the third largest pool of technically skilled manpower in the world, next only to the United States and Russia: In 1982-83, India had 322,000 graduate engineers, 464,000 diploma holders in engineering, and two million science graduates and post-graduates—a total of 2.8 million technically qualified people, not counting medical and agricultural graduates.[26]

It should, however, be noted that the emphasis in India's science and technology policy was on the creation of a scientific infrastructure. The Draft Fifth Five Year Plan (1974-79) recognized for the first time the weakness in India's approach to science policy and pointed out that the earlier plans had lacked a technology policy. Although the five year plans had underscored the importance of science and technology in India's development, in none of the plans was the relationship between science and technology clearly brought out. The Fifth Five Year Plan document, which was prepared by the planning commission in close cooperation with the National Committee on Science and Technology (NCST),[27] therefore emphasized the need for a clearly articulated technology policy:

More importantly, perhaps, the structuring of the effort has been such that the goals of R&D programmes and projects have, often, not been derived directly from the technological needs of development projects, whether in industry or other areas. At the same time, the scope of "science planning" has not covered the whole of the "innovative chain." As a result, successful research results at the laboratory level have often failed to be linked to such elements as pilot plan work, design engineering, plant erection, and commissioning and marketing, which are essential if the nation is to secure real and substantial social and economic benefits from science and technology. . . . The task involved is really "planning the promotion of Science and Technology and their application to the Development and Security of the nation. . . ." What we are primarily interested in, is not a plan merely for education and research in various scientific and technological disciplines but a plan to harness science and technology for achieving the goals and programs of the Fifth Plan.[28]

The Fifth Five Year Plan had thus identified the central problem in India's science and technology policy—the country's inability to apply scientific knowledge successfully to increase productivity in the industrial sector. India's first Science and Technology Plan (1974-79) drew attention to the socioeconomic and political aspects of the import of technology. The absence of integration between development planning and technology planning was found to be the main shortcoming of the science and technology policy in India.[29] Accordingly, the government announced the Technology Policy Statement (TPS) in January 1983.

The basic objectives of the TPS are the attainment of technological self-reliance, the development of indigenous technology, and the efficient absorption and adaptation of imported technology appropriate to national priorities and resources.[30] The statement carefully made a distinction between self-reliance and self-sufficiency. It maintained that India would continue to import know-how selectively, taking into account its needs, capabilities, and the time required to develop indigenous technology. Although the TPS did not lay down modalities for its implementation, the government has since taken steps to formulate a simplified, liberalized scheme to encourage technology imports for modernizing identified thrust industries. The government addressed for the first time the problems of inefficiency, technological obsolescence, and the lack of international competitiveness in the industrial sector.

The specific measures taken by the government include (1) selective enhancement of royalty rates and lump-sum payments; (2) modification of rules with regard to the period of agreement; (3) enhancement of limits of imports made for promoting technological upgrading and modernization under the Technical Development Fund; (4) import of select machinery and equipment "not domestically available" under Open General License (OGL)—that is, import without specific license—"for creation of new capacities in the export sector as well as to upgrade technology and improve the quality of products"; (5) fiscal incentives to encourage in-house R&D by the private sector firms; and (6) delicensing of several industries.

Although it is beyond the scope of this study to discuss in detail India's industrial policies, trade policies, and the policies of economic liberalization in the 1980s, it is important to underline a few significant changes in government policies following the announcement of the TPS. Recognizing that the excessive regulation and control of the economy—popularly known as the permit-quota raj—throughout the 1960s and 1970s had resulted in slow growth in the industrial sector,[31] technological lag, and industrial products not being internationally competitive, the government decided to introduce a series of measures of trade liberalization. The liberalization of the import regime, which began in the early 1980s, gave particular attention to the import of technology. In the 1982 *Import and Export Policy*—a Union Ministry of Commerce annual publication—the import of technology was for the first time given a separate category with a chapter of its own. The strategy of a liberal technology import was based on the belief that if the government simplified rules and procedures and liberalized inputs of foreign exchange to the Indian private sector for acquisition of imports of know-how, designs, consultancy, capital goods, and so on, it would upgrade Indian products to international standards.

A stable, long-term import-export policy was adopted in 1985 when the government decided to formulate import and export policy every three years instead of annually. The first three-year import and export policy (1985-88) liberalized the import regime further, "providing easy access to imports essential for maximizing production and exports." The second three-year policy (1988-91) provided continuity of the earlier policy. Encouraged by India's trade performance toward the end of the first three-year period, the policymakers carried the process of trade liberalization a step further by expanding the regime of OGL. In spite of a difficult balance of payments situation, 745 items were added to the existing OGL list, and the imports of capital goods were further liberalized.[32] Since the industrial policy of the Rajiv Gandhi government in the late 1980s was growth-oriented,

India concentrated on increasing production and generating employment, with a particular focus on the organized industrial sector. It was believed that by simplifying procedures and removing bottlenecks to technology improvement, India's industrial sector would grow and become competitive by international standards. The entry of foreign technology was made easy in the 1991 New Industrial Policy, which gave automatic approval for technology agreements and foreign investment (and foreign equity participation up to 51 percent) for most industries. Therefore, India has substantially strengthened its trade liberalization policy in the 1990s.

RESEARCH AND DEVELOPMENT (R&D)

India has recognized the importance of in-house R&D for the absorption of imported technology and for the development of new processes and products. To encourage the setting up of R&D centers recognized by the Department of Science and Technology (DST), the government started a scheme in 1974 that provides a number of fiscal incentives—for example, R&D expenditures being 100 percent tax-deductible. Such incentives have had a positive effect on the growth of R&D units in the private sector: The number of industries with recognized R&D centers has risen from 106 in 1973 to 930 in 1986. (Of this 930, 89 belonged to the public sector.) There has been a steady increase in R&D manpower employed by in-house R&D units. In 1975-76, about 13,000 R&D personnel were employed by about 400 units. During 1981-82, the number increased to over 41,000 for about 750 units, and by 1986 the manpower for 930 units had reached 45,000.[33]

India's expenditure on R&D and related science and technology (S&T) activities has grown rapidly since 1951, from the annual average of Rs. 4 crores during the First Five Year Plan period to Rs. 1,507 crores during the Seventh Five Year Plan period to the expected annual average of Rs. 4,000 crores in the Eighth Five Year Plan (see Table 3.6). As Table 3.5 indicates, the national expenditure on S&T activities has increased from Rs. 4.68 crores in 1951 to Rs. 173.37 crores in 1971 to 1,003.45 crores in 1981 to Rs. 3,303.55 crores in 1988, which represents 0.02, 0.47, 0.66, and 1.10 percent, respectively, of the GNP. India's allocation of resources to R&D and S&T activities, measured in terms of the percentage of the GNP, is higher than other NICs with the exception of South Korea and is comparable to many developed countries such as Canada, Australia, and Italy.[34] The difference in per capita R&D expenditure between India and most industrialized countries, however, is enormous. For example, India's $2.78 per capita R&D expenditure in 1984 was 57 times less than the average of $159 per capita for developed countries.[35]

Furthermore, India spent only 23 percent of its total R&D resources on industrial R&D, compared to 50 percent or more spent on nuclear energy, space,

Table 3.5
Trends in National Expenditure on Science
and Technology Activities

Year (March end)	S&T Expenditure (Rs. Crores)	As percentage of GNP
1951	4.68	0.02
1956	12.14	0.12
1959	28.81	0.23
1966	85.06	0.39
1971	173.37	0.47
1976	397.99	0.60
1981	1,003.45	0.66
1986	2,223.91	0.96
1988	3,303.55	1.10

Source: *R&D Statistics*, 1986-87 (New Delhi: Department of Science and Technology, 1988), cited in V. Govindarajulu, "India's Science and Technology Capability: SWOT Analysis," *EPW*, Feb. 17-24, 1990, p. M-35.

Table 3.6
Trends in the Growth of Science and Technology
Expenditure in India

Five Year Plan Period	Total S&T Expenditure (Rs. Crore)	Average Per Annum
1st FYP	20	4.0
2nd FYP	67	13.4
3rd FYP	144	28.8
4th FYP	375	75.0
5th FYP	1,381	276.2
6th FYP	3,716	743.2
7th FYP	7,535	1,507.0
8th FYP	20,000	4,000.0

Source: Same as Table 3.5

and defense research. In 1982-83, for example, India spent Rs. 286 crores out of Rs. 1,237 crores on industrial research, which was a mere 0.63 percent of the sales turnover. The level of expenditure has also differed significantly between public and private sector companies. According to the RBI Fourth Foreign Collaboration Survey, the average annual difference in R&D expenditure between the private and public sector companies was 1:4.

A number of empirical studies on technology transfer have suggested that the companies that did their own R&D received a better return on their technology import.[36] The government has recognized the importance of in-house R&D in accelerating meaningful absorption and adaptation of imported technology in the private sector, and has sought to bring production and R&D sectors in the country closer. Accordingly, in August 1986, it announced four stringent conditions for foreign collaboration agreement for technology payments of more than over Rs. 2 crores. First, it is now obligatory for Indian entrepreneurs wishing foreign collaboration to involve competent R&D personnel from within the enterprise, or from any other competent R&D institutions in the relevant area, in the process of technology acquisition from the negotiating stage. Second, the Indian entrepreneur will have to submit a time-bound program for technology absorption/adaptation/improvement (TAAI) within six months of the issue of the foreign collaboration approval. Third, it is compulsory for technology units registered with the Department of Scientific and Industrial Research to set up in-house R&D facilities or to enter into long-term consultancy agreements with any relevant R&D institution in the country within two years of receiving the foreign collaboration approval letter. Finally, the collaboration agreement to be executed by the Indian party and the foreign collaborator will not deny an indigenous R&D institution, identified for the purpose of examining the TAAI plans, any access to the production unit of the Indian enterprise.[37]

The government unfortunately has not strictly adhered to these conditions in technology transfer negotiations. The data on R&D in industry available from the Ministry of Science and Technology suggest a general trend toward stagnation in R&D efforts of the private sector in the 1980s: "R and D expenditure as a percent of sales turnover of firms in the private sector as a whole has declined on an average from 0.78 per annum during the period 1975-76 to 1979-80 to 0.68 in the period 1980-81 to 1986-87."[38] However, there seems to be some agreement among policymakers and academic analysts that India should raise its R&D- and S&T-related expenditure to as high as 2 percent of the GNP. A higher allocation of resources to R&D would indeed modernize India's industrial sector and make its products internationally competitive in a global economy.

TECHNOLOGY EXPORTS

A growing body of literature has emerged in the last decade considering NICs as suppliers of technology to other developing nations, and India has figured prominently in the debate. The pioneering studies of Sanjaya Lall pointed out that even though India was not a major exporter of technology by means of direct foreign investment (Hong Kong was the leader),[39] nor a major exporter of capital goods (South Korea topped the list),[40] among the NICs, India had emerged by the late 1970s as the largest exporter of industrial technology. Lall's comparative data on South Korea, India, Brazil, and Argentina reveal that India's main strength was in industrial projects exports, rather than product exports, where it leads the other NICs in absolute and deflated values.[41]

India's technology export is the most diversified and sophisticated and has the largest indigenous technology content among the NICs. By contrast, Brazil, which is more industrialized than India and is a bigger exporter of sophisticated industrial products, was "surprisingly weak in all forms of industrial technology exports, with the exception of disembodied service exports in relation to its manufactured exports."[42] The difference between the two NICs was due mainly to the fact that, whereas India emphasized self-reliant development through the creation of an S&T infrastructure and the development of indigenous technological capability, Brazil greatly relied on imported technology, which limited its technological development and self-reliance.

India's direct foreign investment abroad in the industrial sector, which has been on the rise in the last two decades, has taken mainly the form of joint ventures. Government restriction on the expansion of large industrial houses under the Monopoly and Restrictive Trade Practices Act (1969) has given an impetus to large business houses to invest abroad in joint ventures. The 1970s witnessed a boom in the setting up of joint ventures abroad, mainly by MRTP firms with a minority equity share capital. As Table 3.7 indicates, in 1982 there were 228 Indian joint ventures in 38 countries. The MRTP firms have remained dominant in direct foreign investment from India.[43]

India can provide a wide range of services to other developing nations including project studies and engineering, process know-how, erection, commissioning and setting up of units, training of local work force, and so forth. It can supply plants and equipment for industries such as textiles, cement, sugar, structural fabrications, power transmission lines, blast furnaces, thermal power plants, fertilizer plants, general purpose machine tools, and others. In the field of engineering, in particular, India's capabilities include the manufacture, supply, and installation of turn-key projects sharing technology and technical services.[44]

Among the NICs, India is an important supplier of capital goods and technology. It has developed a competitive position in the export of some intermediate and light capital equipment. Because India has 150 consulting firms, it can offer a wide range of consulting services to other developing countries. The UNIDO has recognized the strength of India in these areas and has encouraged many less industrialized nations to acquire "appropriate" technology from India instead of from the West.

CONCLUSION

The Indian government's efforts to develop S&T infrastructure and its restrictive policy frame for the transfer of technology has allowed India to develop technological capability not found in any other NIC. However, the strict regulation and control of the industrial sector (and the economy) until 1991 has resulted in poor industrial growth, technological obsolescence in many industries, and a decline in India's share of the total export in the world.

India has acquired industrial technology through a large number of technical collaboration agreements. In the first two decades of independence, the government followed a liberal policy and, as in other developing nations, DFI was the important mode of technology transfer. In the late 1960s, the tight regulation of technology import began, which lasted until the late 1970s. To make the country technologically self-reliant, the government preferred pure technical collaboration agreement to DFI, which allowed the development of indigenous technological capability. The strict regulations regarding technology transfer did

Table 3.7
Indian Joint Venture Abroad: Countrywise Breakup

No	Country	In Operation	Under Implementation	Total
1.	Australia	1	-	1
2.	Bahrain	1	1	2
3.	Bangladesh	1	-	1
4.	Botswana	1	0	1
5.	Cyprus	0	1	1
6.	Fiji	1	-	1
7.	France	1	-	1
8.	Gibraltar	-	1	1
9.	Greece	-	2	2
10.	Hong Kong	2	1	3
11.	Indonesia	11	4	15
12.	Kenya	8	4	12
13.	Kuwait	1	1	2
14.	Liberia	-	1	1
15.	Malaysia	27	1	28
16.	Mauritious	3	1	4
17.	Nepal	1	6	7
18.	Netherlands	1	-	1
19.	Nigeria	7	14	21
20.	Oman	1	2	3
21.	Philippines	2	-	2
22.	Saudi Arabia	3	3	6
23.	Senegal	-	1	1
24.	Seychelles	-	1	1
25.	Singapore	16	11	27
26.	Sri Lanka	10	13	23
27.	Sudan	-	1	1
28.	Switzerland	-	2	2
29.	Tanzania	-	1	1
30.	Thailand	8	4	12
31.	Tonga	1	-	1
32.	Uganda	1	-	1
33.	U.A.E.	9	2	11
34.	U.K.	9	3	12
35.	U.S.A.	11	3	14
36.	W. Germany	3	-	3
37.	Yugoslavia	-	1	1
38.	Zambia	-	1	1
Total		141	87	228

Source: India, *India Offers Technology* (New Delhi: India Investment Center, 1983), p. vi.

keep the cost of technology import down. However, the late 1970s witnessed the beginning of a period of relaxation of regulations. India's approach to reforms in the 1980s was incremental, but it changed qualitatively in 1991 under Prime Minister Rao, when his government accelerated the process of liberalization by radically liberalizing the import regime, industrial policy and foreign investment, and the trade and exchange rate policy.

India's five year plans have emphasized the importance of science and technology in the process of development. Although the plans lacked an integrated approach to development and technology planning, the planned expenditure on S&T has created a scientific infrastructure and technological capability that is unparalleled in the Third World. India's achievements in nuclear energy, space, and defense research are excellent. Because R&D in the private sector was found to be lagging, the government has given fiscal incentives to encourage R&D at the firm level. To modernize India's industries, the import of technology has been liberalized in the 1990s. India is an exporter of a wide range of technology, and it is least dependent on foreign-licensed technology. Although many industries are facing the problem of technological obsolescence, India's technological capability is the largest and most diverse among NICs.

NOTES

1. India, *Seventh Five Year Plan*, vol. II (Government of India: Planning Commission), p. 167.

2. Sanjaya Lall, "Technological Learning in the Third World: Some Implications of Technology Exports," in Frances Stewart and Jeffrey James (eds.), *The Economics of New Technology in Developing Countries* (London: Westview Press, 1982).

3. India, *Sixth Five Year Plan 1980-85* (Government of India: Planning Commission), p. 319.

4. India's annual growth rate in manufacturing, which was 7 percent from 1956 to 1966, declined to 5 percent from 1966 to 1982. See Isher Judge Ahluwalia, *Industrial Growth in India: Stagnation Since the Mid-Sixties* (Delhi: Oxford University Press, 1985).

5. M. R. Bhagavan, "Technological Implications of Structural Adjustment: Case of India," *Economic and Political Weekly*, 30, Nos. 7 and 8 (1995): M2.

6. Baldev Raj Nayar, *India's Quest For Technological Independence: The Results of Policy*, vol. II (New Delhi: Lancers Publishers, 1983), p. 107.

7. Sanjaya Lall, "Trade in Technology by a Slowly Industrializing Country: India," in Nathan Rosenberg and Claudio Frischtak (eds.), *International Technology Transfer: Concepts, Measurements, and Comparisons* (New York: Praeger, 1985), p. 50.

8. *Foreign Collaboration in Indian Industries: Fourth Survey Report*, pp. 129-130.

9. Indian Investment Center, *Changing Forms of Foreign Investment in India* (New Delhi: Indian Investment Center, 1982), p. 24.

10. Lall, "Trade in Technology", p. 51.

11. V. N. Balasubramanyam, *International Transfer of Technology to India* (New York: Praeger, 1973), p. 129.

12. After the enactment of the Patent Law—discussed in Chapter 5—patent protection was significantly reduced in the early 1970s. See Ashok V. Desai, "Indigenous and Foreign Determinants of Technological Change in Indian Industry," *EPW*, Special Number November, 1985, p. 2086. Also see NCAER, *Foreign Technology and Investment: A Study of Their Role in India's Industrialization* (New Delhi: National Council of Applied Economic Research, 1971).

13. J. L. Enos, "The Transfer of Technology," *Journal of Asian-Pacific Economic Literature*, 3, No. 1 (March 1989).

14. Ibid.

15. *The Economic Times*, November 6, 1986.

16. World Bank, *World Development Report*, 1982, quoted in Sanjaya Lall, "Trade in Technology," 1985, p. 49.

17. FICCI, "Some Questions Related to Import of Technology and Domestic R&D," Technology Sub-Committee, Federation of Indian Chambers of Commerce and Industry, New Delhi, August 1986.

18. K. K. Subrahmanian, "Technology Import: Regulation Reduces Cost," *EPW*, XXI, No. 32 (August 9, 1986).

19. Ghayur Alam, "India's Technology Policy and Its Influence on Technology Imports and Technology Development," *Economic and Political Weekly*, Vol. XX, Nos. 45, 46, and 47, Special Number 1985, p. 2075.

20. Ibid.

21. Lall, "Trade in Technology."

22. V. Govindarajulu, "India's S and T Capability: SWOT Analysis," *EPW*, Feb.17-24, 1990, pp. M39-40.

23. Lall, "Trade in Technology," pp. 52-53.

24. Planning Commission, Government of India, *The First Five Year Plan* (New Delhi, 1952), pp. 12-13.

25. See A. Rahman, "Evolution of Science Policy in India after Independence," in A. Rahman and P. N. Chowdhury (eds.), *Science and Society* (New Delhi: Center of R&D Management, CSIR, 1980).

26. India, *Draft Five Year Plan, 1978-83*. Also see F. A. Long, "Science and Technology in India: Their Role in National Development," in John W. Mellor (ed.), *India: A Rising Middle Power* (Boulder, Colo.: Westview Press, 1979).

27. The government established a number of policy-level bodies to guide science and technology programs. The Scientific Advisory Committee to the Cabinet (SACC) was established in 1956 to advise the cabinet in the formulation and implementation of the government's science policy. The SACC worked for about a decade under the chairmanship of Homi J. Bhabha. After Bhabha's death, however, the cabinet secretary became its chairman, and its style of functioning became more bureaucratic. In 1968, the SACC was replaced by the Committee on Science and Technology (COST), which had its own secretariat, and its members included economists, a few independent scientists, and industrialists. The COST was replaced by the National Committee on Science and Technology (NCST) in 1971, which produced the nation's first S&T Plan (1974-79) in 1973. In the early 1980s the apex organization of S&T underwent some changes again: SACC was restored in 1981; in addition, there is a Cabinet Committee on Science and Technology.

28. India, *Draft Fifth Five Year Plan—1974-79* (New Delhi, 1974), pp. 216-218.

29. For a critique of India's science and technology policy, see V. V. Bhatt, "Development Problem, Strategy and Technology Choice: Sarvodaya and Socialist Approaches in India," in his *Development Perspectives: Problem, Strategy and Policies* (New York: Pergamon Press, 1980), Ch. 6.

30. Text of Technology Policy Statement reprinted in *The Economic Times*, Jan. 4, 1983.

31. For two divergent explanations of the slow industrial growth in India since the mid-1960s, see Isher Judge Ahluwalia, *Industrial Growth of India: Stagnation since the Mid-Sixties* (Delhi: Oxford University Press, 1985) and Pranab Bardhan, *The Political*

Economy of Development in India (Oxford: Basil Blackwell, 1984).

32. See Charan Wadhva, "Import and Export Policy 1988-91: A Provisional Appraisal," *EPW*, June 25, 1988.

33. *The Economic Times*, Feb. 25, 1987.

34. See Surendra J. Patel, "Main Elements in Shaping Future Technology Policies for India," *Economic and Political Weekly*, March 4, 1989.

35. V. Govindarajulu, "India's S&T Capability: SWOT Analysis," *EPW*, Feb. 17-24, 1990, pp. M37-38. It is interesting to note that the nondefense R&D expenditure of the United States in 1988 was 1.7 percent of GNP compared to W. Germany's and Japan's 2.5 to 2.7 percent. See Lester C. Thurow, "Maintaining Technological Leadership in a World Economy," *MRS Bulletin*, 14, No. 4 (1989): 43-48.

36. According to one study, the companies that did their own R&D "unpackaged their technology requirements and imported only those components they could not generate economically or fast enough, they were better informed about the technology market before entering it as buyers, and they received greater benefit from technology imports in terms of their own product and process development." See Ashok V. Desai, "The Origin and Direction of Industrial R&D in India," *Research Policy*, 9, No. 1 (Jan. 1980): 75.

37. Ibid., August 29, 1986.

38. K. K. Subramanian, "Technological Capability under Economic Liberalization: Experience of Indian Industry in the 80s," in Yoginder K. Alagh et al. (eds.), *Sectoral Growth and Change* (New Delhi: Har-Anand Publication, 1993), p. 17.

39. It has been estimated that out of the total direct foreign investment of the Third World firms amounting to $5 to 10 billion in the early 1980s, the total stock of DFI of firms from India, Brazil, Hong Kong, and Argentina was over $2 billion. See Louis Wells, Jr., *Third World Multinationals: The Rise of Foreign Investment from Developing Countries* (Cambridge: MIT Press, 1983) and Sanjaya Lall, *The New Multinationals: The Spread of Third World Enterprises* (Chichester and New York: John Wiley & Sons, 1983).

40. In 1978, India exported capital goods worth $421 million compared with $1.5 billion for South Korea and $1.4 billion for Brazil. Argentina and Mexico, however, exported fewer capital goods than India: $407 million and $364 million, respectively. See Sanjaya Lall, "Trade in Technology by a Slowly Industrializing Country: India," pp.54-55.

41. Sanjaya Lall, "Exports of Technology by Newly-Industrializing Countries: An Overview," *World Development*, 12, No. 5/6 (1984), p. 475.

42. Ibid.

43. See Sebastian Morris, "Foreign Direct Investment from India: Ownership and Control of 'Joint Ventures' Abroad," *EPW*, Feb. 17-24, 1990.

44. India, *India Offers Technology* (New Delhi: India Investment Center, 1983).

4

The Structure of the Pharmaceutical Industry and Its Development in the Third World

The modern pharmaceutical industry is relatively young compared with other industries; it has grown rapidly worldwide since aspirin was introduced in 1899. The drug industry was stimulated by the advent of the new "wonder drugs," the sulfa drugs in the late 1930s and penicillin in the mid-1940s. The pharmaceutical industry before 1930 was a commodity business; the major drug companies were full-line houses manufacturing and selling a complete range of all the medicaments the pharmacists needed to fill the doctors' multi-ingredient prescriptions.

By the end of the 1950s, however, the pharmaceutical industry had transformed itself into an R&D- and advertising-intensive business. This transformation was brought about by a revolution in drug therapy made possible by new drug technologies. The discovery of sulfa drugs and penicillin was followed by other breakthroughs in the 1950s: tranquilizers, steroids, oral contraceptives, oral antidiabetic drugs, and cardiovascular drugs. Large drug firms grew rapidly. They concentrated on specialty products and discontinued the manufacture of hundreds of commodity items.

The growth of the industry has been phenomenal in the past three decades. It has been estimated that there are more than ten thousand pharmaceutical manufacturers around the world.[1] The vast majority of these firms are very small. Production has been dominated by a few large transnational firms in the United States, Switzerland, West Germany, Great Britain and, more recently, Japan. In 1970, the top 100 transnational firms produced about 90 percent of the total pharmaceuticals output, worth $50 billion.[2] The top 50 drug companies account for "nearly two-thirds of the total production, while the leading twenty-five firms account for about one-half."[3] Among nonmilitary industries, the pharmaceutical industry is highly research-intensive—the top firms spend about 10 percent of their turnover on research and development.[4]

In recent years, the U.S. drug companies have come to dominate international pharmaceutical production and sale. As Table 4.1 indicates, of the top 15 pharmaceutical firms, only three have their headquarters in Switzerland, two in West Germany and one in Japan, whereas nine are in the United States.

The concentration in the pharmaceutical industry can be further observed at the level of bulk drug (active ingredient) production. While there are many companies involved in the production and marketing of formulations, there is a high degree of concentration in bulk drug production. A UN study found that of the 650 bulk drugs manufactured in the United States in 1972, 500 were available from a single domestic source and, by 1975, "the concentration at the bulk level was even more extreme." For example, ascorbic acid (vitamin C) in dosage form is offered by more than 100 firms, but the entire output of the vitamin itself is produced by Merck, Pfizer, and Hoffmann-LaRoche.[5]

The pharmaceutical industry is highly visible because it is one of the most profitable industries in the developed world. The largest pharmaceutical companies are not nearly as large as giant oil and banking transnationals. For example, in 1981, the American Home Products Corp., the largest U.S. pharmaceutical company, had $4.1 billion in sales compared to Exxon's $108 billion.[6] However, the rate of return on investment and on equity has been higher in this industry than the overall manufacturing industry average. In the United States from 1958 to 1975, the average return on equity was 18.1 percent, ranging from a low of 16.7 percent in 1961 to a high of 20.3 percent in 1965 and 1966, whereas the average for all manufacturing industry in that period was 11.1 percent. In Britain, the return on employed capital for three leading drug firms in 1972 ranged between 22

Table 4.1
The World's Top Pharmaceutical Corporations, 1984-85

Company	Pharma. Sales ($ Million)	Pharma. as % Total Sales
Merck & Co. (U.S.)	2,657.8	74.7
Amer. Home Products (U.S.)	2,416.8	53.9
Hoechst (West Germany)	2,378.3	16.3
Bayer (West Germany)	2,192.8	14.5
Ciba-Geigy (Swiss)	2,156.9	29.0
Pfizer (U.S.)	1,891.0	49.1
Abbott (U.S.)	1,706.0	55.0
Eli Lilly (U.S.)	1,664.0	53.5
Bristol-Myers (U.S.)	1,586.6	37.9
Smith Kline (U.S.)	1,542.2	52.3
Roche (Swiss)	1,477.6	41.9
Sandoz (Swiss)	1,472.3	46.5
Upjohn (U.S.)	1,449.0	66.5
Warner-Lambert (U.S.)	1,409.0	44.5
Takeda (Japan)	1,297.8	56.7

Source: "Scrip Pharmaceutical Company League Tables, 1984-85," cited in OPPI Bulletin, Jan.-June 1986, pp.12-13.

and 45 percent: Beecham Group (41 percent), Glaxo (22 percent), and Boots (45 percent).[7] Even during the 1970s, when many industries, notably the U.S. auto and steel industries, underwent a period of profit squeeze, the pharmaceutical industry showed a consistent profit margin of 20 percent.[8]

The drug multinationals have maintained high rates of profit due, partly, to overpricing their products in the Third World. In Colombia, for example, prices for the tranquilizers Valium and Librium were found to be 82 and 65 times higher, respectively, than the estimated world market price.[9] In general, the industry has been successful in maintaining its high rates of profit because of technological innovation and monopoly patents.

Pharmaceutical production is overwhelmingly concentrated in a few countries. Of an estimated total output of $87 billion in 1984, the developed countries accounted for nearly 70 percent. The share of developing countries was a meager 10 percent and the other 20 percent was produced in centrally planned countries. Within the developing world, the distribution of production is quite uneven. Whereas Asia and Latin America produced 5.6 percent and 5.2 percent of world output, respectively, Africa contributed only 0.6 percent. Two-thirds of the total Third World production comes from Argentina, Brazil, Egypt, India, Mexico, and the Republic of Korea. Developing countries' share of world consumption is also quite low—only 13 percent compared to 86.2 percent for the developed world (including the then centrally planned economies), and per capita consumption varies a great deal from one country to another. As Table 4.2 indicates, the difference in drug consumption between South Korea and India in 1984 was 13:1.

THE PHARMACEUTICAL INDUSTRY IN THE THIRD WORLD

The pharmaceutical industry in the Third World represents a formidable challenge to policymakers. In the absence of adequate sanitation, nutrition, and primary health-care facilities for the bulk of their population, developing countries rely on pharmaceuticals as the first line of defense against a wide range of disease. A recent study reports that "pharmaceutical expenditures constitute around one-sixth of health expenditures in developed countries but one-third to one-half of the health expenditures in developing countries."[10]

Policy Options and Strategies of Developing Nations

In the pharmaceutical industry, multinationals have held a virtual monopoly on sales to the Third World. Given the crucial role that the industry plays in maintaining national health, most developing countries sought to regulate and control the industry. The regulatory efforts were taken at both international and national levels.

Table 4.2
Annual Per Capita Consumption of Drugs--1984, Selected Countries

Country	Figures in Indian Rupees
India	26 (rural 6)
Pakistan	43
Indonesia	42
Nigeria	70
Philippines	95
Taiwan	159
Turkey	165
Egypt	190
South Korea	346
Japan	1,650

Source: OPPI, Annual Report, 1985

In the last two decades, several UN agencies such as the World Health Organization (WHO), United Nations Industrial Development Organization (UNIDO), United Nations Conference on Trade and Development (UNCTAD), United Nations Center on Transnational Corporations (UNCTC), and United Nations Children Education Fund (UNICEF) have made significant contributions to the development of an appropriate drug and pharmaceuticals policy in the Third World.

WHO has been concerned for more than 25 years with the quality and safety of drugs in international commerce. Since 1978, its main organ, the World Health Assembly, has actively discussed the problem of developing appropriate drug policies. The technical concept of "essential drugs" was introduced, and a WHO action Program on Essential Drugs and Vaccines was established in 1981. The WHO expert Committee on the Selection of Essential Drugs has developed a list of 258 active ingredients as "essential" drugs and has urged developing countries to come up with their own list of essential drugs in accordance with their own needs and health policies. The then director general of WHO, Dr. Halfdan Mahler, has been highly critical of the activities of the drug multinationals and has accused them of carrying on "drug colonialism" in the Third World. While WHO's declared goal of Health for All by the Year 2000—adopted in 1981—seems difficult to attain, it has nonetheless made the developing countries more aware of the problems associated with the pharmaceutical industry and the ways they could overcome some of the problems.

In an effort to reduce prices for the developing countries, UNCTAD has advocated the idea of bulk purchase through either "centralising all drug imports within a single state buying agency" or buying through "organizations like UNICEF with an international drug procurement system."[11] Many countries in the Third World, notably Sri Lanka, Pakistan, and Bangladesh, have experimented with varying degrees of success with the system of bulk purchase by a centralized state agency. It has also been suggested that small countries may find it profitable to pool their drug imports with other countries. The concept of regional bulk buying, although not very successful, was tried by the Caribbean Community (CARICO-M), which started its pooled purchasing of formulations in 1977-78.[12]

The UN agency that has most actively been advising and assisting the developing nations in the development of the pharmaceutical industry is UNIDO. It has been providing technical assistance and holding workshops and seminars in various countries in order to disseminate information regarding transfer of technology and technical know-how between developed and the developing countries. More recently, UNIDO has tried to promote South-South technology transfer, that is, the less industrialized countries should acquire pharmaceutical (and other) technology from the more industrialized developing countries. An important step was taken by the United Nations Development Program (UNDP) when it organized the Technological Cooperation among Developing Countries (TCDC) conference at Buenos Aires, Argentina, in 1978. The conference led to the formulation of the UN pharmaceutical strategy to improve the developing countries' self-reliance in drugs and pharmaceuticals.[13] The strategy consists of four elements:

1. identifying a short list of essential drugs needed by the majority of a country's population;

2. promoting bulk purchase of drugs to reduce prices;

3. developing a local drug industry; and

4. developing policies and legislation for Third World countries on transfer of technology and foreign investment.[14]

These objectives of the UN agencies were further articulated by the Third World through the Non-Aligned Summit meetings—in the 1976 Colombo Conference and the 1979 Havana Conference of Heads of State or Government. Since the mid-1970s, the pharmaceutical question has been linked to the set of demands for the creation of the New International Economic Order. However, the efforts made by the international organizations have had serious limitations. Although they raised general awareness and made technical information available to many developing countries, the UN agencies lack enforcement and monitoring power.

The ineffectiveness of the international efforts to reduce the dependency of the Third World on the drug multinationals is evident by the fact that the latter still dominate the industry in most developing countries. In Mexico, for example, of the top 40 pharmaceutical companies, 38 are foreign-owned; of these, 35 firms have no national participation and their share of the national market is 68 percent.[15] In Argentina, although the pharmaceutical industry is characterized by a strong national sector, the industry is almost totally dependent on foreign supply of bulk drugs, since 95 percent of all active ingredients consumed are imported by both national and foreign-owned companies. In Egypt, the industry remains heavily dependent on imports for bulk drugs and chemical intermediates, although the government has moved steadily toward self-reliance in the production and delivery of drugs since the nationalization of the industry in 1962-63. Furthermore, since 1975, the Egyptian government has followed more of an open-door policy toward foreign investment, leading to the establishment of wholly owned transnational firms. Squibb, for example, established a manufacturing plant in Egypt in 1979.

Third World governments, policymakers, social activists, and radical academics therefore turned to national-level policy as a possible solution. Once the pharmaceutical question became politicized, it was given special attention at the highest political levels in the Third World. The pharmaceutical multi-nationals have been accused of dumping worthless or needlessly dangerous products, of bribing physicians and key government officials, of selling irrational drugs, of transferring inappropriate technology, and of hindering the development of indigenous technology. In order to regulate the activities of the multinationals more effectively, the developing countries turned to national-level policy. Their regulatory efforts were based on the objective of "the establishment of explicit bargaining structures involving specific criteria and policy instruments," which will allow the developing host country to "evaluate, negotiate, approve, regulate, and monitor TNCs operations."[16]

The effort to regulate the pharmaceutical industry was carried out more successfully by larger, more industrialized developing countries. In most cases, it was an effort on the part of the state to increase its bargaining power vis-a-vis the multinationals. The Sri Lankan experience of the establishment of a State Pharmaceutical Corporation (SPC) in 1972, which pooled procurement of drugs through global tendering for large quantities of drugs, did result in a reduction of the number of imported drugs from 2,100 to 600[17] and a drop in the nation's drug bill by 40 percent.[18] The government policy was clearly designed to stop the selling of "overpriced" raw material by the multinationals to their Sri Lankan subsidiaries.[19] These policies, however, were changed in response to the pressure exerted by the U.S. government just as the Sri Lankan government was about to nationalize Pfizer and, after the election of a nonsocialist government in 1977, the SPC was dismantled.

In Pakistan, the effort to introduce generic drugs and stop the use of brand names was not successful either. Introduced in 1973 by a left-wing minister, the scheme was not well conceived. The government had paid no attention to the questions of adequate testing of generic drugs, quality control, and re-education of doctors.[20] Faced with the serious problem of illegal imports of the branded drugs, due mainly to the unavailability of quality drugs in the country, the government soon abandoned the scheme.

The Bangladeshi drug policy and drug legislation, inspired by India's Hathi Committee Report, was adopted under martial law in 1982. The Bangladeshi policy went much further in regulating market structure than the essential drug policy advocated by the World Health Organization. Social activists, policymakers, and leftist academics in many developing countries have given strong support to the policy and have argued that other Third World countries should emulate the Bangladeshi rational drug policy. While the Bangladeshi experiment of establishing grassroots primary healthcare projects—Gonoshasthaya Pharmaceuticals Limited (GPL),[21] for example—were quite successful, the shortcomings of the policy were revealed shortly after the policy went into effect. Empirical studies suggest that the Bangladeshi attempt to rationalize the drug supply was overambitious as it led to a shortage of many lifesaving drugs. The rational drug policy of Bangladesh, therefore, became self-defeating.[22]

The experiences of the developing countries with either advanced pharmaceutical industry (UNIDO category IV and V countries—Egypt/Argentina and Mexico/Brazil, respectively) or with less-developed pharmaceutical industries (such as Bangladesh and Sri Lanka) suggest that despite all efforts to regulate and control the industry, the drug transnationals continue to play a dominant role in these countries. However, the international and national efforts have evoked some response from the multinationals. Recognizing that they had a "public image problem"[23] in the Third World, the multinationals sought to change that image. In 1981, the International Federation of Pharmaceutical Manufacturers Association (IFPMA) issued a "Code of Pharmaceutical Marketing Practices."[24] More important, drug multinationals in recent years have shown a willingness to be more flexible on questions such as the dilution of foreign equity and have agreed to increase their expenditure on in-house R&D activities. They have also shown sensitivity to the social problems in developing countries. However, they remain resolute in trying to maintain, and perhaps expand, their domination of manufacturing and marketing in the Third World.

There are pressing economic reasons why foreign firms are eager to expand in the Third World. They recognize the trend in the pattern of consumption of pharmaceutical products in the Third World and the developed countries: Whereas drug expenditures in the developed countries—already close to a saturation level—are likely to decelerate,[25] they are expected to increase by almost 50 percent in the Third World by the year 2000.[26] It is predicted that, by the turn of the century, one-third of the total turnover by international pharmaceutical firms will come from Third World markets. It is not surprising, therefore, that the Third World still remains an attractive area for the pharmaceutical multinationals. Yet, ironically, a few developing countries have succeeded in breaking the monopoly of the multinationals by revising their patent laws.

PATENT LAWS

Patent protection in most developed countries is granted for periods of 16 to 20 years—16 years in the United Kingdom and 17 years in the United States. In the pharmaceutical field, however, a distinction is made between process patents and product patents.[27] While the United States and Great Britain permit both, Switzerland and Canada permitted only process patents until 1995. Italy, from 1939 until 1978, permitted no pharmaceutical product or process patent at all. It is important to note that in most countries with strong patent systems, the law either omits compulsory licensing, as in the United States,[28] or provides for licensing only under extreme conditions.

Patent laws in the Third World have undergone significant changes in the 1960s and 1970s. The drug industry is considered vital in maintaining the health of a nation. But there has been a virtual monopoly of multinationals over this industry. In order to remedy this situation, many Third World countries—notably Brazil, Mexico, Colombia, and India—sought to revise their patent laws in the late 1960s and early 1970s. Consequently, the patent protection in these countries has been very weak until the passage of the Uruguay Round.

Brazil took the lead in 1969 by completely abolishing patent protection for pharmaceuticals. Such a radical step generated a widespread fear that in the absence of patent protection the country would not be able to attract foreign investment. Yet the actual foreign investment figures in the 1970s reveal that the Patent Law had hardly any effect on the flow of investment into the pharmaceutical industry—it rose from $113 million in 1971 to $646 million in 1979, making it "one of the highest growth rates of any industry in Brazil."[29] The Brazilian government also tried to limit the "evil" of the nonworking of patented inventions to public advantage by providing that the patent would lapse by itself or on the petition of any interested party if not expanded within four years of grant. After the enactment of the Patent Law, the United States retaliated against Brazil (and Thailand) because of its refusal to protect patents on American drugs.

Mexico's Law on Inventions and Trademarks, enacted in 1976, reduced the patent period from 15 to 10 years and provides that the patent will automatically expire if not exploited within a period of four years. Accordingly, the government enacted various laws—the Law on the Transfer of Technology (1972), the Law to Promote Mexican Investment and Regulate Foreign Investment (1973), and the Law on Inventions and Trademarks (1976)—to "increase domestic control of the industry."[30]

The Colombian government revised its patent law in 1967 and limited it to processes.[31] The duration of the patent protection was reduced to five years. In 1971, the government adopted the Uniform Regime for Industrial Property of the Andean Group, thereby imposing all the regulations incorporated in this document. Colombia also decided to remain outside the Paris Convention following a careful assessment of the costs and benefits of membership.

The Indian Patent Act of 1970 replaced a previous act of 1911 and granted patents for new processes instead of products—product patents, it was thought, would allow companies to gain a monopoly market by combining drugs and chemicals in different formulations. The patent was limited to a period of seven years in drugs and pharmaceuticals, and there was a provision of compulsory licensing. Furthermore, the law made mandatory a worldwide search of patent literature to establish the novelty of a product or process; in the past, patents had been granted for processes outdated elsewhere. The new law therefore provides a very weak patent protection in India.

The West, particularly the United States, expressed its displeasure with the Indian law from the time it was enacted. In the 1980s, the Reagan and Bush administrations demanded that the Indian government strengthen its patent protection laws. In May 1989, the Bush administration retaliated by excluding India from the trade "priority countries" list under the Super 301 provision of the 1988 Omnibus Trade and Competitive Act.[32] Although India resisted United States pressure in the 1980s, the Rao government's policy of economic liberalization in the early 1990s and India's decision to sign the Uruguay Round of multilateral trade treaty in 1994, despite the strong opposition in parliament from non-Congress M.P.s, intellectuals, and consumer groups, will make patent protection in the pharmaceutical industry stronger in the late 1990s and especially after the year 2005.

THE PHARMACEUTICAL INDUSTRY IN INDIA

The modern pharmaceutical industry in India is the largest and among the most developed of the developing countries. Although the foundation of the modern pharmaceutical industry was laid in 1901 with the establishment of Bengal Chemical and Pharmaceutical Works, and the two World Wars gave a boost to the development of the industry, the progress made under British rule was insignificant and India depended largely on imports from Britain, France, and Germany for its requirements of drugs and medicines. At the time of independence, pharmaceutical operation involved merely simple packaging and bottling; it could hardly have been termed an industry. Since then, progress has been substantial.

Starting from repackaging and formulations from imported bulk drugs, the Indian pharmaceutical industry has progressed to the integrated production of complex synthetic drugs and antibiotics involving high technology. The industry's present production covers a broad spectrum of drugs, including everything from simple headache pills to the most sophisticated antibiotics and cardiac compounds. The UNIDO has recognized these achievements and has classified the Indian pharmaceutical industry in category V, which means a near self-sufficiency in raw materials to start production from basic stages, a capability to produce bulk drugs belonging to a wide range of therapeutic groups, an endowment of competent developmental and process research, and an effective distributive system.

The capital investment in the industry has risen from Rs. 24 crores in 1952 to Rs. 650 crores in 1984-85; about one-third of the investment is in the public sector. The value of drug production increased from Rs. 10 crores (almost solely formulations) in 1948 to Rs. 445 crores in 1973, Rs. 1,376 crores (Rs. 226 crores bulk drugs and Rs. 1,150 crores for formulations) in 1979-80 and Rs. 2,204 crores (Rs. 337 crores bulk drugs and Rs. 1,827 crores for formulations) in 1985. The sales value of pharmaceutical production increased over 150 times in less than 35 years. However, India today accounts for only 1.7 percent of the world's production of drugs and pharmaceuticals even though it ranks eleventh (see Table 4.3).

The number of drug manufacturing units has increased from 1,643 in 1953-54 to an estimated 9,000 in 1986. Although the industry is composed of four sectors—foreign (FERA and ex-FERA) sector, private Indian sector, public sector, and small-scale sector—250 Directorate General of Trade and Development (DGTD) firms in the organized sector, both public and private, dominate the industry. Within the organized sector, the bulk of pharmaceutical production lies in the private sector where until recently the foreign firms have been dominant. In 1973, for example, 33 foreign-controlled firms supplied about 65 to 75 percent of the total pharmaceutical demand in the country.[33] The remaining 25 to 35 percent was shared by 116 large and 2,500 small manufacturing companies.

An important characteristic of the industry is that no single company has a market share of more than 10 percent. There are at least 50 different companies in the organized sector that share the market among themselves. As can be seen from Table 4.4, Glaxo (Glindia), which enjoys the highest sales for an individual firm, had a market share of 6.29 percent in 1981-82.

In recent years, however, the foreign sector has slipped from a position of dominance to that of a minor partner in the Indian pharmaceutical scene. The Indian private sector, on the other hand, has emerged as the largest segment of the industry, accounting for 52 percent of production capacity. Yet the foreign sector remains, at least in the area of technology, the most important and critical segment of the industry. The foreign sector has not only been a vehicle of large-scale transfer of pharmaceutical technology to India in the last three decades, but it is also expected to play an important role in the area of high-technology drugs and in the introduction of new chemical entities in the country in the coming years.

Table 4.3
World Drug Market in 1984 (In Million $)

U.S.A.	24,200
Japan	13,000
West Germany	5,400
France	3,900
Italy	3,100
U.K.	2,500
Canada	1,500
Spain	1,300
Brazil	1,200
Argentina	1,100
India	1,100
Mexico	1,000
South Korea	1,000
Total market	87,000

Source: OPPI Newsletter, August-Oct. 1985

Table 4.4
Major Manufacturers of Pharmaceuticals and Their Share in Total Production (Rs. crores)

No.	Name of Company	1977-78		1981-82	
1.	Alembic	29.15	(3.17)	44.84	(2.61)
2.	Boots	13.35	(1.34)	23.86	(1.39)
3.	Burroughs Wellcome	16.64	(1.81)	32.33	(1.88)
4.	Cadila	2.59	(0.28)	18.73	(1.36)
5.	Cynamid	17.27	(1.88)	23.35	(1.86)
6.	E. Merck	10.17	(1.11)	17.12	(1.00)
7.	German Remedies	12.01	(1.31)	24.34	(1.41)
8.	Geoffrey Manner	25.25	(2.75)	37.77	(2.20)
9.	Glaxo	65.44	(7.13)	108.17	(6.29)
10.	Hoechst	32.97	(3.59)	56.41	(3.28)
11.	Parke Davis	15.69	(1.71)	24.19	(1.41)
12.	Pfizer	38.31	(4.17)	46.33	(2.70)
13.	Ranbaxy	8.12	(0.88)	23.02	(1.34)
14.	Richardson Hindustan	13.89	(1.51)	20.12	(1.17)
15.	Standard Pharma	10.20	(1.11)	19.02	(1.10)
16.	Others	607.95	(66.22)	1199.35	(69.77)
Total:		918.00	(100.00)	1719.00	(100.00)

Note: Figures in parentheses denote percentage share of each company in total production.
Source: Adapted from P. L. Narayana, *The Indian Pharmaceutical Industry: Problems and Prospects* (New Delhi: NCAER, 1984), pp. 335-360.

THE POLICY FRAME

The growth of the pharmaceutical industry in India, like that of most other basic and heavy industries, has taken place within the overall policy of industrialization announced by the government from time to time, as well as its policy regarding foreign investment and collaboration. The beginning of economic planning marked the entry of foreign firms into several key industries, where it was found that indigenous effort would not lead to rapid development. The Industrial Policy Statement of 1948, which was the declaration of the government's policy toward the private sector, recognized that "participation of foreign capital and enterprise, particularly as regards industrial technique and knowledge, will be of value to the rapid industrialization of the country," and the First Five Year Plan specifically permitted foreign investment wherever "new lines of production are to be developed or where special types of experience and skill are required or where the volume of domestic production is small in relation to the domestic demand and the indigenous industry is not likely to expand at a sufficiently rapid pace."

In a policy statement made in Parliament in April 1949, Nehru explained the government's policy regarding foreign investment and collaboration as necessary for India's industrialization, not only because national savings were found to be inadequate for rapid development of the country but also because, in many cases, "scientific, industrial, and technical knowledge and capital equipment [could] be best secured with foreign capital." Furthermore, the Industrial Policy Resolution of 1956 had classified "antibiotics and other essential drugs" in category II, which allowed the private sectors to participate in the growth of the industry—although the public sector was to take initiative in the industries in this category. These pragmatic government policy pronouncements were based on the domestic capabilities in key industries in terms of financial and technological resources.

Until 1985, when 94 bulk drugs were delicensed, licensing was an important instrument through which the government controlled the development, diversification, and expansion of the pharmaceutical industry. The emphasis put by the government on regulation of the industry has varied according to the ideological orientation of the national leadership and the expected growth of the industry envisaged in order to meet the projected demand of drugs and pharmaceuticals. While in the mid-1960s and the early 1970s there was liberalization of the licensing policies,[34] in the late 1970s the government reserved certain products exclusively for the Indian public sector and certain products for the private sector. The government's policy of sectoral reservation announced in the New Drug Policy of March 1978 (to be discussed in detail in Chapter 5) had been at the center of debate in the Indian pharmaceutical industry.

Government regulation of the pharmaceutical industry is also to be found in the area of price control. Like many developed and developing countries,[35] the government of India has made a sustained effort since the early 1960s to fix the price of formulations and bulk drugs. Although introduced as an emergency measure in the wake of the Sino-Indian border war of 1962, controls on drug prices continued even after the end of the emergency in 1966. The Drugs (Display and Control) Order of 1966, which fixed the sale price of essential drugs at certain levels, was followed by the Drug Price Control Orders of 1970, 1979, and 1987. The latter fixed the prices of bulk drugs and formulations based on cost and allowable margin of profit. The list of drugs covered under price control has, therefore, changed several times.

The system of price control in India, which is highly complex and pervasive, has been a subject of controversy. In the 1970s, especially after the enactment of the New Drug Policy in 1978, there were strong supporters of the government policy, both in India and outside. In the 1980s and early 1990s, there was much criticism of the system of licensing, price controls, and other regulatory measures.[36] The emphasis of the government thus shifted from regulation to encouraging the growth of the industry. In the 1980s, the decision to delicense 94 bulk drugs (1985), the "new" drug policy (1986), and the price liberalization in the "new" DPCO (1987) were moves toward liberalization of the industry and efforts to increase productivity.

What has been the effect of government policy on the growth, profitability, and indigenization in the Indian pharmaceutical industry? Did government regulation and control of the industry in general, and of the multinationals in particular, reduce India's dependence on the multinationals? These questions will be addressed in Chapter 5. Whether the policy frame of the government had a positive effect on technology transfer or contributed to the development of the technological capability in the drug and pharmaceutical industry will be discussed in Chapter 6.

NOTES

1. Gary Gereffi, *The Pharmaceutical Industry and Dependency in the Third World* (Princeton: Princeton University Press, 1983), p. 169.

2. Anil Agarwal, *Drugs and the Third World* (London: Earthscan, 1978), p. 6.

3. Gereffi, *The Pharmaceutical Industry*.

4. Sanjaya Lall, "The International Pharmaceutical Industry and Less-Developed Countries, with Special Reference to India," *Oxford Bulletin of Economics and Statistics*, 56, No. 3 (August 1974): 146.

5. United Nations Center for Transnational Corporations, *Transnational Corporations and Pharmaceutical Industry* (New York: United Nations, 1979), pp. 37, 78.

6. "The 500 Largest Industrial Corporations", *Fortune*, May 3, 1982, pp. 260-273.

7. Lall, *The International Pharmaceutical Industry*, p. 155.

8. *Standard and Poor Industry Survey*, 1982, p. 431.

9. Richard J. Barnet and Ronald E. Muller, *Global Reach: The Power of the Multinational Corporations* (New York: Simon and Schuster, 1974), p. 158.

10. Aurelie Von Wartensleben, "Major Issues Concerning Pharmaceutical Policies in the Third World," *World Development*, 11, No. 3 (March 1983): 170.

11. Agarwal, *Drugs and the Third World*, p. 6.

12. For details regarding the limitations of the CARICOM measures see Lori Ann Thrupp, "Technology Policy and Planning in the Third World Pharmaceutical Sector: The Cuban and Caribbean Community Approaches," *International Journal of Health Services*, 14, No. 2 (1984): 189-216.

13. Supported by the Non-Aligned Movement. See David Carney, "Conditions and Perils of Nonalignment: An Interpretation of Events Since Bandung," *The Nonaligned World*, 2, No. 4 (Oct.-Dec. 1984): 609-617 and Ali Mazrui, "The Non-Aligned Movement: Changing Focus from Detente to Development," *The Nonaligned World*, 1, No. 2 (April-June 1983): 255-257.

14. Agarwal, *Drugs and the Third World*, p. 6.

15. See Gereffi, *The Pharmaceutical Industry*, pp. 53-61.

16. Constantine V. Vaitsos, "Government Policies for Bargaining with Transnational Enterprises in the Acquisition of Technology," in Jairam Ramesh and Charles Weiss, Jr. (eds.), *Mobilizing Technology for World Development* (New York: Praeger, 1979), pp. 99-100.

17. John Braithwaite, *Corporate Crime in the Pharmaceutical Industry* (London: Routledge and Kegan Paul, 1984), p. 271.

18. Sanjaya Lall and Seneka Bibile, "The Political Economy of Controlling Transnationals: The Pharmaceutical Industry in Sri Lanka (1972-76)," *World Development*, 7, No. 8 (August 1977): 677-697.

19. Ibid. Lall and Bibile have reported that subsidiaries of Pfizer and Hoechst were paying four to eight times more for buying tetracycline and chlorpheniramine, respectively, from their parent companies than what SPC paid for the same products from the same companies.

20. Agarwal, *Drugs and the Third World*, pp. 28-29.

21. For details, see Andrew Chetley, "Drug Production with a Social Conscience: The Experience of Ganoshasthaya Pharmaceuticals," *Development Dialogue*, No.2 (1985): 96.

22. D. C. Jayasuriya, *The Public Health and Economic Dimensions of the New Drug Policy of Bangladesh*, Pharmaceutical Manufacturers Association, n.d.

23. Braithwaite, *Corporate Crime in the Pharmaceutical Industry*, p. 244.

24. In 1981, the Council of the International Federation of Pharmaceutical Manufacturers Association approved its own code of pharmaceutical marketing practices and was voluntarily accepted by member associations of 48 countries, more than half of them developing countries. But the code did not include other important issues such as trade, prices, transfer of technology, and prescription and distribution. See *Development Dialogue*, No. 2 (1985): 1-4 and *Financial Express*, December 3, 1983.

25. Wartensleben, "Major Issues Concerning Pharmaceutical Policies in the Third World," p. 199.

26. Surendra J. Patel, "Editor's Introduction," to the Special Issue on Pharmaceuticals and Health in the Third World, *World Development*, 11, No. 3 (March 1983): 166.

27. Whereas a product patent is for a newly invented end product, a process patent "protects a new method of manufacturing an existing product."

28. The idea of compulsory licensing was strongly suggested by the Senate Subcommittee on Antitrust and Monopoly chaired by Senator Estes Kefauver. Senate bill no. S.1552 proposed that a manufacturer, instead of retaining patent rights for 17 years, would have these rights for only three years; "for the remaining 14 years the manufacturer would be required to license any qualified applicant to produce the drug, at a royalty not to exceed 8 percent of sales." The concerted lobbying by the Pharmaceutical Manufacturers Association (PMA), however, resulted in the removal of the section governing patents and licensing procedures from the bill. See Ronald W. Lang, *The Politics of Drugs* (England: Saxon House, 1974).

29. Gereffi, *The Pharmaceutical Industry*, p. 229.

30. Ibid., p. 224.

31. The countries granting only the process patent include Argentina, Chile, Egypt, India, Pakistan, Yugoslavia, Ghana, Cameroon, Central African Republic, Chad, Congo, Dahomey, Gabon, Ivory Coast, Madagascar, Mauritania, Niger, Senegal, Togo, and Upper Volta.

32. See Sanjoy Hazarika, "India and the U.S. Disagree on Patents," *The New York Times*, April 17, 1989, and *India Abroad*, June 2, 1989.

33. Lall, "The International Pharmaceutical Industry."

34. For example, the provision of the Industrial Licensing Policy of 1973 allowed both the MRTP and FERA companies to participate in the "core industries."

35. Among the developed countries, Great Britain and Italy have the system of "voluntary" price control. But the government does not regulate prices in the United States, West Germany, Japan, and Switzerland.

36. See, for example, Sanjaya Lall, "Pharmaceutical Industry: Economic Costs of Regulation," *Economic Times*, September 20 and 21, 1982.

5

From Dependence to Relative Self-Reliance in the Indian Pharmaceutical Industry

Dependency theory is generally critical of multinationals' operations in the Third World. Drug multinationals have been criticized for monopolizing a very profitable industry; repatriating huge profits out of the Third World through transfer pricing, royalty payments, and dividends; producing profitable lines such as cough syrups and vitamin pills instead of lifesaving drugs; making Third World doctors prescribe unnecessary drugs; spending three times more on sales promotion than on research; and not allowing the national sector of the industry to grow in most developing countries.[1] The bargaining school, on the other hand, believes that prolonged contact between the multinationals and the host country works to the advantage of the latter in the long run. It posits that after the multinational has remained in the host country for some time, a shift in the bargaining power of the two will be brought about, and the initial advantage enjoyed by the multinational will shift in favor of the host country.

The objective of this chapter is to test the validity of some of these propositions by analyzing the case of the pharmaceutical industry in India. In particular, the study will focus on an analysis of the monopoly enjoyed by drug multinationals in independent India and how the state succeeded in bringing about a basic change in the structure of the industry. The pharmaceutical industry in India has gone from a state of total dependence on transnational firms in the first two decades of independence to one of relative self-reliance in the 1980s and early 1990s, mainly because of the emergence of a strong national sector and the state control and regulation of the industry. A survey of the growth of the pharmaceutical industry in the last four decades, within the framework of government control and regulation of the various segments of the industry, will suggest that there is a real possibility of the development of technological capability in a research-intensive industry in India. At the same time, the case study will also indicate the limitations of the Indian state in influencing the behavior of drug multinationals.

FOUR PHASES IN THE DEVELOPMENT OF THE PHARMACEUTICAL INDUSTRY

The pharmaceutical industry in India has gone through four distinct phases, and it is only in the last phase that the national sector of the industry has acquired the capability to compete with the multinationals and that the country has achieved a degree of self-reliance not found in most Third World countries.

Phase I (1948-1968): Toward the Multinational Monopoly of the Industry

Most of the leading transnational drug companies established their trading and manufacturing operations in India in the 1950s. The monopoly of the new drug technology by a handful of transnational firms led to their entry into India either as subsidiary companies or as collaborators with Indian entrepreneurs. Although these firms began by importing the finished drugs and simply marketing them, they slowly moved, under the government's pressure, to the importation of formulations in bulk drugs and started processing them into tablets, capsules, and syrups.

The pharmaceutical industry in India has been broadly planned by the government, which has rigid control over every stage of licensing, import, collaboration, and extension. Because the drug market was expanding and the national sector was almost nonexistent, the government encouraged the trading and manufacturing activities of the foreign firms in the beginning. To meet the growing demand for drugs, the government granted "permission letters"/no-objection letters/registration certificates to 15 leading transnational firms, which allowed them to manufacture 364 items (360 formulations[2] and 4 bulk drugs) in the country. These permission letters were in the nature of "blanket orders which allowed the unit to manufacture drugs and pharmaceuticals. In many cases neither the capacities nor the drugs that a unit can produce were mentioned."[3] Such a liberal policy led to a substantial growth of the foreign firms. As Table 5.1 indicates, not only was the initial investment of most of these firms small compared to their turnover, but they also succeeded in building up large reserves and assets within the country. Glaxo Labs, for example, with an original equity of Rs.150,000, had a turnover of Rs. 120 million by 1973, and its reserves stood at Rs. 48 million.

The liberalization of licensing policy—and of the economy—in the mid-1960s, although short-lived, gave further impetus to the growth of the foreign sector. In 1966, the government, responding to the prevailing shortages of the various commodities, permitted drug manufacturers to diversify into the manufacture of "new articles." The following year, it also allowed them to expand production of licensed or registered capacities up to 25 percent without any amendment to the licenses under the Industrial Development and Regulations Act (IDRA).

Table 5.1
Growth of Assets of Important Units Having Foreign Equity

Name of the Firm	Original Equity Rs.	----Turnover---- Year	Rs. Lakhs	Reserves Rs. Lakhs
1. A.C.C.I.	35,34,000	1972-73	3316	298
2. Anglo-French Drug Co.	10,000	1973	227.69	49
3. Bayer(I) Ltd.	4,00,000	1973	1578	368
4. Beechem(I) Ltd.	1,00,000	1973-74	127	1
5. Boehringer-Knoll	15,00,000	1972-73	346.86	54
6. Boots Co. Ltd.	10,00,000	1973	778.43	126
7. Burroughs Wellcome & Co.	5,00,000	1973	419.10	103
8. Ciba of India Ltd.	3,00,000	1973	3,122.00	403
9. Cyanamid (I) Ltd.	1,50,200	1973	1,201.00	485
10. Glaxo Labs	1,50,000	1973-74	3,639.00	758
11. Johnson & Johnson	20,00,000	1973	489.36	92
12. Merck Sharp & Dohme	180,00,000	1973	1,051	93
13. Parke Davis Ltd.	87,50,000	1973	1,062	291
14. Pfizer Ltd.	2,00,000	1973	2570	823
15. Reckitt & Colman	30,00,000	1972-73	802.74	144
16. Richardson Hindustan Ltd.	2,000	1972-73	546	93
17. Roche Product Ltd.	100,00,000	1972-73	926	330
18. Sandoz (I) Ltd.	10,00,000	1973	1,556.42	489
19. Searle (I) Ltd.	60,00,000	1973	185.33	36
20. Wyeth Labs Ltd.	33,30,000	1973	393	63
21. Abbott Labs Ltd.	1,00,000	1973	824.07	159
22. C.E. Fulford Ltd.	4,00,000	1973	159.48	11
23. Dental Products of India	2,00,000	1973	19.00	8
24. E. Merck Ltd.	20,00,000	1973	477.28	34
25. Criffon Labs.	2,00,000	1973	243.00	30
26. Indian Schering Ltd.	83,500	1973-74	414	81
27. Roussel Pharm.	1,96,000	1973	233.66	49
28. Dupher Interfran	8,00,000	1973	324.86	64
29. Goeffrey Manners & Co.	1,000	1973	1,536.69	218
30. Hoechst Pharm.	20,00,000	1973	2,172.48	619
31. Martin & Harris	NA	1973	12	NA
32. Organon (India) Ltd.	97,54,900	1973	316	25
33. Suhrid Geigy Ltd.	7,20,000	1972-73	1,500.51	262
34. Synbiotics Ltd.	60,00,000	1972-73	313.80	99
35. Uni-Sankyo Ltd.	1,00,000	NA	NA	NA
36. Wander Ltd.	9,70,000	1973	127.77	17
37. Warner Hindustan Ltd.	70,00,000	1973	639.00	154

Source: Government of India, Ministry of Petroleum and Chemicals, *Report of the Committee on Drugs and Pharmaceutical Industry,* 1975; adapted from Annexure 1, pp. 108-109.

The structural imbalance that was taking place in the industry was emphasized by the government during the drafting of the Second Five Year Plan. It was found that the industry was formulating medicines solely from imported bulk drugs and there was no in-country production of new drugs such as antibiotics, antidiabetics and most vitamins. The Pharmaceutical Enquiry Committee was appointed in 1953 to examine the structural imbalance in the industry and to suggest remedial measures. The committee, which submitted its report in 1954, highlighted the importance of producing bulk drugs from basic stages and recommended that no licenses should be granted unless the production of basic drugs formed part of the license. This recommendation, along with those related to foreign collaboration, foreign capital participation, distribution, and prices, led to a rapid and diversified growth of the industry in the ensuing decades.

One of the suggestions of the government to the industry, based on the recommendation of the committee, was that the production of basic drugs could be phased out through penultimate stages to a total integration in a period of five years. Foreign firms, however, did not comply. The government was becoming increasingly aware of the reluctance of foreign firms to start manufacturing bulk drugs from basic stages in India, and it recognized the inability of the Indian private sector to undertake the manufacture of such drugs because of the Patent Law and for want of the requisite know-how.

The government therefore decided to establish a basic drug industry in the public sector. Although the Industrial Policy Resolution of 1956 grouped the pharmaceutical industry under the category (B) where both state and private industry could operate, it was the state that was to establish new undertakings in "Antibiotics and other essential drugs" with a view to accelerating their future development. The new industrial strategy adopted in the Second Five Year Plan further emphasized the important role that the public sector was to play in the industrial development of the country. In the Nehru-Mahalanobis strategy of industrialization, investment in basic and heavy industry was given the top priority. With a view to making the country self-reliant in antibiotics and other essential drugs, two public sector firms were established: the Hindustan Antibiotics Limited (HAL) in 1954 and the Indian Drug and Pharmaceutical Limited (IDPL) in 1961, with a total investment outlay of Rs. 56 crores.

Hindustan Antibiotics Limited, set up with the technical assistance of WHO and the financial assistance of UNICEF, started production in 1955 and was the first company to manufacture a number of lifesaving antibiotics from basic stages: penicillin, streptomycin, Sulfate, ampicillin, anhydrous, gentamicin. The other public sector firm, IDPL (which is the largest in the Third World, with a total turnover of Rs. 117 crores in 1973), was set up with Soviet technical and financial assistance. It has five plants: an antibiotic plant at Rishikesh, a synthetic drug plant at Hyderabad, a surgical instruments plant at Madras, a formulation plant at Gurgaon, and a drug and chemical intermediates plant at Muzaffarpur. The IDPL antibiotic plant, equipped to produce eight different antibiotics and with an initial installed capacity of 290 tons per year, is one of the largest in Asia. The synthetic drug plant at Hyderabad, having an initial installed capacity of 851 tons of sulfa drugs and other synthetic drugs, is again one of the largest of its kind in Asia. The company claims to meet some 40 percent of India's requirement for essential bulk drugs.[4]

The establishment of the two public sector firms for the production of antibiotics and bulk synthetic drugs marked the beginning of India's move toward self-reliance in basic drugs. It had the effect of reducing the country's technological dependence on foreign firms in the long run. The industrial strategy of the Second Five Year Plan was thus crucial for India's self-reliance in drug and pharmaceuticals and other industries. This, along with the policy of sectoral reservation announced by the government in the Drug Policy of 1978, made the Indian pharmaceutical industry much more self-reliant than that of any other country in the Third World.

Phase II (1969-1978): Effort to Curb the Monopoly of Drug Transnationals

As discussed earlier, the transnational firms had an extremely favorable climate in India, and they attained a position of dominance in the drug industry in the first two decades of independence. Their success could be attributed partly to the antibiotics and synthetic drugs that they introduced in the Indian market. However, the patent law concerning drugs prevented the Indian firms from entering into synthetic drugs. One finds, therefore, that by 1970, there were not more than two Indian private companies—Standard Pharma and Alembic Chemical Works—that had taken the initiative in the production of penicillin and other antibiotics. The RBI survey covering the period 1960-70 also shows that foreign subsidiaries were particularly important in the pharmaceutical industry.[5] Thus, the government's effort in the second phase was to curb the monopolistic position of the foreign firms by enacting legislations.

In 1970, the government withdrew the concessions it had granted to foreign firms in 1966 permitting them to diversify. Such diversification as had already taken place between 1966 and 1970 was required to be regularized by specific applications for "carrying-on-business" licenses (COB licenses). The Hathi Committee Report (1975) found that 12 foreign companies and five Indian companies had obtained COB licenses covering 215 formulations and 20 bulk drugs. More important, some of the most profitable drugs, such as Librium and Valium, the two largest-selling tranquilizers in the world at the time, were marketed in India under COB licenses. In January 1972, Indian firms were permitted to increase their licensed capacities on the basis of maximum utilization of plant and machinery and to diversify up to 100 percent. Furthermore, the government, by enacting antimonopoly legislation, subjected the expansion of foreign and large Indian firms to the new set of laws.

There seems to have been a sudden shift in the government policy following Indira Gandhi's split of the Congress Party and her massive electoral victory in 1971. In order to bolster Gandhi's leftist image, her government moved quickly to curb the growth and monopoly power of big business and industrial houses in general and the foreign firms in particular, by emphasizing the need to develop self-reliance and a strong national sector over economic considerations such as economies of scale and efficient utilization of scarce resources.

In the late 1960s, following the Report of the Monopolies Inquiry Commission (1964) and the Reports of Hazari (1966) and the Industrial Licensing Policy Enquiry Committee (1969), which reviewed the industrial licensing system, the government came to the conclusion that the existing licensing apparatus was not effective in controlling the "monopoly and concentration of economic power" in a few hands. As a result, the Monopoly and Restrictive Trade Practices Act (MRTP Act) was passed in 1969. This act sought to check the expansion of large industrial houses with gross assets exceeding Rs. 20 crores in interlinked undertakings or of dominant undertaking with assets of more than Rs. one crore (the definition of "dominance" being a market share exceeding 33 percent until 1982 and exceeding 25 percent since then).

The enactment of the Foreign Exchange Regulation Act (FERA) in 1973 put further restrictions on foreign equity holdings, which had to be diluted to a maximum of 40 percent of the total holdings except in the case of core sector industries (as listed in Appendix I of the 1973 policy statement). The Industrial Licensing Policy, however, included drugs and pharmaceuticals in the list of "core" industries, which allowed both MRTP and FERA companies to participate in the growth of the industry. Once again pragmatism prevailed over ideological considerations. The projection made by the planning commission that there would be a large expansion in the production of pharmaceuticals during the Fifth Five Year Plan—a 100 percent increase in the production of formulations and a 400 percent increase in the production of bulk drugs—underlined the importance of the active participation of all the sectors allowed by the government at this stage.

The pharmaceutical industry had become highly visible by the early 1970s. A few instances of overpricing by drug multinationals, reported in the press and journal articles,[6] led to an intense debate in Parliament between 1971 and 1973. Recalling the investigations made by the Kefauver Committee in the United States and the Salisbury Committee in the United Kingdom into the workings of the pharmaceutical industry, including the question of drug prices, suggestions were made that the questions of the transnational firms' stronghold in this industry, the performance of the public sector units, and the prices of locally produced drugs should be examined by an expert committee.

In response, a Committee on Drugs and Pharmaceutical Industry (popularly known as the Hathi Committee) was set up under the chairmanship of Jaisukhlal Hathi in February 1974. Although the committee had 14 members—including three influential Congress members of parliament: Yashpal Kapur, Vasant Sathe, and C. M. Stepan—it did not include any representatives from the industry. The committee's report, submitted in April 1975, is the most comprehensive document on the Indian pharmaceutical industry. It recommended a policy of sectoral reservation in order to provide a leadership role to the public sector and to foster and encourage the growth of the Indian sector.

Despite such regulatory measures, the growth of the industry was spectacular in the 1970s. There was between 13 and 22 percent turnover annually—and the foreign firms continued to dominate the industry.

Phase III (1978-1985): The Emergence of a Strong National Sector

The third phase witnessed a dramatic decline in the foreign sector's share of the industry and a rapid growth of the Indian private sector. The policy of sectoral reservation adopted in the New Drug Policy of 1978 gave the necessary protection that the latter needed in order to grow and to compete technologically with the foreign sector. The developments during this period must also be viewed against the achievements India had made in science and technology during 25 years of independence.

India had made sustained efforts in building a fairly elaborate institutional and infrastructural base in science and technology and had acquired indigenous capacity, which enabled the government to strive for a greater degree of self-reliance. For example, whereas India had a corps of roughly 375,000 scientists and engineers in 1956, the number had increased to a million by 1979 out of which 140,000 scientists and engineers were engaged in organized R&D.[7] Moreover, it had established a network of laboratories which allowed Indian scientists to undertake innovative and adaptive process and product research in a large number of disciplines (metallurgy, chemistry, electronics, medicines, etc.). In the pharmaceutical industry, private industry—not the CSIR labs—had already demonstrated that it had the capacity to develop process technology through in-house R & D if the proper environment were created by the government (e.g., by drastic revisions in the Patent Law). The government responded favorably and gave the Indian sector the necessary protection, which accelerated the growth and development of this sector.

The Indian Patent Act, drawn up by a joint committee of the two Houses of Indian Parliament in 1970, was an important step taken by the government to break the monopoly of drug multinationals. The act, which replaced the old Indian Patents and Designs Act of 1911, lowered the period of validity of patents in general from 16 to 14 years, and of patents in the field of food, drugs, and medicines to a period of seven years, and raised the scales of fees payable for renewing the patent. An important feature of the new law is the provision that grants patent protection only to processes and not products.[8] The rationale was that product patents allowed companies to gain a monopoly market by combining drugs and chemicals in different formulations. Indeed, the legislation, inspired by the reports of various enquiry committees,[9] diluted patent rights in an effort to promote local development work, process research, and manufacture. Other important provisions of the act were:

1. to broaden considerably the grounds for the issue of compulsory licensing;

2. to give the Controller wide powers in determining the terms of settlement;

3. to allow the unrestricted use of patented inventions by the government for its own purposes; and

4. to provide for the automatic endorsement of patents in the field of foods, drugs and medicines and patents for the methods or processes for the manufacture or production of chemical substances with the words "licenses of rights" after a period of three years from the date of sealing of the patent.[10]

The provisions of the act were thus far-reaching and reflected the thinking of policymakers in the late 1960s, particularly Prime Minister Indira Gandhi. Addressing the 34th World Health Assembly in Geneva in May 1982, she reiterated the stand she had taken more than a decade before with these words: "The idea of a better-ordered world is one in which medical discoveries will be free of patents and there will be no profiteering from life and death."[11] Although the analysts and policymakers do not agree on the pros and cons of the Patent Act, and the debate still continues, it will be useful to examine the salience of the act for the development of the national sector in the Indian pharmaceutical industry.

It is a widely accepted view that the enactment of the Patent Act has contributed significantly to the growth of the national sector—both public and private—in the Indian pharmaceutical industry. The managing director of a leading Indian company has described it as "the most significant milestone in [India's] aim to achieve self-sufficiency and self-reliance in the drug industry."[12] Indeed, the decade following the implementation of the Patent Act in 1972-73 witnessed unprecedented progress and development of bulk drug manufacture by both the private (Indian) and public sector drug companies. Using indigenously developed technology, the national sector of the industry began to produce a number of bulk drugs and their formulations such as ampicillin, amoxycillin, erythromycin, ethambutol, metronidazole, propranolol and trimethoprim.[13] By 1984, the contribution of the national sector of the industry had reached 65 percent of the drug formulations and 83 percent of the bulk drug production in the country, and this sector also contributed to over 65 percent of the exports of drugs and pharmaceuticals from India.[14] In 1983-84, this sector produced Rs. 295 crores' worth of bulk drugs as compared with Rs. 60 crores by the foreign sector and Rs. 1,000 crores' worth of formulations as compared with Rs. 760 crores by the foreign sector.

The growth of the national sector was further accelerated by the New Drug Policy (NDP) announced by the Janata government in March 1978. The NDP, which was based primarily on the recommendations of the Hathi Committee Report, divided drugs into three groups for purposes of reserving items for production by various sectors. Whereas the production of 17 essential drugs was reserved for the public sector and production of 27 items was reserved for the Indian sector, public and private, 64 items were open for licensing to all sectors, including the foreign sector (see Table 5.2).

The NDP imposed restrictions on the growth and expansion of FERA companies. Those firms not manufacturing bulk drugs and those producing "low technology drugs" were required to bring down their foreign equity holding to 40 percent; however, those foreign companies producing "high technology" drugs were allowed to retain foreign equity in excess of 40 percent subject to dilution formulas linked to expansion projects. In the case of product mix, the FERA companies were required to maintain a ratio of 1:5 in the production of bulk drugs to formulations, whereas the ratio for Indian companies was 1:10. Furthermore, FERA and MRTP companies were required to make 50 percent of their bulk drug production available to nonassociated formulators (the ratio being 40 percent and 30 percent for the public and Indian companies, respectively).

The NDP achieved at least one of its major objectives, namely, the growth of the national sector. In the post-1978 period, there has been an enormous growth of wholly owned Indian companies. The Operational Research Group (ORG) Survey of retail sales between 1980 and 1986 has consistently ranked five Indian companies among the top ten, with Sarabhai Chemicals ranking first or second in the last seven years. Other Indian firms such as CIPLA, Cadila, Lupin, and Ranbaxy have emerged as major pharmaceutical manufacturers since 1979-80. There has been, for example, a three-fold increase in the sales turnover of CIPLA between 1979 and 1985 (see Table 5.3). The progress that the company has made in the manufacture of bulk drugs and intermediates has been partly due to the government bias against foreign firms in granting industrial licenses for drugs even in the category open for all sectors. In the much publicized controversy over Glaxo's application for the manufacture of salbutamol, an antiasthma drug, the government decided to grant the license to CIPLA, which had indigenously developed the technology.

Another Indian firm, Ranbaxy Laboratories, doubled its sales turnover in three years (from Rs. 3,695 crores in 1983 to Rs. 7,099 crores in 1985), and the ORG survey has ranked it as ninth in 1983 and sixth in 1985. The company's leading product, Compos, a tranquilizer reserved for the Indian sector under the NDP, captured the market of Valium and Librium marketed earlier by the foreign firm, Roche. The drug output of Lupin Laboratories has recorded a similar growth pattern: Its bulk drug output alone increased from Rs. 3.74 crores in 1983 to Rs. 10.33 crores in 1985 and reached Rs. 30.50 crores in 1987.

The range of products manufactured by the Indian sector has also become increasingly sophisticated in recent years. A number of these firms have undertaken the production of bulk drugs and have started producing high-technology drugs, which until recently was the domain of foreign firms. For example, Standard Medical and Pharmaceutical Limited, a relatively new Indian company, announced in February 1987 that it would manufacture cephalexin, an advanced antibiotic not produced by any other Indian or foreign company.[15] Cephalexin is considered to be superior to many semisynthetic penicillins including

Table 5.2
The New Drug Policy

Items Reserved For Public Sector	Items Reserved For Indian Sector (S.No. Name of Drug)	
1. Penicillin	1. Ampicillin	15. Pethidine
2. Streptomycin	2. Doxycycline	16. Diethylcarbamazine-
3. Tetracycline	3. Sulfacetamide	Citrate
4. Oxytetracycline	4. Vitamin C	17. Xylocaine
5. Gentamycin	5. Nicotinamide	18. Phenylbutazone
6. Sulfaguanidine	6. Halogenated-	19. Oxyphenbutazone
7. Sulfadimidine	Oxyquinolines	20. Caffeine (Natural)
8. Sulfamethoxy-	7. Metronidazole	21. Vaccines & Toxoids
Pyridazine	8. Glybenclamide	22. Diazepam
9. Sulfadimethoxine	9. Chlorpropamide	23. Erythromycin
10. Vitamin B-1	10. Thiacetazone	24. Griseofulvin
11. Vitamin B-2	11. Sodium PAS	25. Piperazine
12. Folic Acid	12. INH	26. Phthalyl-
13. Quinine	13. Bephenium Hydro-	Sulfathiazole
14. Analgin	xynaphthoate	27. Tolbutamide
15. Phenobarbitone	14. Paracetamol	
16. Morphine		
17. Polio Vaccine		

Items Open For All the Sectors
(Including Foreign Sectors)
(S.No. Name of Drug)

1. Chloramphenicol	23. Chloropromazine	44. Framycetin
2. Neomycin	24. Caffeine (synthetic)	45. Bacitracin
3. Rifampicin	25. Xanthinol-Nicotinate	46. Cyclophosphamide
4. Sulfamethoxazole	26. Theophylline	47. Mepacrim
5. Sulfasomidine	27. Aminophylline	48. Imipramine
6. Sulfamoxole	28. Ephedrine	49. Amitriptyline
7. Vitamin B-12	29. Nitrofurantoin	50. Diphenyl
8. Vitamin A	30. Furazolidone	Hydantoin
9. Vitamin B-6	31. Chloroquine	51. Methyl Dopa
10. Vitamin D-3	32. Nitrofurazone	52. Triamcinolone
11. Vitamin K	33. Succinylcholine	53. Phenyl Ephedrine
12. Panthenols	Chloride	54. Salbutamol
13. Diloxamide-	34. Hydrochlorothiazide	55. Oxytocin
Furoate	35. Clofazimine	56. Rutin
14. Insulin	36. DDS (Dapsone)	57. Prenylamine
15. Ethambutol	37. Prednisolone	Lactate
16. Primaquine	38. Dexamethasone	58. Thioridazine
17. Amodiaquine	39. Betamethosone & all other	59. Phenothiazine
18. Chlorpheniramine	Corticosteroids and Hormones	60. Allopurinol
19. Aspirin incl.	40. Ibuprofen	61. Trimethoprim
Salicylic Acid	41. Dextropropoxyphene	62. Fursemide
20. Indomethacin	42. Thiabendazole	63. Sulfadiazine
21. Pheniramine	43. Tetramisole	64. Sulphaphenazole
22. Procaine		

Source: India, Ministry of Chemicals and Fertilizer, *New Drug Policy*, 1978.

Table 5.3
CIPLA Sales, 1979-80 to 1984-85

Year	Rs. Crores	Percentage increase over previous year (of pharmaceutical division)
1979-80	10.43	40
1980-81	13.35	29
1981-82	16.5	32
1982-83	20.16	25
1983-84	25.35	25.7
1984-85	33.21	

Source: Compiled from the *Bombay Stock Exchange Official Directory.*

ampicillin and amoxycillin in its efficacy in treating penicillin-resistant infections and gastrointestinal disorders. The technology of this drug has been indigenously developed by the scientists of Standard Medical, which indicates the maturity attained by this sector.

Government policy has had a positive effect on the outflow of foreign exchange because of remittances and the import of raw materials. The multinational companies have been criticized for taking more out of the Third World by way of profits than they bring in as investable capital. It would therefore be useful to compare the foreign exchange earnings of the multinational firms through exports with their remittances abroad by way of dividends. Table 5.4 reveals that the foreign exchange earnings of the international companies located in India totaled more than three times their remittances by way of dividends, which was about Rs. 8 crores per annum. For an earlier period (1970-75), the Hathi Committee Report had found the remittance of profits by multinationals to be Rs. 5 crores annually, which was "less than the actual exports by firms having foreign equity of more than 50 percent."[16]

The government's introduction of the system of "drug canalization"—the importation of bulk drugs through the use of a government agency, the state Chemical and Pharmaceutical Corporation (CPC), in order to prevent transfer pricing and to ensure a reliable supply of raw materials to indigenous manufacturers at fair prices[17]—further curtailed one of the worst abuses that multinationals have been accused of practicing in most Third World countries. The CPC started importing essential raw materials on a bulk purchase basis, pooled them with the same raw materials produced domestically by the public sector company (IDPL), and distributed the pooled stock to domestic manufacturers at a pooled (fair) price. The system, which worked well according to most industry analysts, was designed to counter the transfer pricing methods used by drug multinationals importing active ingredients and drug intermediates from parent companies. These constraints imposed by the government on the behavior of drug multinationals in India hardly resemble the situation found in most Third World countries. Case studies of the multinational drug firms in the Third World have shown weaker government regulations in a number of African and Latin American countries.[18] A recent study of Mexico's steroid industry suggests that foreign control of the

Table 5.4
Export and Remittances of International Drug Companies (Rs. in Lakhs)

	1979	1980	1981
Export	2,909.52	2,541.50	2,514.43
Remittances	813.55	786.64	789.16
Net Gain	2,095.97	2,754.86	2,725.27

Source: Minister's Answer to Lok Sabha unstarred Question No. 2570 on August 3, 1982 (for remittances), *Annual Reports* of International Companies and Basic Chemicals, Pharmaceuticals and Cosmetics Export Promotion Council (for export).

industry has wider implications for the country; it "restrict[s] the choice among local development options."[19]

In the last decade there has been a rapid decline in the shareholding of the transnational subsidiaries. A comparison of the foreign shareholding in the period before and after the enactment of FERA/NDP is quite revealing. The official statistics indicate that up to March 1964, over half the foreign subsidiaries operating in India had a 100 percent foreign ownership, which remained as high as one-third of all the subsidiaries between 1964 and 1970. In 1974, a year after the enactment of the FERA, the total number of drug companies holding foreign equity was 66, of which 10 had 100 percent equity holding, 24 held 50 to 59 percent equity and 15 held 40 to 50 percent. The number of companies holding equity below 40 percent was only 17. As late as 1978, when the NDP was announced, there were 31 FERA companies. By contrast, by the late 1980s, there were only half a dozen FERA companies—Bayer, Johnson & Johnson, Roche, Wyeth, IEL and Sandoz—in the drug sector.[20] There was also a significant decline in the market shares of the FERA and ex-FERA companies—to be discussed later in this chapter. Therefore, the foreign sector has been reduced to a position of minor partner in the Indian drug and pharmaceutical industry.

Phase IV (1985-1995): The Growing Competitiveness in the Industry

The above discussion suggests that by the mid-1980s the pharmaceutical industry in India had grown into a vertically integrated manufacturing enterprise producing almost all essential drugs and meeting the country's requirements of formulations in full and of bulk drugs very substantially. Moreover, the Indian pharmaceutical industry was no longer dominated by multinationals, which was unquestionably due to the New Drug Policy and the Patent Law. Do these developments in the pharmaceutical industry provide enough evidence to support the dependency hypothesis that states intervention and regulation of an industry in the Third World would not only reduce dependence on foreign multinationals but also facilitate the growth of the national sector in the industry? As the following discussion will suggest, it would be a mistake to conclude that India has succeeded fully in overcoming its dependence on drug multinationals. The situation is much more complex than what dependency theory would have us believe about the possibility of "dependency reversal" due to state intervention. Nor does the Indian case fully support the proposition of the bargaining school that states prolonged contact with the multinationals necessarily results in increased bargaining for the host country. On the one hand, the analysis in the previous section partially supports the hypothesis that the regulation and control of the multinationals will allow the growth of the national sector and eventually reduce dependence on the multinationals. On the other hand, the inadequate production of drugs in India in the last decade and the liberalization in price increases, delicensing, and broad-banding[21] to encourage market economy, and India's signing of the Uruguay Round with its controversial TRIPS provisions, will suggest that in the Third World there is a definite limit to state intervention and control of an industry that is highly research-intensive and in which there is a high level of product obsolescence.

The government's decision to delicense 94 bulk drugs and related formulations in 1985 brought an end to the sectoral reservation system introduced in the New Drug Policy in 1978. While the NDP did result in the growth of the national (private) sector of the industry and the Drug Price Control Order (DPCO) of 1979 made the price of drugs in India among the lowest in the Third World,[22] they also had many negative consequences for the industry. The most important among them was the consistent shortfalls in the level of production of drugs, especially essential drugs, in the years following the implementation of the DPCO.

The DPCO brought under its control the price of 347 bulk drugs, of which about 225 were domestically produced. It divided the price-controlled formulations into four categories.[23] Categories I and II consisted of essential drugs, and the markups—which included distribution cost, promotional expenses, trade commission, and the manufacture's margin—were fixed at 40 percent and 55 percent, respectively. Category III formulations, considered less essential, carried a markup of up to 100 percent, and category IV formulations were outside price control. It has been estimated that "4,000 formulations, marketed in 25,000-odd packs" were brought under the control of the 1979 DPCO.[24]

The drug manufacturers, particularly the FERA and ex-FERA companies, responded by diverting their production into nonessential and decontrolled products, thereby flooding the Indian market with category IV formulations such as "unnecessary" vitamins, tonics, mineral supplements, and cough and cold preparations, which are top-selling drugs and account for a large percentage of the total market for drugs in the country.[25] It is not surprising, therefore, that by the early 1980s, the Indian pharmaceutical industry was producing between 40,000 and 60,000 formulations, most of which were considered superfluous and some harmful.[26] As Table 5.5 indicates, the multinationals' share of the production of simple formulations far exceeded that of the national sector. Discussing the proliferation of drugs in India, a commentator observed in a recent article that "backed by an aggressive advertising and marketing campaign, the drug companies have

Table 5.5
Comparative Position of Contributions of MNCs (FERA and ex-FERA) and National Sector in Critical and Noncritical Areas (Rs. crores)

	Top 20 Companies			Top 85 Companies		
	Total (20)	MNCs (12)	National (8)	Total (85)	MNCs (36)	National (49)
Total turn-over	713	420	293	1,450	734	716
A. Turnover in critical areas like antibiotics, etc.	242 (100%)	92 (38%)	150 (62%)	463 (100%)	163 (35%)	300 (65%)
B. Turnover in simple areas like vitamins, etc.	202 (100%)	147 (73%)	55 (27%)	377 (100%)	245 (65%)	132 (35%)

Source: ORG Survey.

successfully promoted the concept of a pill for every ill, even if imaginary."[27] This has resulted in the shortfall in production of several essential drugs such as antibiotics, sulfas, analgesics, corticosteroids, anti-T.B. drugs, antimalarials, cardiovascular drugs, and anesthetics.

The total imports have increased from Rs. 16.14 crores in 1970-71 to Rs. 162.16 crores in 1983-84. Imports of bulk drugs in the same period have gone up from Rs. 11.52 crores to Rs. 123.06 crores, and the proportion of bulk drugs in total imports is around 75 percent since 1980.[28] The government objective of self-sufficiency in drug production was thus far from being realized. According to many analysts, this situation came about mainly because of the new pricing policy of the government. Nitya P. Anand, the former director of the Central Drug Research Institute (CDRI), Lucknow, was one of the vocal opponents of the government pricing policy. He believed that the market forces alone, not price control, could bring the prices down. Therefore, he argued that "major changes were needed in the existing pricing policy, as the low mark-up was unrealistic."[29]

From the beginning there were skeptics within the government who doubted the usefulness of the policy of price control. On the eve of the announcement of the DPCO, Nitya Anand sent a long telegram to the concerned ministry (the Ministry of Petroleum and Chemicals) urging the government not to announce the DPCO in 1979.[30] As the Director of CDRI and a consultant to the UNIDO and other international agencies for many years, Anand had actively participated in the formulation of the DPCO and was dissatisfied with its provisions, especially with markups in category I and II drugs. The reservations expressed by him and many others were not unfounded. As it turned out, the critics of the NDP proved to be more farsighted than the supporters of the policy. The implementation of the DPCO soon resulted in the distortion of the production of essential drugs. Due to the serious shortfalls in production, the Sixth Five Year Plan targets had to be revised downwards—to Rs. 500 crores from Rs. 665 crores for bulk drugs and to Rs. 1,950 crores from Rs. 2,400 crores for formulations—and even the revised plan targets were not achieved.[31] The magnitude of the shortfall in production in the Sixth Five Year Plan period was quite serious compared to the production figures of the Fifth Five Year Plan; the latter had not only attained the production target of bulk drugs but it also exceeded the target by 57 percent in formulations, mainly because of the high tempo of growth produced by the industry between 1975 and 1979.

The production of the wholly owned Indian private companies was far below the target. Out of 27 items reserved for them, production of 19 bulk drugs had been inadequate to meet the country's total requirements in the early 1980s. The shortfalls in production were not only in the private sector—the record of the public sector had been far from satisfactory. The production data on different sectors of the industry further reveal that of the 17 drugs reserved for the public sector, the production of almost all of them had been below the targets set for them, and in the cases of three reserved items—morphine, polio vaccines and sulfamethoxy-pyridazine—production had not even commenced. The public sector, in general, was also suffering from high cost of production mainly because of technological obsolescence—a subject to be addressed in the following chapter.

Public discussion of the New Drug Policy and the DPCO (1979) started shortly after they went into effect. The government started receiving complaints from the industry and consumers, and several MPs belonging to both the ruling party and the opposition parties started raising questions in Parliament regarding the unavailability of many essential drugs, lower capacity utilization by many companies, and the proliferation of "irrational drugs" in the country. The government responded by setting up the National Drug and Pharmaceuticals Development Council (NDPDC) in 1983 for the purpose of reviewing the working of the drug policy of 1978 and to suggest necessary changes toward formulating a new policy. The main objective was to find ways to increase the production and ensure availability of essential and lifesaving drugs in abundance. NDPDC, which had representation from the industry but not from people and consumer groups, submitted a report in 1984, which formed the basis of the 1985 delicensing decision of the government and the 1986 drug policy.

Among the various areas of the drug policy, the council paid special attention to the operation of price controls. It recognized that the pricing system was distorting the production pattern because of the shift in the production away from the more essential category I and II formulations, which carry a lower markup. The 1984 NCAER study also found that the pricing policy of the government was the major impediment to the growth of the industry. Based on the data collected from 23 companies, the study concluded that the break-even markup of the sample units ranged from 63.3 percent in 1978 to 62.5 percent in 1980. Thus the mark-up prescribed by the DPCO (1979) for certain categories of formulations

(I and II) was lower than the break-even markup.[32]   On the question of the government's pricing policy, therefore, there emerged a consensus in the industry, and throughout the early 1980s there was an intense lobbying effort on the part of both the national sector (through IDMA—Indian Drugs Manufacturers Association) and the multinationals (through OPPI—the Organization of the Pharmaceutical Producers of India) to change the existing drug policy. Both sectors of the industry have argued vigorously that the profitability in the industry had been declining and was at an all-time low in 1985-86. As Table 5.6 suggests, the profitability of the industry as a whole had decelerated rather sharply from 15.47 percent in 1969-70 to just 4.0 percent in 1985-86.

The concerted lobbying by the industry coupled with the shortfalls in the production of essential drugs led to the revision of the drug policy announced by the government in December 1986. This revision raised the markup—called Maximum Allowable Post Manufacturing Expenses (MAPE), the difference between the cost of production and the final selling price—on a small number of essential drugs from rather unattractive levels (40 and 55 percent) to a profitable 75 to 100 percent and cut the categories under which drugs are grouped from three to two. According to the 1986 Drug Policy, whereas for the FERA companies the ratio of bulk drugs to formulations had been raised from 1:5 to 1:4, the ex-FERA companies were treated for the first time as national companies. In order to liberalize the industry, broadly in accordance with the general liberalization of the

Table 5.6
Profitability in the Pharmaceutical Industry

Year	Profitability before Tax as Percentage of Sales
1969-70	15.47
1971-72	10.19
1972-73	8.53
1974-75	10.7
1975-76	10.4
1977-78	11.7
1978-79	12.0
1978-80	12.4
1980-81	8.8
1981-82	8.0
1982-83	7.5
1983-84	6.7
1984-85	5.8
1985-86	4.0

Sources:	1969-70 to 1973-74:	Hathi Committee Report
	1974-75 to 1980-81:	RBI Bulletins
	1981-82 to 1983-84:	NCAER Study
	1984-85:	A. F. Ferguson Survey
	1985-86:	OPPI estimates

economy, the government decided to dismantle physical controls. The decision taken under the liberalized Drugs (Price Control) Order (DPCO) of August 1987 to slash the number of bulk drugs and their formulations governed by price controls by more than half—from 371 to 166—was a move in that direction.

These changes in the government policy were made primarily to encourage investment in the industry in order to meet the projected demand of drugs by the turn of the century, as computed by IDMA, NCAER, and the planning commission. NCAER has estimated the demand for drugs by the year 2000 at Rs. 16,000 crores. To meet this projected demand, it was thought that the industry must grow at an annual rate of 15 to 20 percent. With the public sector out of the reckoning, the government had very little choice but to attract the private sector "with the carrot of higher profits being the lure for increased investment and production."[33]

However, it would be a mistake to conclude that there is no effective control of the industry by the government. Based on a survey conducted by ORG[34] in 1987, it was estimated that 72.8 percent of the formulations market will remain under price controls, a reduction of just 3.2 percent from the old DPCO. It is a testimony to the effectiveness of the pressure exerted by consumer groups, intellectuals, and many experts in the field of community health and social medicine who wanted to maintain the effective control of the government over the industry.

CONTRIBUTION OF THE NATIONAL SECTOR VS. THE MULTINATIONALS

In recent years, the wholly owned Indian companies have emphasized the contribution made by the national sector, which includes the public, private, and small-scale industry companies as compared with the international companies (both FERA and ex-FERA). They emphasize that the national sector has achieved all-around growth in the production of bulk drugs and formulations while the contribution of the international companies in the production of formulations has been quite disproportionate to their production of bulk drugs. Such claims are supported by the growth figures of the private national sector of the industry.

The senior managers and the managing directors of the two leading national companies I interviewed (CIPLA and Ranbaxy) were emphatic in pointing out the positive effect of the Patent Law and the sectoral policy of the government on the growth of the private national sector of the industry. In general, they argued that the national sector, including the public sector, has made the country "not only self-sufficient in a number of essential and life-saving drugs such as Ampicillin, Sulphamethoxazole, Trimethoprim, Metronidazole, Ethambutol, etc., but has also helped India emerge as a major exporter of these drugs the world over."[35] The international companies, on the other hand, claim that their contribution to the development of the industry is crucial because they have brought to India the latest drug technology from the parent companies and, in many cases, without paying any royalty or technical fee.[36] These competing claims, however, are not mutually exclusive. In fact, there is enough empirical evidence cited by both in support of their claims.

The role of the government's sectoral policy in the growth of the national sector has already been noted. However, a few important developments must be underscored. By 1986, the national sector was contributing about 83 percent of the bulk drug production, of which 60 percent was by the private national sector. The country has thus become self-sufficient in a number of bulk drugs, and some of these drugs are now exported to sophisticated Western markets. Some of the large Indian companies such as Sarabhai Chemicals, Unichem, Alembic, Cadila, CIPLA, and Ranbaxy have grown to the extent of successfully competing with the very best of the international companies in terms of the quality, quantity, and efficacy of drugs manufactured. Many of these companies have their factories approved by the U.S. FDA so that they could export their products to the markets of the developed countries. A few national sector companies, notably Sarabhai Chemicals and IDPL, have been selling turnkey plants and technical and training services to other developing countries.

In the manufacture of formulations, the share of the Indian sector increased from 58.29 percent in 1976-77 to 70.61 percent in 1984-85, while that of the foreign sector declined from 41.71 percent to 29.39 percent over the same period.[37] Compulsory licensing under the Patent Law, as already discussed, was largely responsible for the progress made by the Indian private sector. For the first time it became possible for the Indian companies to manufacture drugs legally although they were still under patent in the developed countries by paying not more than 4 percent royalty on total sales to the original patent-holder. A number of lifesaving drugs still under patent in the West, such as rifamycin (an anti-T.B. drug) and salbutamol (an antiasthma drug), are now being manufactured by Indian companies from basic stages. Such possibilities were unthinkable until the revised Patent Law went into effect in 1973.

The data on growth of the industry further reveal that the production of bulk drugs has increased at a rate higher than the rate of growth in production of formulations. The rate of growth of bulk drugs between 1970 and 1984 is 19.5 percent while that of formulations is only 12.5 percent.[38] This is mainly because the formulations market is highly competitive and the Indian manufacturers find it difficult to compete with the brand name drugs marketed by international firms. As a result, a number of Indian private sector units, both in the organized and unorganized sectors, have concentrated on the production of bulk drugs.[39]

Notwithstanding the growing share of the national sector in the production of both bulk drugs and formulations, the performance data of the Indian sector between 1980-81 and 1984-85 reveal that in the reserved categories (i.e., items reserved for both the public sector and the Indian sector) it failed to achieve the targets set in this regard. As Tables 5.7 and 5.8 suggest, for four consecutive years, the national sector's production of most of the essential bulk drugs under categories I and II was consistently far below the target.

Another problem with the national sector has been the horizontal growth of the small-scale sector. According to the DPCO (1979) small-scale companies with annual turnovers of up to Rs. 5 million were exempt from price control. Although the price control did not directly apply to the small-scale drug manufacturers, they were brought under the scheme indirectly by being required to follow the "leader price" principle—the price charged by the most efficient manufacturers in the country for the particular product. This was done, in accordance with government policy, to encourage the small-scale sector in each industry. The small-scale manufacturers were required only to register with the state government instead of securing industrial licenses from the Ministry of Industry (DGTD). (It has therefore been very difficult to get reliable data and statistical information about this sector of the industry.) The NDPDC found that a large number of small companies floated associated companies, allegedly to circumvent the provisions of the DPCO. Such developments were obviously not in the interest of the growth of the industry.

The multinationals have emphasized their contribution to the production of basic drugs in India. They claim to have introduced a number of basic drugs dating back to the 1950s, including liver extract from Rallies (1941); INH from Pfizer (1956); vitamin A from Glaxo (1958) and Roche (1959); prednisone from Glaxo (1958), MSD (1959), and Wyeth (1963); vitamin B-12 from MSD (1959); and amodiaquin from Parke-Davis (1959).[40] Since the enactment of the NDP, multinationals maintain, international companies have continued to manufacture the high-technology[41] bulk drugs used in category I and II formulations, from basic and intermediate stages.[42] For example, in the late 1980s, Glindia launched a new drug, Normadate, which was an entirely new and unique concept in cardiovascular treatment.[43]

After the announcement of the NDP, however, the international companies started concentrating on the production of category III (with 100 percent markup) and category IV (outside price control) drugs. They emphasized that the low markups in categories I and II were the reason why they found it necessary to reduce the production of drugs in the essential categories and correspondingly increase the production of more profitable drugs. Despite such a move on the part of the international firms, they are still considered crucial for the future development of the industry and in meeting the demand of drugs and pharmaceuticals in India. Neither the public sector nor the wholly owned Indian companies have ever suggested the nationalization of the multinationals. Perhaps it is a recognition of the fact that in the area of high technology, India cannot do without the multinationals. In fact, what is ailing the public sector pharmaceutical companies in India is technological obsolescence, and serious efforts are being made to overcome that. It has been acknowledged that the latest and most efficient drug technology is available from the multinationals, but they do not want to sell it at any price without having financial participation in a company. This has led the government

Table 5.7
Performance of Indian Sector (Category I & II Bulk Drugs)
(All these drugs are included in those reserved for the Indian sector)

Name of Drug	Unit	1980-1981		1981-1982		1982-1983	
		Target	Prodn.	Target	Prodn.	Target	Prodn.
CATEGORY I							
Halogenated Oxyquinolines	T	265	184	267	206	258	271
Thiacetazone	T	20	8	16	14	21	25
PAS and salts	T	480	405	475	262	400	288
INH	T	154	129	140	110	158	125
Triple Vaccine	KL	11	14	15	17	23	19
Tetanus Antitoxin	MU	not fixed	12,867	not fixed	11,902	16,000	12,633
Diptheria Antitoxin	MU	-do-	612	-do-	870	1,200	654
CATEGORY II							
Diethylcarba-mazine Citrate	T	30	19	28	16	18	14
Piperazine and salts	T	20	25	6	8	not fixed	19
Phthalyl Sulfathiazole	T	11	12	30	5	55	13
Tolbutamide	T	not fixed	24	not fixed	40	44	34

Name of Drug	1983-1984		1984-1985		
	Target	Prodn.	Target	Prodn. April-Dec. 84	Prodn. 84-85 (est.)
CATEGORY I					
Halogenated Oxyquinolines	400	233	435	200	267
Thiacetazone	53	38	55	32	43
PAS and salts	250	217	250	100	133
INH	240	153	290	127	170
Triple Vaccine	23	19	26	19	25
Tetanus Antitoxin	13,000	11,012	13,000	6,425	8,567
Diphtheria Antitoxin	800	568	800	682	909
CATEGORY II					
Diethylcarbamazine Citrate	50	50	55	31	41
Piperazine and salts	210	108	220	61	81
Phthalyl Sulfathiazole	240	17	250	26	34
Tolbutamide fixed	40	24	40	29	38

Sources: 1. Ministry of Chemicals and Fertilizer, *Annual Reports*, 1981-82, 1982-83, 1983-84, and 1984-85.
2. *IDMA Bulletin*, May 7, 1985.

Table 5.8
Performance of Public Sector (Category I & II Bulk Drugs)
(All these drugs are included in those reserved for
the public sector)

Category & Drugs	Unit	1980-1981		1981-1982		1982-1983	
		Target	Prodn.	Target	Prodn.	Target	Prodn.
CATEGORY I							
Penicillin	MMU	370	337	408	361	628	358
Streptomycin	T	302	227	320	256	320	239
CATEGORY II							
Tetracycline	T	234	167	209	189	248	209
Oxytetracycline	T	120	130	135	114	135	120
Sulfadimidine	T	600	444	500	375	550	513
Analgin	T	400	390	450	484	500	239
Phenobarbitone	T	29	16	30	23	30	29

Category & Drugs	1983-1984		1984-1985		
	Target	Prodn.	Target	Prodn. April-Dec. 84	Prodn. 84-85 (est.)
CATEGORY I					
Penicillin	390	317	410	172	229
Streptomycin	270	238	270	182	243
CATEGORY II					
Tetracycline	300	209	330	177	237
Oxytetracycline	150	105	160	101	135
Sulfadimidine	630	481	660	253	337
Analgin	1,000	576	1,000	789	1,052
Phenobarbitone	37	13	39	3	4

Sources: 1. Ministry of Chemicals and Fertilizer, *Annual Reports* 1981-82, 1982-83, 1983-84, 1984-85
       2. *IDMA Bulletin*, May 7, 1985.

to consider the possibility of allowing the multinationals to have equity share in a public sector company, an idea selectively implemented in the late 1990s. The multinationals' strength in the area of technology and marketing has also allowed them to continue the domination of the lucrative formulations market in return for meeting the government's requirement of producing a certain proportion of high-technology bulk drugs.

THE LIMITS OF THE TWO THEORIES

Based on the knowledge of the growth and development of the pharmaceutical industry in India, we can make some generalizations and examine the validity of the two theories we set out to verify in the first chapter. It is of utmost significance to note that the multinationals, which dominated the industry for three decades in independent India, have been reduced to the level of junior partners, so far as their shares of the total production of both bulk drugs and formulations are concerned. The domination of the multinationals in the first two phases lends support to some of the hypotheses of dependency theory: their profitability was high, they concentrated on the manufacture of simple formulations as opposed to bulk drugs and were reluctant to produce drugs from the basic stages, their R&D investment (to be discussed in Chapter 6) was low, and there were reported cases of transfer pricing.[44] But the analysis of the third and fourth phases presents problems for dependency theory as well as for the bargaining school. The nationalist phase, which witnessed the unprecedented growth of the national sector, making it the largest segment of the industry, seems to fit the dependency reversal prescriptions advanced by a few dependency theorists. Yet, the shortfall in production in public and private national sectors made the government decide to eliminate many restrictions on multinationals imposed in the third phase.

If the hypothesis of the bargaining model, on the other hand, were to be applied, one would expect a gradual increase in the power of the state vis-a-vis the multinationals. To some extent, it happened in the 1970s: The revision of the Patent Law (1970), the NDP (1978), and DPCO (1979) were steps taken by the state to increase its regulatory and bargaining power. But the drug policies announced by the government in December 1986 and the DPCO the following year, mainly guided by the consideration of growth in the industry, seem to suggest a slight erosion in the bargaining power of the state.

THE MULTINATIONALS' STRATEGY

There were definite limits to the state's bargaining power set by the technological advantage enjoyed by the multinationals. For example, the possibility of nationalizing the pharmaceutical multinationals was never considered a viable option because they controlled the rapidly changing technology that generates new and improved drugs often at lower costs. The Hathi Committee Report recognized the salience of the multinationals for the Indian pharmaceutical industry when it stated:

Several instances can be quoted to show [how] the vast resources of the multinational corporations [had] secured for the country the kind of production and the type of technology which otherwise would not have been available. For instance, as far back as 1959-61, the manufacture of Vitamin A was established within the country, using indigenously available lemongrass oil. From 1963, Vitamin C and B-12 had been produced from the basic stages. The same is true of many other drugs such as chloraphenicol, insulin, a wide range of cortocosteroids, Erythromycin, Penthonal, ampicillin, etc. Many other products such as PAS, INH, oral antibiotics, calcium gluconate and other calcium salts and iron salts also came into commercial production as a result of the activities of the multinational corporation in this country.[45]

Taking advantage of its monopoly of the latest technology, the drug multinationals responded to government regulations and controls in ways that often frustrated the policymakers and the consumer groups. They devised innovative strategies to get around new state regulations. All but eight multinationals accepted the government policy and decided to dilute their equity up to 40 percent. Since these companies then became legally Indian companies, they could no longer be discriminated against.[46] They are referred to as ex-FERA companies. Most of them decided to change their names—for example, Glaxo became Glindia, MSD became Merind. They were quick to recognize that 40 percent ownership will virtually guarantee the control of the company. At the same time, they kept lobbying for changing the existing laws.

All FERA and ex-FERA companies are members of OPPI.[47] The ex-FERA companies have been involved in an intense and sophisticated lobbying effort since the enactment of the NDP in 1978. OPPI advertisements countering the charges of the critics have appeared regularly in English daily newspapers in major cities, especially around the time when drug issues were being debated in the national capital. OPPI's Delhi office has a full-time, well-paid lobbyist who remains in constant touch with the concerned ministries and tries to influence the policymakers. While interviewing public sector managers, I often heard them complain that the government bureaucrats are usually favorably inclined toward the multinationals and tend to protect their interests. This view is consistent with the findings of the Hathi Committee Report, which pointed out, for example, the close relations between high-ranking ministry officials, who have enormous influence over policymaking, and the OPPI lobbyists in Delhi in day-to-day interaction. Although it is difficult to prove the degree to which such closeness influences government decisions, the public sector managers nonetheless emphasized the point by noting that when the ministry brings out a new circular, the multinationals are usually the first to receive it because "the bureaucrat will personally take a copy of the circular to the office/home of the OPPI representative in Delhi whereas we receive it in the mail."

The OPPI has also produced a videotape program titled "Health for All," which gives the highlights of the industry and shows how it has grown in the last three decades. This program underscores the contribution made by the multinationals in the area of technology transfer and how crucial this sector has been in making the Indian pharmaceutical industry among the most developed in the Third World. This publicity videotape has been used extensively by the association in conferences and seminars and in other lobbying efforts. OPPI effectively lobbied against the Patent Act of 1970 and mobilized enough support within the government and the bureaucracy; it led to India's signing of the Uruguay Round, which has a strong patent protection provision.

Many multinational drug firms evaded successfully the government regulation regarding the production ratio of bulk drugs to formulations. Even when they met the government-required ratio of bulk drug and formulation production, very often they produced bulk drugs from the intermediate stages and not from the basic stages. Table 5.9 shows how six multinational companies were involved in the production of bulk drugs from intermediate stages. This data was revealed by the Ministry of Chemicals and Petrochemicals only after a series of questions were asked in Parliament by the MPs who were sympathetic to the national sector.[48]

A few multinational firms took advantage of the legal system in India and filed injunctions in the Delhi court against drug price controls for bulk drugs and their formulations in essential categories. After getting a stay order from the Delhi High Court on prices fixed by the government, they continued selling the drugs at much higher prices. In 1978, the government had changed its earlier (DPCO, 1970) pricing policy. After examining cost data, the government started setting prices. Because the differential between the declared prices and the prices set by

Table 5.9
Bulk Drug Production from Intermediate Stages
by Multinational Corporations

Name of Company	Name of the Bulk Drug
1. Glaxo Labs	Megestrol acetate
	Methdilazine Hc1
	Chlorphenesin
	Ethinyl estradiol
	Hydrocortisone acetate
	Hemi-succinate
2. Hoechst Pharma	Pyrrolidine Methyltetracycline
	Piperidinoethyl Chlorine Hc1
	Novelgin Calcium
	Novelgin Quinine (Analgin)
3. Pfizer	Chlorpropamide
4. Bayer	Chloroquine phosphate
	Restoren Substance (Chloquinate)
	Detigon Substance (Chlorphedianol Base)
	Incidal Substance
	(Mebhydrolin)
	Badional
	Uvilon (Piperazine phosphate)
5. Roche	Sulfamethoxazole
	Vitamin E acetate
	Chlordiazepoxide
6. M.S.D.	Cyproheptadine
	Dexamethasone 21 phosphate
	Dexamethasone

Source: IDMA, *Voice of the National Sector Annual, 1986* and Ranbaxy, Company File.

the government was quite substantial, the concerned international firms obtained stay orders from the High Courts. For example, the difference in price declared by Glaxo on its product, betamethasone, and that set by the government was more than 50 percent and in the case of Hoechst's Baralgan Ketone it was even higher.[49] It has been estimated by a consumer group that between 1980 and 1986, the multinational firms overcharged the consumers on essential drugs by about Rs. 400 crores.[50] However, it is important to emphasize that the private national sector and consumer groups played up the few instances of multinationals charging high prices through court stay orders in the national press and through sympathetic members of Parliament. They were highly successful in putting the multinationals on the defensive.

Furthermore, the provisions of the Drugs and Cosmetics Rules, 1981, requiring that five commonly used drugs containing single active ingredients (analgin, aspirin and its salts, chlorpromazine and its salts, ferrous sulfate, and piperazine and its salts) be marketed only under generic names, which were challenged in the Delhi High Court by some foreign companies, were also publicized by the private national sector. The Delhi High Court in a judgment on the brandname petition filed by Hoechst Pharmaceuticals Ltd. declared in August 1982 that certain provisions of the government notification were illegal and ultra vires of both the act, other laws, and certain articles (14 and 19 [1] [g]) of the constitution. The judgment stated:

In our view brand names are absolutely essential to identifying each drug to the consumer. When brand names are used the formulations of different manufacturers are made known to the consumer leaving the choice with the doctor to prescribe a particular drug manufactured by a particular party. . . . If brand names are not allowed to be used, it interferes with the right to carry on trade or business. . . . The argument about high-powered marketing techniques and advertisement has no relevance in modern India.[51]

In this instance again, the nationalist-minded industry leaders pointed out,[52] foreign firms through legal recourse succeeded in frustrating the objective of the government to promote a limited number of generic drugs in India.[53] It should, however, be remembered that since the government was more concerned with the shortfalls in production due to the multinationals' strategy, it did not strictly enforce the provisions of the NDP and DPCO (1979).

CONCLUSION

What emerges from our analysis of the effect of government policies on the structure, profitability, sectoral growth, and production in the Indian pharmaceutical industry is that it is neither a categorical validation of the dependency hypotheses nor a clear confirmation of the assumptions of the bargaining school. Sensitive to the possible threats of multinationals to its national autonomy, the Indian government tried to control the expansion, growth, profitability, and ownership of the multinationals through legal and administrative measures. As a result, most of the criticisms found in the empirical studies on the behavior of the drug multinationals in the Third World—high profits, transfer of inappropriate technology, hindering the development of indigenous technology, transfer pricing, and so on—do not apply to India.

The Patent Act (1970), especially its provision of compulsory licensing, and the policy of sectoral reservation in the NDP (1978) did contribute significantly to the growth and expansion of the national sector, both public and private. Once the new Patent Law, which allowed process patent only, went into effect in 1973, it became possible for Indian companies to manufacture the patented drugs legally by paying 4 percent royalty on sales to the patent holder, or to manufacture the patented drug themselves through a different process. Many companies decided to develop their own process through in-house R&D instead of paying the royalty; they did so by simply altering the molecular structure of a drug. The introduction of the system of "drug canalization" almost eliminated the problem of transfer pricing so widespread in the pharmaceutical industry. The foreign exchange earnings of the drug multinationals were much higher than their remittances by way of dividends.

By 1984, multinationals had been dislodged (to use a term from Dennis Encarnation's study[54]) from their dominant position to become junior partners in the industry. In that year, the national sector's contribution to the total production of formulation and bulk drugs had reached 65 percent and 83 percent, respectively. The range of products manufactured by the Indian sector also became sophisticated, and its contribution to the growth of bulk drug production was significant. The private national sector seems to have benefited most from the protective policies of the government. In less than a decade, the private national sector reached maturity and became competitive with the foreign sector in a highly research-intensive industry. Many private sector Indian firms acquired the technological capability to manufacture bulk drugs from the basic stages.

However, sectoral reservation and price control created many problems for the industry in the ensuing years. While DPCO (1979) had made the price of drugs in India among the lowest in the Third World, the pricing policy of the government became the major impediment to the growth of the industry. The low markups in categories I and II drugs led to the multinationals' shift of production from essential and lifesaving drugs to more profitable nonessential drugs in categories III and IV. The low production of essential drugs resulted in a ten-fold increase in their import between 1970 and 1984. The problem was recognized by the NDPDC and NCAER study and addressed in the 1986 Drug Policy, which reduced the categories under which drugs are grouped from three to two and increased the markup in the essential drug category (from 40 to 55 percent to 75 to 100 percent). It was expected that a "reasonable" profit margin in the production of essential drugs and the end of sectoral reservation with the government decision in 1985 to delicense 94 bulk drugs and related formulations would encourage new investments, which would help the industry attain 15 to 20 percent annual growth rate in order to meet the projected demand for drugs.

Although the government policies have succeeded in dislodging multinationals in the drug and pharmaceutical industry, the strategies adopted by the latter were such that many of the intended benefits of government control and regulation were not realized, which frustrated policymakers as well as consumer groups and intellectuals. The complexity of the situation is mainly due to the nature of the industry, which is research-intensive and has a high rate of technological innovation and obsolescence. The salience of the multinationals in drugs and pharmaceuticals, not only in India but all over the Third World, is closely related to their domination of the latest technology—which is the subject of Chapter 6.

NOTES

1. Milton Silverman, Philip R. Lee, and Mia Lydecker, "The Drugging of the Third World," *International Journal of Health Services*, 12, No. 4 (1982): 591-92 and Anil Agarwal, *Drugs and the Third World* (London, Earthscan, 1978).

2. These formulations included household remedies containing vitamins and minerals, many of which did not require a doctor's prescription, such as cough mixtures, ring worm ointments, "health salts," "gripe mixtures," laxative tablets, eye drops, malted tonics, digestive tablets, ointments for burns and piles, tonics containing calcium, alcohol-based tonics, and others.

3. Government of India (Ministry of Petroleum and Chemicals), *Report of the Committee on Drugs and Pharmaceutical Industry* (hereafter the Hathi Committee Report), 1975, pp. 56-57.

4. *Scrip*, Jan. 1986, p. 87.

5. Reserve Bank of India, *Foreign Collaboration in Indian Industry: Second Survey Report 1974* (Bombay: RBI, 1985).

6. Sanjaya Lall, "Multinational Companies and Concentration: The Case of the Pharmaceutical Industry," Social *Scientist*, March-April, 1979, pp. 3-29; UNCTAD, *Case Studies in the Transfer of Technology: The Pharmaceutical Industry in India* (New York: United Nations, 1977); P. L. Badami, "The Pharmaceutical Industry: A Survey," *Commerce*, No. 116, 1968, pp. 12-13; P. S. Agarwal et al., "Anomalies in Drug Prices and Quality Control," *Economic and Political Weekly*, Nov. 18, 1972, pp. 2282-2292.

7. Ashok Parthasarathi, "India's Efforts in Building an Autonomous Capacity in Science and Technology for Development," *Development Dialogue*, No. 1, 1979, pp. 46-59.

8. Other countries that allowed only process patents are: Australia, Brazil, Bulgaria, Canada, China, Chile, Czechoslovakia, Denmark, former East Germany, Hungary, Italy, Japan, Netherlands, Pakistan, Poland, Spain, Sweden, Switzerland, former Soviet Union, and Yugoslavia.

9. The most important among them was the Ayyangar Report (1959), which argued for abolishing the existing Indian Patent and Design Act of 1911. The old patent act had been amended from time to time, one of the notable amendments being the provisions introduced in 1952 relating to the compulsory licensing of patents in the field of food or medicines at any time after the sealing of the patent. See N. Rajagopala Ayyangar, *Report*

on the Revision of the Patents Law (New Delhi, 1959).

10. For an excellent discussion of the Indian Patent Act see Amiya Kumar Bagchi et al., "Indian Patents Act and Its Relation to Technological Development in India," *Economic and Political Weekly*, Feb. 18, 1984, pp. 287-302; and S. Vedaraman, "The New Indian Patent Law," *IDMA Bulletin*, 10, No.8 (Feb. 29, 1984): 115-124.

11. Quoted in *IDMA Bulletin*, 15, No. 25 (July 4, 1984): 391.

12. The Managing Director of CIPLA, Dr. Y. K. Hamied, in an address to a gathering in Pune on December 2, 1983, to commemorate the transfer of technology for manufacture of vinblastine and vincristine from NCL to CIPLA.

13. In India, unlike some other countries—China, for example—burden of proof of infringement is on the patentee even for a process patent; this is practically impossible to prove in the case of imported items.

14. Y. K. Hamied, "Address to a Gathering in Pune on Dec. 2, 1983."

15. *The Economic Times*, February 16, 1987.

16. *Hathi Committee Report*, p. 98.

17. UNIDO, *Appropriate Industrial Technology for Drugs and Pharmaceuticals* (New York: UNIDO, 1984), p. 20.

18. See, for example, Andrew Barnett, Andrew Lacey Creese, and Eddie C. K. Ayivor, "The Economics of Pharmaceutical Policy in Ghana," *International Journal of Health Services*, 10, No. 3 (1980): 479-499; John S. Yudkin, "The Economics of Pharmaceutical Supply in Tanzania," *International Journal of Health Services*, 10, No. 3 (1980): 455-477; Harold Glucksberg and Jack Singer, "The Multinational Drug Companies in Zaire: Their Adverse Effect on Cost and Availibility of Essential Drugs," *International Journal of Health Services*, 12, No. 3 (1982):381-387; Owen T. Adikibi, "The Multinational Corporation and Monopoly of Patents in Nigeria," *World Development*, 16, No. 4 (1988): 511-528; and Daniel Chudnovsky, "The Challenge by Domestic Enterprises to the Transnational Corporations' Domination: A Case Study of the Argentine Pharmaceutical Industry," *World Development*, 7, No. 1 (1979): 45-58.

19. See Gary Gereffi, *The Pharmaceutical Industry and Dependency in the Third World* (Princeton, N.J: Princeton University Press, 1983).

20. Bayer and IEL are not strictly drug companies because drugs comprise less than half their turnover.

21. Broad-banding means that the description of items of manufactures in the Industrial License would be in terms of broad characteristic categories instead of rigidly defined specific products. For example, if a drug company gets industrial licence/permission for the production of penicillin, it can produce all types of penicillins and chemically related analogues like ampicillins, and others. See S. K. Jain, *The Drug Policy 1987-88* (Delhi: India Investment Publication, 1987), p. 78. This book is a collection of all the documents, statements, and press notes related to the drug industry that were issued by the government since 1973.

22. According to OPPI (Organization of Pharmaceutical Producers of India), drug prices in India are lower than those prevailing in most developing and developed countries, mainly because of government price control since the early 1960s.

23. "Speech of Vasant Sathe, Union Minister of Chemical and Fertilizers, at the Meeting of Expert Group on Nov. 29, 1984, to Discuss the NDPDC's Recommendations of 5 September 1984," in *IDMA Bulletin* 15, No.48 (December 31, 1984): 755.

24. K. Jayaraman, "Drug Industry: A Crisis of Confidence," *Economic Times*, August 21, 1987.

25. It is interesting to note that 30 percent of the total sales of Glaxo—the name was changed to Glindia in 1987—consisted of baby formula.

26. "Farce of Drug Policy," *Economic and Political Weekly*, March 8-15, 1986, p. 409.

27. Anand P. Raman, "Strong Medicine," *Business World*, December 7-20, 1987, p. 45.

28. "Review of Pharmaceutical Industry in India," *Industrial Research*, 12, No. 3 (Oct. 1975): 201.

29. Personal interview in Lucknow on September 19, 1986.

30. Communicated to the author in a personal interview on September 19, 1986.

31. The actual production of bulk drugs and formulations was Rs. 377 crores and Rs. 1827 crores respectively.   Government of India, Department of Chemicals and Petrochemicals, *Annual Report 1985-86* (New Delhi: Ministry of Industry), p. 16; also see Arvind Nair, "Drug Industry: Prospects for the Seventh Plan," *Chemsearch and Industry*, 1, No.2 (August 1986): 30.

32. The NCAER study has been widely accepted as an "objective" study of the industry. P. L. Narayana, *The Indian Pharmaceutical Study: Problems and Prospects* (New Delhi: NCAER, 1984), p. 158.

33. *Business World*, December 7-20, 1987.

34. Cited in Ibid., p. 38.

35. In a statement made by C. I. Gandhi, the President of IDMA, in his speech at the IDMA Day Celebrations held at Bombay on Jan. 25, 1986. *Drugs and Pharma: Industry Highlights*, 9, Nos. 4-5 (April-May, 1986): 114.

36. This point was emphasized by Pfizer managers in a personal interview on October 6, 1986. Unlike many international firms such as Glaxo (Glindia), Pfizer does not pay any royalty or technical fee to the parent company.

37. *Guidelines for Industries*.

38. "Review of Pharmaceutical Industry in India," *Industrial Research*, 12, No. 3 (October 1985): 199.

39. Sudip Chaudhuri, "Manufacturing Drugs Without TNCs: Status of Indigenous Sector in India," *Economic and Political Weekly*, Annual, August 1984, p. 1361.

40. Data based on the following sources: *Indian Pharmaceutical Industry*, 1961, 1965, 1969, 1973, *Tariff Commission Report*, 1968 and *Hathi Committee Report*, Chapter 2, Appendix 4.

41. The criteria adopted for classification of bulk drugs were defined by the government Committee on High Technology in March 1982. Although the definition adopted was quite exhaustive—it involved 12 different criteria—some of the committee members expressed their dissatisfaction with the government decision. For example, Nitya P. Anand, a member of the committee, told me in a personal interview that because of the way high and low technology drugs were defined, it became possible for multinationals to get most of their drugs classified in the category of high technology drugs.

42. K. Jayaraman's "Multinationals: Sinners or Sinned Against?" (unpublished paper, Bombay, 1986?) provides a list of category I/II bulk drugs manufactured by FERA and non-FERA companies.

43. *Glaxo News*, May 1987.

44. When multinationals are involved in intrafirm trade (i.e., trade between associated units of a company operating in several countries), they can move profits clandestinely "by changing intra-firm prices" instead of declaring profits and paying taxes in a host country. Empirical studies have shown that transfer pricing in imported

intermediates is more likely to occur in the pharmaceutical and automobile sectors. See Sanjaya Lall, "Transfer Pricing and Developing Countries: Some Problems of Investigation," *World Development*, 7, No. 1 (Jan. 1979): 59-71, and Constantine C. Vaitsos, "Government Policies for Bargaining with Transnational Enterprise in the Acquisition of Technology," In Jairam Ramesh and Charles Weiss, Jr. (eds), *Mobilizing Technology for Development* (New York: Praeger, 1979).

45. *Hathi Committee Report*, p. 97.

46. The national sector opposed the government formula of 40 percent equity criterion qualifying the ex-FERA companies to be treated legally as Indian companies. A senior manager of a leading national company whom I interviewed (Nov. 19, 1986) emphasized that "in Japan, if the foreign shareholding is more than 10 percent and in Australia if it is more than 15 percent, these companies are treated differently than their national sector companies. Why in India do we have to be so lenient toward the foreign firms?"

47. The OPPI is an association of pharmaceutical manufacturers established in 1965. Although the membership is open to all drug manufacturers, OPPI has been the organization of the international companies. By the mid-1980s, the membership of the organization consisted of both the Indian and international companies. In 1985, out of a total of 54 members of the organization, there were no less than 17 wholly owned Indian companies as full members. Membership dues are based on the total sales of a company; for companies having a total turnover of more than Rs. 15 crores, the membership costs Rs. 60,000 per annum and there is a minimum membership fee of Rs. 5,000. Despite the participation of the Indian companies, OPPI is still considered to be the Organization of the drug multinationals. See *OPPI Annual Report*, 1985.

48. The sympathetic MPs included Rajni Ranjan Sahu (Rajya Sabha), Pravin Kumar Prajapati (Rajya Sabha), Usha Malhotra (Rajya Sabha), Maimoona Sultan (Rajya Sabha), Nand Kishore Bhatt (Rajya Sabha), Ramkrishna More (Lok Sabha), and Krupasindhu Bhoi (Lok Sabha).

49. B. K. Keayla, "MNCs Charging High Prices Through Stay Orders Obtained from High Courts," (unpublished paper), New Delhi: 1986.

50. In a statement given by Consumers' Forum President, Gyan Chand Pandit, in September 1986 in New Delhi. *Hindustan Times*, September 21, 1986.

51. The Delhi High Court Judgment, quoted in *OPPI Bulletin*, Jan.-June 1985, p. 5.

52. Y. K. Hamied and B. K. Keayla, for example.

53. For details, see *OPPI Bulletin*, No. 2, May-July, 1985, pp. 5-6.

54. See Dennis J. Encarnation, *Dislodging Multinationals: India's Strategy in Comparative Perspective* (Ithaca: Cornell University Press, 1989).

6

Development of Technological Capability in the Indian Pharmaceutical Industry

Technological development in the drug and pharmaceutical industry displays the classic symptoms of dependence in developing countries. The industry is almost totally dependent on the imported technology from the West. There is very little effective research and development (R&D) that is actually conducted in the Third World. Yet, pharmaceutical development has been rapid in many developing countries in the last two decades. This chapter examines the nature of the technological dependence of India in the drug and pharmaceutical industry and analyzes whether the country has become technologically self-reliant and, if so, to what degree. India's technological capability and technological dependence is evaluated by examining the roles of the two leading public sector firms (HAL and IDPL), public-funded research institutes, and in-house R&D of the private sector.

This discussion suggests that there is a paradoxical situation in the Indian pharmaceutical industry: Technologically, it is the most advanced in the Third World, yet there is a growing technological obsolescence in the industry, especially in the public sector, which has created a situation of continued dependence on the drug multinationals for high-technology modern drugs. This chapter suggests that some of the factors that have contributed to technological obsolescence in the pharmaceutical industry—public sector firm inefficiencies, R&D organization that separates research from user units, suboptimal plant size, and others—have not been taken into account by either dependency or bargaining theory. The concept of organizational involution, as advanced by the Rudolphs,[1] will help clarify how lag in technology in the pharmaceutical industry is due, at least in part, to government policies and inefficiencies at the firm level.

TECHNOLOGY AND THE PHARMACEUTICAL INDUSTRY

For nearly half a century, the pharmaceutical industry has been one of the major innovative industries in the West. The technological advancements made by the discovery of new drugs that could actually cure disease has revolutionized the pharmaceutical industry. The discovery of Prontosis by Gerhard Domagk in the mid-1930s was followed by the discovery of sulfa drugs, penicillins and tetracyclines. In the 1950s, "wonder drugs" (tranquilizers, steroids, oral contraceptives, oral antidiabetic drugs, and cardiovascular drugs) were discovered. Further technological advances have been made in the drug industry in the last 25 years although discovery of new drugs has been slow.

Research and development is the key to success in the pharmaceutical industry. Competition in the industry takes the form of rivalry in innovation.[2] In order to maintain the competitive edge, most large drug firms have made high rates of investment in R&D. The R&D expenditure of the leading drug firms has therefore been fairly high compared to other industries.[3]   The pharmaceutical industry spends more on R&D than most other industries. The leading companies spend between 10 and 16 percent of their annual sales turnovers on R&D, which is more than 50 percent of their recorded profits.

In pharmaceutical research, the company concerned has to take substantial risks, and there is an additional factor of lengthy time requirements. Since the early 1960s (i.e., after the passage of the 1962 Kefauver-Harris amendments to the Food, Drug and Cosmetic Act of 1938), R&D in the pharmaceutical industry, especially in the United States, has become more costly and more risky.[4] In the last 25 years, there has been a sharp decline in the rate of introduction of pharmaceutical innovations. In the 1950s, the annual average of new products was 358, of new chemicals 42; in the 1960s, these averages dropped to 160 and 22; in the 1970s through the 1980s, the numbers have been much lower than in the 1960s.[5] This decline is due partly to the depletion of research opportunities and partly to costs. Many major therapeutic areas have currently reached a point where the probability that a new discovery will be an advance over existing therapies is quite low. For every drug that is introduced on the market today, there are approximately 8,000 that are tested. Investment in research in the pharmaceutical industry in 1989 was more than $7 billion. The R&D investment of research-based companies has doubled every five years since 1970. It has been estimated that in the 1960s a new drug took, on the average, seven years to develop and its development cost about $15 million, but in the 1980s a new drug can take from 7 to 10 years to develop (i.e., move from discovery through testing, development, and FDA approval) and cost up to $125 million.[6]

In the drug industry, a distinction is made between three types of technology: product technology, process technology, and formulation and packaging technology. Product technology refers to the discovery of new drugs, which is difficult, expensive, and time consuming. Process technology means the improvements or adaptations in production methods for given drugs. Formulation and packaging technology involves innovations in dosage forms, packaging, storage, and so forth. In the Third World, however, only two components of drug manufacturing technology have been considered relevant by experts of UNIDO and other UN agencies: bulk drugs production (production of the active ingredients in drugs) and formulations production (the processing of bulk drugs into finished dosage forms such as tablets, capsules, ointments, etc.). Although the development of new drugs still remains the monopoly of multinationals, a number of developing countries have made tremendous progress not only in the development of formulation and packaging technology, but also in the indigenous development of technologies for manufacturing existing drugs.

The drug industry can operate at any of the following stages:

1. Import finished medicines and repack them;

2. Import bulk materials and formulate them;

3. Import penultimate and intermediate products in bulk and formulate them;

4. Import basic raw materials and produce bulk drugs from various stages;

5. Produce bulk drugs from locally available raw materials.[7]

The stage from which drugs are produced will depend on the degree of industrialization, infrastructural development, technological capability, the availability of technical skills, and the existence of chemical industry in the country. Production policies, therefore, will vary from country to country. A UN study has advised:

All [developing] countries should establish their own formulation and packaging units. Large or relatively more industrialised countries should consider the production of large-tonnage chemical intermediates and chemopharmaceuticals, whereas small or less industrialised countries may find it advisable to cooperate in setting up subregional or regional pharmaceutical production units. The public industrial sector should concentrate on the production of essential drugs; private sector units should be encouraged to reserve a portion of their production capacity for the manufacture of essential drugs through special incentives.[8]

However, the primary technology for production of drugs and pharmaceuticals is the technology for bulk drugs production, which most developing countries lack.

TECHNOLOGY AND THE INDIAN PHARMACEUTICAL INDUSTRY

Technological development in the Indian pharmaceutical industry presents a paradox. On the one hand, India has the second largest and most modern pharmaceutical industry in the Third World (Brazil is first). It produces about 400 to 500 bulk drugs and is almost self-sufficient in its drug formulation technology.

The country has acquired a greater degree of self-reliance in pharmaceutical technology through its development of domestic capabilities and skills, which are unrivaled in the Third World. On the other hand, the industry, particularly the public sector, is suffering from technological obsolescence, which has increased India's dependence on multinationals for the latest technology in some critical areas.

In the pharmaceutical industry, a large mass of technology was imported into India in the postindependence period. The imported technology was adapted to local conditions and, in many cases, improved on by Indian scientists, technologists, and engineers. Technology transfer was effected through international collaboration, technical or financial. The contribution of multinationals in providing the most effective and economic method for the transfer of technology in a field in which technological and product obsolescence is quite significant has been recognized by the government and various committees. Given the disease pattern and the requirement of drugs to combat it,[9] the Hathi Committee Report strongly favored the continued operation of multinationals in India. The report explained why the outright purchase of technology was not the preferred mode of technology transfer in the Indian pharmaceutical industry.

It is often argued that instead of permitting foreign firms to operate in this country, technology can be purchased outright. This is claimed to be cheaper and would also assist the development of domestic Research and Development. While in appropriate cases outright purchase of technology may be the most suitable method for the transfer of technology, this mode of transfer of technology cannot be generalised.

In highly specialised fields or where the new technology is confined to one or two sources, it may not always be possible to purchase the know-how. Moreover, it is one thing to buy know-how and quite another to have continuing access to improvements in technology which are taking place all the time.

Pointing out the advantages of foreign equity participation in the pharmaceutical industry, the committee argued that if the

foreign party which has provided the technology has an equity participation, the Indian company can have access to the continuing improvements in technology. There would be instances, therefore, where continuing association in the form of equity participation is the only way of securing access to new technology. . . . If the objective is to provide for the masses in this country drugs and pharmaceuticals at reasonable prices, this can only be done by constant improvements in products technology based on researches which are continuing elsewhere.[10]

The views expressed by the Hathi committee confirmed the general thinking found in the literature on technology transfer at the time, which suggested that foreign firms are less keen on transferring technology under pure technical collaboration agreements than under direct investment or minority participation agreements. The assumption of the committee was that India should take advantage of the existing

R&D of the multinationals in the West. Since the pharmaceutical industry relies heavily on R&D-based product innovation, the committee realized that it is extremely unlikely that India, or even a developed country, could achieve technological self-sufficiency. Other studies supported this view. The Reserve Bank of India (RBI) studies on foreign collaboration found that technology transfer has been "regular, up-to-date and cost-effective when effected through the subsidiaries of the foreign companies, as against those under purely technical collaboration agreements."[11] Empirical studies on technology transfer in other industries further confirm that imported technologies have often been adapted to meet local needs and were even improved on.

The experts and the expert committees in the 1960s and early 1970s thus recognized the technological advantages enjoyed by the multinationals and the national sector's inability to meet the growing demand of drugs and pharmaceuticals on its own, without the full participation of the multinationals. However, the government was determined to overcome India's technological dependence on the multinationals. From the early 1950s, India's development strategy emphasized accelerating economic growth and self-reliance through industrialization, with stress on basic and heavy industry to be located mainly in the public sector.

In the pharmaceutical industry, it was found that the technology imported from multinational corporations by their subsidiaries in the country were often from penultimate or intermediate stages and not from basic stages. In other words, multinationals were not interested in the production of bulk drugs from basic stages in India. The R&D expenditure of the industry, which was very low compared with the developed countries, reflected this attitude: It was estimated at 1.1 percent of the total turnover in 1961,[12] dropped to below 1 percent of total sales in 1973,[13] and rose to a mere 1.5 percent of the sales turnover in 1981-82.[14] These figures compare very unfavorably with those of the developed countries where R&D expenditure in the drug industry remained on average about 5.6 percent of the sales value of the drug.[15] The top 25 companies in the world spend over $100 million each per annum on R&D as compared to around $40 million spent by the entire pharmaceutical industry in India in 1984. The Hathi Committee Report found that out of 45 FERA companies, only seven performed R&D in the manufacture of basic drugs. Even as late as 1976-77, only about one-half of all the multinational companies—32 out of 63—were producing bulk drugs.[16]

In order to make the country relatively self-reliant in essential drugs, the government decided to start the production of bulk drugs from basic stages in the public sector and allocated more resources for R&D activities in this sector of the industry. It is significant to note that India recognized the importance of bulk drugs production, which had been a monopoly of the West,[17] quite early on after independence and started emphasizing its development in the public sector beginning with the Second Five Year Plan. At the same time, publicly funded research institutes were assigned the role of drug development, and it was expected that the processes developed in government institutes would be successfully commercialized. The government started giving encouragement and incentives to industries in the organized sector to invest more in in-house R&D—especially after the announcement of the Technology Policy Statement in January 1983.

THE PUBLIC SECTOR AND PHARMACEUTICAL TECHNOLOGY

The decision of the government to start the production of essential bulk drugs in the public sector was an effort on the part of the government to make India more self-reliant in a research-intensive industry. The public sector, with about one-third of the industry's total investment, is an important segment of the pharmaceutical industry. This case study of the two public sector companies would suggest two rather contradictory tendencies. On the one hand (as noted in Chapter 5), the government policies enabled the country to achieve a higher degree of technological capability. On the other, the public sector companies have experienced technological obsolescence from the beginning; their in-house R&D has not been satisfactory in bringing about improvements in process technology, nor have they been able to buy the latest technology they want from the international sources because of the unwillingness of the multinationals to transfer technology on an arm's-length basis. This has resulted in an enormous loss for the two public sector companies, HAL and IDPL, which are discussed in the next section.

Hindustan Antibiotic Limited (HAL)

Realizing the pressing need for producing pharmaceuticals, particularly antibiotics, Hindustan Antibiotics Limited (HAL) was set up by the government in Pimpri, Maharastra, in 1954 with the assistance of WHO and UNICEF. The company, a pioneer in antibiotics, has grown over the years into a vast complex supplying a wide array of lifesaving drugs. HAL became the first company to manufacture a number of drugs in India: penicillin, streptomycin sulfate, ampicillin anhydrous, and gentamicin.[18] HAL's main achievement was its emphasis on basic research from the very beginning. A full-fledged R&D laboratory with specially trained scientists and the latest sophisticated equipment was established in 1955.

The experience of HAL in connection with the import of technology on a one-time basis, however, has been far from satisfactory. The initial American technology for the manufacture of penicillin and ampicillin, transferred through WHO at an estimated cost of $350,000,[19] became obsolete, resulting in low yields. The company then acquired an upgrading package from Toyojozo of Japan. The Japanese technology—acquired after a lump-sum payment of about $1 million—was not a full technology but was designed only to increase yields by 300 percent. However, the actual result of the new technology was an improvement of the strain yields by only 58 percent.

Likewise, the gentamicin technology, for which the company shopped for many years, was acquired from Medimpex of Hungary at a cost of Rs. 1.8 million. Because HAL was unable to buy the best technology from Schering, an American company, due to the unwillingness of the latter to give the technology without financial participation in the company, HAL bought the inferior technology available from the Hungarian firm. HAL believed that through in-house process development, it could make the second-rate technology more efficient and would eventually catch up with the best technology. In reality, however, as HAL tried to catch up, the international technology advanced, and soon the company found that the production of gentamicin with obsolete technology was not economically viable. Since the import of gentamicin was allowed by the government, HAL could not compete with the international price of this essential drug.

The importance of innovation in the drug and pharmaceuticals industry and the advantage enjoyed by the multinationals, at least in a few key areas, have been emphasized by the public sector managers. During the course of my interviews, the senior managers of HAL underscored the point that the multinationals are willing to sell only second-generation, and not new, drug technology. One manager commented that since the early 1980s "we have been going around the world hunting for the best technology but with little success. . . . We have reached a point where the government should consider allowing foreign firms to have financial participation in a public sector company if they are willing to give the latest (fermentation) technology in return." Others cited the example of the difficulty they faced in obtaining the streptomycin technology for many years; HAL finally got the high-yielding strain of streptomycin-producing organism from Glaxo, U.K., free of cost in 1981.[20]

According to HAL managers, technological obsolescence and government policy were two important reasons why the public sector pharmaceutical company has been unable to attain its declared goal of providing lifesaving drugs in abundance and at a low price. A recent study suggests that in the field of antibiotics, India is lagging behind the developed countries by almost a decade "with respect to the introduction of newer antibiotics and also the yields and process efficiency."[21]

The production of penicillin and other antibiotics, which begins with biological fermentation, consists of three steps: seed growth, production fermentation, and harvesting the fermented broth. From the fermented broth, the mycelium is separated and penicillin is recovered from the filtrate by the solvent extraction process. The problem HAL has always faced is that of low yield in fermentation technology. The Committee on Public Undertaking in its report expressed dissatisfaction with the performance of the company and noted that the expected titer yield[22] of penicillin in different categories had mostly been lower than the standard yield.[23] In order to overcome the problem of low yield, HAL entered into an agreement with and bought technology for the manufacture of streptomycin from an American firm (Merck). However, it has been reported that even after the use of new technology, the company was getting lower titer yield than the supplier of the technology. After a thorough investigation of the matter, it was found that

Merck was using a different strain—supplied by Glaxo, U.K.—than the one it sold to HAL. HAL scientists have, therefore, concluded that in order to be competitive, what they need most is the latest technology for the production of antibiotics. The company, in particular, needs to modernize in different areas including improvement in the media, fermentation process and extraction procedures, and the computerization of the fermentation process to minimize human errors.

The modernization and updating of antibiotic technology is, however, a difficult process, especially in a public sector company, for two reasons. First, the technology in this area is not available off the shelf, and second, the in-house R&D, which is a slow process, did not bring about process improvement within a reasonable period. By the time the company's R&D effort showed signs of promise and it appeared that it was catching up with the existing technology in the West, the international technology had moved further ahead at a much faster pace making the gap between the two even wider. Moreover, the R&D program of HAL, as the NCAER study points out, has been directed mainly toward "discovering new antibiotics rather than on up-grading the obsolete technology used in the manufacture of penicillin and streptomycin."[24] The then managing director of HAL, Y. H. Gharpure, in an interview in 1982, commented:

Although we were pioneers in R&D activity, the main emphasis on the Research and Development aspect was not given adequate importance. We did not have adequate pilot plant facilities; even our testing facilities required much to be desired.[25]

The problem of the high cost of penicillin and other bulk drugs, which is about two to three times more than imported drugs, is also related to the scale of production. The government policy of discouraging larger production in the name of "monopoly" has resulted in the fragmentation of capacity between a multitude of small units. The inefficiencies that result from what the Rudolphs have called "organizational involution"—"the multiplication of more and smaller enterprises" because of government policies[26]—could be observed in this case. In the production of penicillin, for example, the minimum economic-size plant is said to be around 800 MMU per annum. Thus, whereas Gist Brocades, the world's leading manufacturer of penicillin, has a capability of 3,000 MMU per annum, a total licensed capacity of 530 MMU is shared by four manufacturers in India.[27] The maximum plant capacity of 200 MMU at HAL is about one-fifth the capacity of an economically viable international penicillin manufacturing unit.

Although there are other reasons[28] for the high cost of bulk drugs in India, experts agree that uneconomic plant capacities and inefficient technologies are the most important. As a result, HAL entered into a joint venture with a private company, Max-GB, which took over its penicillin plant on lease in 1993.

Despite the technological and other problems experienced by HAL, its in-house R&D has resulted in the discovery of two very effective antifungal antibiotics—Hamycin and Aureofungin. The products have been licensed for production in the United States, bringing a small royalty for the company. It is important to emphasize that the establishment of the company in the public sector made India perhaps the only country in the Third World capable of producing antibiotics, both bulk and formulations, in the 1950s; HAL started production of its bulk penicillin in 1955. The company claims that its participation in the production of bulk drugs has brought down the retail price of many essential drugs. Gentamicin, for example, used to be sold at Rs. 35 a vial and its price came down to Rs. 7 or 8 a vial after HAL started manufacturing the drug.

Indian Drug and Pharmaceutical Limited (IDPL)

Indian Drug and Pharmaceutical Limited was set up as a government company in November 1961 for the manufacture of antibiotics, synthetic drugs, and surgical instruments, with the technical assistance of the Soviet Union. The Soviets provided a loan of Rs. 9.52 crores to cover technical services including the training of Indian technicians at the Soviet plant and the cost of machinery and equipment to be imported for these plants. During the formulation of the Second Five Year Plan, Prime Minister Nehru emphasized the need to produce bulk drugs from basic stages and was personally involved in the decision to set up IDPL. The production of essential bulk drugs by a public sector company was expected to eliminate the outgo of foreign exchange and to bring down the prices by larger production. But the company has experienced problems related to the Soviet technology from the very beginning. Today its cumulative losses of about Rs. 170 crores have reduced its net worth to zero. The company is saddled with obsolete machinery, an obstinate labor force, and high inventories. Although the government of India entered into an agreement with the Soviet Union in May 1959 and the company was incorporated in 1961, the commissioning of the plant was delayed by several years because of the snags of supply and installation of equipment, frequent design changes, and raw material procurement. The three units of IDPL were completed only by 1967-68, and production did not start until 1970-71.

The Rishikesh plant, which had an installed capacity of 33 tons of antibiotics distributed over a product-mix of eight basic drugs, was producing far below its rated capacity from the beginning. The Hyderabad unit was to produce 16 synthetic vitamins, analgesics, antipyretics, diuretics, and antitubercular and sulfa drugs. Ironically, whatever the two units were producing did not find a ready market because the imported CIF prices for the range of drugs produced by IDPL were much lower. The Madras unit, which was to manufacture principal surgical instruments with an installed capacity of 2.5 million pieces a year, produced much more than it could sell. By early 1971, the company had thus incurred an accumulated loss of Rs. 29.68 crores against its equity base of Rs. 25.95 crores.[29]

There was, however, a brief period, between 1972 and 1978, when the company's sales increased and for four years—from 1974-75 to 1977-78—it also made some profits. The average capacity utilization, however, was lower than 50 percent. Upon examining the data presented in the annual reports, it was found that the profits of IDPL were on account of trade in canalized items and not because of the sales of its manufactures. The government's decision to give IDPL monopoly over the distribution of imported drugs within the company's range of production kept it in financial health. Following the DPCO (1970), the company was allowed to pool its own products with imports—tetracycline, for example—and then distribute the canalized drugs at "pooled prices." As a result, its sales and profits increased. The company thereafter undertook an ambitious expansion plan: The capacity of the Hyderabad unit was expanded from 1,988 tons to 3,386 tons of bulk drugs, which included the production of 36 new drugs and 5 intermediates, and the capacity in the Rishikesh unit was doubled to 600 tons "in order to undertake production of new antibiotics like tetracycline, semi-synthetic penicillins, erithromycin and doxycyclene."[30] Two new plants were built—a production plant at Gurgoan and an Rs. 14-crore nicotinamide and acetic acid manufacturing plant at Muzaffarpur. However, the government's decision to transfer drug canalization from IDPL to the State Chemical and Pharmaceutical Corporation, a subsidiary of the State Trading Corporation, affected the company adversely. It has not recovered from the shock as yet and has been incurring losses ever since.

The problems faced by IDPL in the last two decades are mainly related to the outdated technology it got from the Soviet Union. At the time India entered into its agreement with the Soviet Union, it knew it was getting second-rate technology. The multinationals had the latest technology, but they were unwilling to give it to a government undertaking that did not allow financial participation by a foreign firm.[31] Nehru had faith in the capabilities of Indian scientists and believed that after getting basic technology from the Soviet Union they would be able to improve its efficiency by international standards.

Shortly after the transfer of Soviet technology for the manufacture of 16 products, the research center of IDPL at Hyderabad started "an all-out effort" to improve its technologies and increase its economic viability and profitability. The company has given priority to this sort of R&D activity, and many improvements on Soviet technology have been successfully implemented in the main plant at Hyderabad to suit the raw materials available in the local markets. This includes sulfa drugs, vitamins, and folic acid.[32] Despite such efforts, it was found that the production of many drugs, especially of penicillin in the Rishikesh unit, was uneconomical, and the company started looking for other sources of improved technology. A six-member team of experts, including the chairman of IDPL and of HAL, went on a "technology hunt." After visiting about two dozen countries, in 1976 the team finally negotiated with Farmafin, an Italian consortium of five companies, a one-time purchase of high-yielding strains and technology for five antibiotics—penicillin, tetracycline, erythromycin, semisynthetic penicillin and doxycycline—at a cost of $1.55 million.[33]

A large number of technical experts were sent to Italy for training in order to ensure a smooth transfer of technology. Yet the company succeeded in fully implementing only one—tetracycline—out of five technologies purchased from

Italy. The production of erythromycin, which was from basic stages, had to be stopped because of the high cost of production; the problem, however, was not so much the technology as the weakness of IDPL's own R&D. In the case of semisynthetic drugs, production was found to be economically unfeasible, as the company did not get the latest technology from Italy. The penicillin technology did not prove to be as efficient as claimed by the consortium. It was reported that during the trial runs, the Italian firms demonstrated that "yields are higher than the minimum stipulated in the original agreement. And yet, after the trial guarantee runs, the production had slumped to low levels."[34]

Being a public sector company, where every decision of the enterprise must be approved by the government, IDPL lacks the dynamism found in the private sector. It has thus continued to manufacture older sulfa drugs, such as penicillin and tetracycline, instead of moving into the production of new antibiotics, such as synthetic penicillin. For example, the demand for IDPL's Sodium PAS, an anti-TB drug, has gone down considerably because of the availability of more effective and efficient drugs such as ethambutol. Yet, the company has an installed capacity of 200 metric tons for the production of Sodium PAS, which has become idle now. Since private doctors prefer to prescribe newer and more effective drugs, one industry insider observed, "the market of IDPL has been reduced to supplying much of its formulations to public hospitals."[35] By contrast, a number of Indian (private) companies—CIPLA, Ranbaxy, Cadila, for example—went into the production of newer drugs in which the market is growing. In the last decade, IDPL also failed to develop a commercially successful technology for the manufacture of 6-aminopencillanic acid (6-APA), which is a key intermediate for preparation of semisynthetic penicillins such as ampicillin and amoxicillin. The level of immobilized enzyme technology in India, which is the most efficient way of producing 6-APA from penicillin-G or penicillin-V, is far from satisfactory and will take several years for its full development by IDPL.[36]

In short, public sector pharmaceutical companies—both IDPL and HAL—are suffering from the problem of outdated technology, long gestation periods, huge accumulated inventories, and outdated marketing methods. In the 1990s, the solution has been found in the joint venture partnership with private companies: In 1993, HAL entered into a strategic alliance with Max-GB, a joint venture between Max India and Gist Brocade of the Netherlands, for the production of penicillin, and in 1995, IDPL was considering joint venture proposals from Ranbaxy and Sol Pharmaceuticals for the production (at the Rishikesh plant) and marketing of penicillin-G. The inefficiency in the public sector in general has been a subject of much debate in recent years, and some of its critics have gone as far as to advocate the idea of privatization of this sector of the industry.[37]

Despite the problems of assimilation and innovation of the imported technology and the staggering cumulative losses of the company,[38] IDPL has successfully developed basic technologies for many well-known drugs and their chemical intermediates, which were earlier imported. Technologies for 24 drugs developed by IDPL, including vitamin B-6, methyldopa and ampicillin trihydrate, have already been transferred to and implemented in the Hyderabad plant. It is important to note that IDPL is the first to produce vitamin B-6 in India, and there are not more than six countries in the world with the know-how to produce this important vitamin. IDPL has also perfected pilot scale technologies for 14 drugs.[39] With an operational annual expenditure of about Rs. 1.8 crores on R&D, which is about 2 percent of its net sales, the company expects to make further advances in assimilation, adaptation, and optimization of the technology transferred and hopes to be able to innovate. Furthermore, IDPL has entered into joint ventures with four state governments, thereby transferring technology horizontally. The UP Drugs and Pharmaceuticals Company in Lucknow, the Jaipur-based Rajasthan Drugs and Pharmaceuticals Limited, and the Orissa Drugs and Chemicals Limited were set up to make formulations mostly out of bulk drugs supplied by IDPL. Punjab Maize Products Limited, another such company, was meant to manufacture dextrose monohydrite and starch.

The technological capability acquired by IDPL in the last two decades is of great significance in the context of the South-South transfer of pharmaceutical technology. IDPL has grown to be one of the largest pharmaceutical manufacturers in Asia. UNIDO has recognized the company's strength in offering to other Third World countries consultancy services for setting up projects for drugs, drug intermediates, organic chemicals, and pharmaceutical specialities in all dosages and forms such as tablets, capsules, syrups, injectable, granulates, and others. Other services offered by IDPL (badly needed by many Third World countries) include feasibility study; technical know-how; design and basic engineering; detailed engineering; erection, supervision, and commissioning including process demonstration, procurement assistance and training of personnel. The company has carried out detailed engineering services for a formulation unit, Royal Drugs Limited, in Kathmandu, Nepal. Through UNIDO, it has also provided consultancy services to Cuba.

ROLE OF PUBLIC-FUNDED RESEARCH INSTITUTES

Inspired by Nehru's vision of an industrial society, the government decided to set up a chain of scientific laboratories in order to build a significant industrial infrastructure in India. Although many scientists had advised Nehru against creating a large research infrastructure under government control, a viable alternative to government-sponsored research was totally lacking in India in the early postindependence period. The private sector lacked the capacity to undertake industrial R&D effort of any significance. In drug and pharmaceutical research, the government thus created the superstructure of institutions for indigenous research through the creation of the Indian Council of Medical Research, two research institutes of the Council of Scientific and Industrial Research (CSIR)—Central Drug Research Institute and the Indian Institute of Experimental

Medicine—and National Chemical Laboratories (NCL) and Regional Research Laboratories (RRLs).

The national laboratories have made a significant contribution to the generation of technology by developing new drugs as well as technologies for drug production. Although the record of India, like other Third World countries, in the discovery of new drugs is not at all impressive, the national laboratories have done as well as, or perhaps better than, the multinationals despite the meager inputs in R&D by international standards. Of the five new drugs discovered in India, three were by national laboratory (two by RRL, Hyderabad) and public sector company (one by HAL) and only two by the international companies (Ciba and Hoechst). Efforts are also being made to discover new drugs for tropical and communicable diseases. More important, the national laboratories have extensive research programs in all priority areas and have successfully synthesized many known drugs by a new route, thereby reducing the time lag between the introduction of new drugs in the international markets and their production in India. By the mid-1980s, 71 CSIR technologies were available for production of drugs and drug intermediates, out of which 63 were licensed and 13 were already under production.[40] The problem, however, remains regarding the commercialization of the indigenous technology.

Although the transfer of technology from laboratory to industry has not been very successful in India—as is the case with CDRI—it has been quite effective in the cases of NCL and RRL (Hyderabad). The long-term association of CIPLA with CSIR, for example, has resulted in the successful implementation and commercialization of processes for a variety of products. In 1959-60, CIPLA obtained and commercialized the technology of diosgenin—developed by the CSIR. CIPLA was the first Indian company to produce steroids derived from diosgenin. More recently, the innovative technology developed by NCL for the manufacture of the anti-cancer drugs vinblastine sulfate and vincristine sulfate was successfully transferred from laboratory to industry. CIPLA has manufactured and marketed the products at half the price charged by Eli Lilly.[41] It has commercialized other drug technologies developed indigenously by the national laboratories such as Salbutamol and Tebutalin (antiasthmatics), Metoprolol and Atenelol (beta-blockers), ibuprofen, Piroxicam and Diclofenac (anti-inflammatory drugs), diazepam and lorazepam (tranquilizers), and sulfamethoxazole and trimethoprim (antibacterial drugs).[42] The company's success in commercializing the CSIR/NCL technologies lies primarily in its ability to identify the products for which there was a market through the involvement of market personnel, production staff, production managers, and the managing director.[43] The council has thus played a significant role in the development of processes for the manufacture of the newer bulk drugs and drug intermediates. The Indian Patent Act of 1970, which denied product patent, has contributed significantly to the indigenous development of technology by the CSIR laboratories. However, the success rate of upscaling of technology from the laboratory to the industry has been very small and the CSIR has recently been criticized for this.

The report of the Fourth Review Committee points out that the CSIR has grown into a massive bureaucracy with all the attendant problems and constraints. With 39 laboratories and 100 extension centers under it, the council has nearly 5,600 scientists and 12,000 technologists working on 1,400 projects. Despite the huge amount spent by the government,[44] the committee argues, very few technologies developed by the council laboratories have been commercially exploited. The committee, after seven months of in-depth study of the functioning of the CSIR, has recommended its complete reorganization.[45]

While it is beyond the scope of this study to go into the details of the functioning of the CSIR, it is important to note that a serious drawback of its R&D efforts is the lack of coordination between national laboratories and public sector R&D centers, which results in duplication of research at the cost of public funds. By contrast, in-house transfer of technology in a unitary industrial setup have been found to be more successful than the transfer of technology from an independent laboratory to industry. For example, in the development of sulfamethoxazole technology by Standard Organic Limited, Hyderabad, the teamwork among chemists, chemical engineers, and managerial personnel facilitated the in-house transfer of technology. The result of such an effort has been phenomenal: Not only did the production of the basic drug increase from 23 tons in 1980 to over 200 tons in 1985, but the large-scale production coupled with continuous technological innovations helped the company to bring down the price of the drug from Rs. 800 kg. in 1980 to Rs. 390 kg. in 1983.[46] A number of new drugs[47] have been introduced in the market through the in-house R&D efforts of the Indian companies within four to five years after they were introduced in the international market. This is in sharp contrast with the earlier time gap of 15 years in technology transfer.

With respect to the utilization of research work done at the national laboratories, the industry has cited various reasons for the nonutilization of the technology developed by the CSIR laboratories. In a survey conducted in the early 1980s, the industry respondents emphasized the communication and credibility gap between the industry and publicly funded research laboratories. Among the major problems they emphasized were the high cost of production in case of utilization of processes developed by the national laboratories, the incomplete technical data supplied by the national laboratories, the lack of communication between laboratory personnel and industry technologists, and the academic nature of most of the work carried out in the national laboratories.[48] Furthermore, although there are about 100 medical colleges, each of which has departments of pharmacology and biochemistry, the interaction between industry and academic institutions in India, unlike that in the West, is very limited. The NCAER study has therefore concluded that "it is unlikely that the universities or CSIR laboratories would be able to develop, on their own, any substantial amount of technology in a form that could easily be transferred to the industry."[49]

IN-HOUSE R&D OF THE PRIVATE SECTOR

There has been little R&D expenditure in Indian industry, but in recent years it has increased, from Rs. 683.9 million in 1965-66 to Rs. 1,396.4 million in 1970-71 to Rs. 4,022 million in 1976-77 to Rs. 7,261 million in 1980-81 to Rs. 13,380 million in 1983-84.[50] Four important features of the rapidly expanding R&D expenditure must be emphasized. First, a high percentage of R&D expenditure is incurred by government sources as compared with the private sector; it was about 87 percent and 13 percent, respectively, in 1982-83. Second, a very high proportion of R&D expenditure goes to expensive and unproductive sectors such as nuclear energy and space; only one-fourth of R&D expenditure is directly devoted to industry. In 1982-83, for example, out of a total R&D expenditure of Rs. 1,237.56 crores, only Rs. 286 crores (23 percent) was spent by the industrial sector. Third, there has been a sharp fall in the share of the CSIR and the industrial associations in total R&D expenditure. In the 1950s, the CSIR laboratories did virtually all the industrial research, but by 1974 their share had fallen to less than a quarter.[51] Finally, in terms of per capita GNP spent on R&D, the figure for India is $1.5 compared to $120 for the developed countries and under $10 for most of the developing countries.[52]

R&D expenditure in the drug and pharmaceutical industry, although low by international comparison, is higher than that in any other industry in India. According to the data compiled by the Department of Science and Technology, R&D expenditure has risen from 1.4 percent (1975-76) to 2 percent (1980-81) of the total sales turnover in the industry (see Table 6.1). Of the total R&D expenditure of about Rs. 300 crores per annum, for all the industries taken together, more than 10 percent is accounted for by the drug industry alone, although it accounts for 5 percent of the entire industrial product in the country. According to the NCAER study, the pharmaceutical industry's R&D success has been "greater than could be expected from the meagre inputs." While the R&D expenditure of companies in different sectors has increased consistently in the last decade, there has been some decline in the expenditure of public sector firms. Table 6.2 gives

Table 6.1
R&D Expenditure in the Indian Drug and Pharmaceutical Industry
(Rs. in crores)

Year	R&D Expenditure	Sales Turnover	Percentage of STO
75-76	8.0	560	1.4
76-77	10.5	700	1.5
77-78	12.0	900	1.3
78-79	14.75	1050	1.4
79-80	18.0	1150	1.5
80-81	29.3	1465	2.0

Note: Total number of companies registered for R&D in 1974 was only 40, while by 1983-84, 78 companies were registered with the Department of Science and Technology.
Source: Department of Science and Technology.

Table 6.2
Drug Research and Development in India
(Major Indian and Multinational Companies Recognized by the Department of Science and
Technology)

Name of Company	Year	R&D Expenditure (Rs. Lakh)
A. Multinationals		
Hindustan Ciba-Geigy	81-82	266
Hoechst Pharmaceuticals	82-83	222
Glaxo	81-82	218
Pfizer	82-83	106
Boots Company	82-83	102
Eskaylabs	81-82	96
Sandoz	82-83	92
Indian Explosives (Alkalis & Chemicals)	82-83	77
Searle	82-83	51
B. Indian/Public Sector		
Ambalal Sarabhai	82-83	348
IDPL	82-83	171
Ranbaxy	82	120
Hindustan Antibiotics	81-8	71
Unichem	82-83	45
CIPLA	82-83	40
Cadilla	82-83	38
Alembic	82	69

Source: Lok Sabha Unstarred Question no. 3379 dated August 14, 1984, and Rajya Sabha Unstarred
Question no. 743 dated March 5, 1984.

details of the R&D expenditure of the major drug and pharmaceutical companies—both multinational and Indian (public and private)—in the early 1980s.

The data published by the Department of Science and Technology further
show that out of the total R&D expenditure of the industry, the share of FERA
companies was about 65 percent. The leading multinational companies spent about
10 percent of their annual turnover on R&D. Table 6.2 also reveals that five
multinational and three Indian companies spend more than Rs. 1 crore per annum
on R&D.

Recognizing the importance of R&D in the pharmaceutical industry, the
government in the New Drug Policy (1978) made it compulsory for companies
whose turnover is more than Rs. 5 crores per annum to spend 4 percent of their
sales turnover on R&D. The Technology Policy Statement, which was announced
in 1983, envisages fiscal and other rewards and incentives for inventions,
innovations, and technological breakthroughs, and for the establishment of in-
house R&D and installations of pilot plants.[53] In recent years, a few companies,
both multinational and Indian, have emphasized basic research and innovation by
investing heavily in R&D efforts. There are four such research centers in the
private sector: Ciba-Geigy (1963), Hoechst (1972), Sarabhai (1967), and Boots

(1981). Whereas Ciba-Geigy's Research Center has successfully marketed two drugs that it developed—Sintamil (R) and Aubril (R)—the Hoechst (India) Center for Basic Research has discovered several new drugs: Magnesidin (an antibiotic); Trequinisn (an antihypertensive vasolidator); Forskolin (an antihypertensive and antiglaucoma agent); HL 640 (a bronchospasmolytic and antiallergic agent); and Cytorhodin S (a new anthracydine antitumor antibiotic). Boots Research Center has concentrated on finding safe and relatively inexpensive drugs for the treatment of amebiasis, a tropical disease.[54] These and other developments have led an industry analyst to draw the conclusion that the pharmaceutical industry in India is "on the threshold of establishing a strong R&D base."[55]

The R&D expenditure of most large companies in the organized sector may further increase as a result of the implementation of the Drug Policy (1986) and DPCO (1987), which are likely to result in higher profitability for most companies. Yet, at the level of small and medium-size companies, what goes on in the name of R&D, industry analysts agree, is in most cases nothing more than quality control work. Furthermore, the horizontal growth of the industry and the government policy protecting the small-scale sector has had a negative effect on the overall growth of R&D in the drug and pharmaceutical industry.

TECHNOLOGICAL CAPABILITY AND TECHNOLOGICAL DEPENDENCE

If technological capability is defined as "the application of scientific knowledge and skills to the setting up, operating, improving and expanding of productive facilities,"[56] the pharmaceutical industry in India seems to have acquired technological capability in the production of both bulk drugs and formulations. The acquisition of technological capability leads to technological development, which has been defined as the growth in the capability of an enterprise "regardless of whether or not [it] is at world technological frontiers."[57] In this sense, technological development in the case of the drug and pharmaceutical industry may look quite impressive. Over the years, India has become almost totally self-sufficient in the production of formulations. In bulk drugs production, it has acquired technical know-how to handle, with a few exceptions, the most sophisticated process technologies. India has developed through indigenous process many new drugs within five years of their introduction in the international market. (It used to take 10 to 15 years.) A few small- and medium-scale companies have also succeeded in bringing down the prices of drugs such as sulfamethoxazole and trimethoprim through process improvement and large-scale manufacture.[58]

These developments and many others have been possible because of the sustained effort made by the government to build a fairly elaborate institutional and infrastructural base in basic research and process development. The public sector and National Laboratories contributed significantly to the development of technological capability for the manufacture of essential bulk drugs from basic stages, and the government policies of sectoral reservation and the revision of the colonial Patent Law further stimulated the development of indigenous technological capability in the Indian sector. In the pharmaceutical industry, India has reached a level of technological maturity whereby it no longer fears the possibility of multinationals' domination. In fact, the government expects that the new competitive phase in the development of the industry will bring about greater technological advancement and improved capability and productivity.

There remain, however, certain areas in which modernization and updating of technology is badly needed. In the manufacture of antibiotics, in particular, the industry is suffering from technological obsolescence and lags behind developed countries by at least a decade in its introduction of newer antibiotics. Some important advances made in the West have not yet been introduced in India, meaning higher cost of production and continued dependence on imports of certain drugs. By the time the original technology for producing penicillin and streptomycin had been introduced in India, it was obsolete and inefficient. In-house R&D made no determined efforts to lower the cost and raise the yield. Recent attempts to upgrade technology with the help of imported know-how have, by and large, failed. The areas needing modernization include the high-yielding mutant strains of molds used in primary fermentation technology; the improved methods of extraction and purification; the manufacture of intermediates for the production of semisynthetic antibiotics such as 6-APA and 7-ADCA; and the production of newer semisynthetic penicillins and cephalosporins (third generation).

The industry's record is not much better with various types of synthetic drugs, a number of which—chlorpropamide, dexamethasone, piperazine, tolbutamide, for example—continue to be made from penultimates. Lately, however, the production of methyldopa and vitamin B-6 was started in India. Although no factual data on the efficiency of technology in the manufacture of synthetic drugs are available, it is well recognized that the prices of locally produced bulk drugs are much higher than the prevailing prices in the international markets. These differences are not entirely due to the higher prices of raw materials and other inputs and taxes on imported intermediates. "A fairly good part of the higher cost [has been] attributed to lower process efficiency and uneconomic scale of manufacture."[59] It should, however, be noted that the weaknesses of synthetic drug manufacture in India are mainly due to historical reasons. In Europe, especially in Germany and Switzerland, the pharmaceutical industry was an offshoot of the organic chemical industry, which could supply the intermediates required by several other industries, but India had to make a beginning with the bulk drugs and work backwards to the basic stages.

The difficulty in exporting bulk drugs at higher prices and the lower prices of imports of many drugs India already manufactures have made the industry and government more aware of the increasing technological obsolescence in several areas of the industry. It is also recognized that in order to be competitive in the international market, the industry must concentrate on process improvement and modern technology. Although patent protection did stimulate the growth of the national sector and allowed the industry to reach a level of maturity, India is now putting more emphasis on acquiring advanced technology, better access to critical raw materials, and optimal productivity and marketing skills. Recent government policies allowing the private sector not only to manufacture antibiotics but also to import the much-needed technology without bureaucratic delays and government interventions and the government decision (1995) to abolish industrial licensing for most drugs (though government controls were not totally abolished) are aimed at curing the malady of technological obsoleteness that has afflicted the industry for many years.

CONCLUSION

The picture that emerges from this discussion is a complex one. The technological development in the Indian pharmaceutical industry does not lend support to the dependency hypothesis that the technological backwardness of a developing country will perpetuate its dependence on the multinationals of the West. Instead, the level of technological capability acquired by the national sector of the industry, especially since the enactment of the Patent Law of 1970, and the infrastructure that now exists in the form of National Laboratories, support the hypothesis of the bargaining school that the developing host country does benefit from the presence of and prolonged contact with multinationals.

The sustained effort made by the government since India's Second Five Year Plan to start the production of bulk drugs in the public sector and the recent growth in the in-house R&D activities of the private sector have significantly increased the industry's technological capability and technological development. India's pharmaceutical industry has emerged as the most advanced in the Third World, and its public sector firms—IDPL in particular, notwithstanding its current status as a "sick" company—have transferred technology horizontally (to many state governments) and offered consultancy and technical services to other developing countries. The country has become totally self-sufficient in the production of formulations, and in bulk drugs it has acquired the know-how for sophisticated process technologies. (IDPL is among a handful of companies in the world that have the know-how to produce Vitamin B-6.) These developments point in the direction of India's growing self-reliance in the drug and pharmaceutical industry.

However, the problems in the public sector companies and public-funded research institutes have set a definite limit on India's technological self-reliance. Although the public sector companies were mainly responsible for India's entry into the bulk drug production and for bringing down the price of many essential drugs, they have faced, among other things, two serious problems: inefficient technologies and uneconomic plant capacities. The experience of HAL and IDPL shows that India is lagging behind the advanced countries by almost a decade in modern antibiotics technology; the problem has been addressed by both companies in the early 1990s in their decision to enter into joint venture partnerships with private sector companies.

The public sector companies failed to upgrade the old technology through in-house R&D efforts, although it was well-known that the latest technology is not available off the shelf because the multinationals are reluctant to share modern technology without financial participation in a company. The problem of high cost of production in the Indian pharmaceutical industry is related to the government policy of suboptimal plant size and uneconomic plant capacities mandated by antimonopoly laws. The inefficiencies that result from what the Rudolphs call organizational involution—the horizontal growth of the industry, the general inefficiencies associated with public sector firms, the problem of up-scaling of technology from laboratory to industry—are impediments to technological self-reliance. India's lag in pharmaceutical technology is thus due to certain factors that have little to do with the relationship to the multinationals.

The lack of technical expertise in areas such as fermentation technology and advanced drug delivery systems has increased India's dependence on imports. It is paradoxical therefore that although the technological gap between Indian and international firms has been narrowed considerably in the last two decades, it is unlikely that India will attain technological parity with the West in the near future.

Comparatively, India's outlook is brighter. If self-reliance means the capability for adoption of acquired technology to suit national requirements, the development of domestic skills and know-how for assimilating imported technology, the indigenous development of science and technology for more effective R&D programs, and the use of indigenous resources and raw materials to optimal levels, India is more self-reliant in the pharmaceutical industry than any other developing country. It has successfully adapted, assimilated, and improved on imported technology and bargained effectively with the drug multinationals in ways that most Third World countries cannot. The technological developments of the last two decades make it almost certain that India will not slip back into the position of technological dependence it experienced in the first two decades after independence.

NOTES

1. See Lloyd I. Rudolph and Susanne H. Rudolph, *In Pursuit of Lakshmi: The Political Economy of the Indian State* (Chicago: University of Chicago Press, 1987), Ch. 1.

2. John E. S. Parker, "Pharmaceuticals and Third World Concerns: The Lall Report and the Otaga Study," in Robert B. Helm (ed.), *The International Supply of Medicines: Implications of U.S. Regulatory Reform* (Washington D.C.: American Enterprise Institute for Public Policy Research, 1980), p. 136.

3. United Nations Center on Transnational Corporations, *Transnational Corporations and the Pharmaceutical Industry* (New York: United Nations, 1979).

4. The Amendment established a mandatory investigational new drug (IND) to be administered by the Food and Drug Administration for the premarket clearance of all new drug compounds. As a result, "the project development costs and gestation times for new drugs have shifted upward" since 1962. See Jerome E. Schnee, "R&D Strategy in the U.S. Pharmaceutical Industry," *Research Policy*, 8, No. 4 (Oct. 1979): 364-382; and Henry G. Grabowski and John M. Vernon, "The Pharmaceutical Industry," in Richard R. Nelson (ed.), *Government and Technical Progress: A Cross-Industry Analysis* (New York: Pergamon Press, 1982).

5. The details of the new products introduced in the ethical pharmaceutical industry between 1950 and 1977 are given in a table in Schnee, "R&D Strategy in the U.S. Pharmaceutical Industry," p. 368.

6. *The Washington Post* (Weekly Edition), Nov. 27-Dec. 3, 1989, pp. 20-21.

7. UNIDO, *Appropriate Industrial Technology for Drugs and Pharmaceuticals*, Monographs on Appropriate Industrial Technology, No. 10 (New York: UNIDO), pp. 91-92.

8. UNCTAD, *Technology Policies and Planning for the Pharmaceutical Sector in the Developing Countries*, Trade and Development Board: Committee on Transfer of Technology (UNCTAD: Oct. 1980), p. ix.

9. Even in the 1980s, the disease pattern in India was catastrophic: The country has approximately 10 million TB patients, of whom 50,000 die every year; 60 million people with goiter, which is the result of iodine deficiency; 40,000 children going blind every year due to lack of vitamin A in their diets; and 1.5 million children dying of diarrhea each year. It is estimated that India loses 73 million man-days a year as a consequence of water-borne diseases.

10. *Hathi Committee Report*, pp. 97-98.

11. "Overall Results of the Third Survey (1970-71 to 1972-73)—Private Sector Companies," in RBI, *Foreign Collaboration in Indian Industry: Fourth Survey Report, 1985* (Bombay: 1985).

12. A. Rahman et al., "Research and Development in the Indian Drug and Pharmaceutical Industry," *Lok Udyog*, July-August, 1970, pp. 635-640.

13. National Committee on Science and Technology, *Report on Science and Technology Plan of Chemical Industry*, 2 vols. (Government of India: 1973), 2: 37.

14. Vasant Deasi, *Indian Industry: Profile and Related Issues* (Bombay: Himalaya Publishing House, 1987), Ch. 12.

15. National Science Foundation, *Research and Development Industry*, Science Resource Series, 68 (NSF: 1966).

16. Sudip Chaudhuri, "Manufacturing Drugs Without TNCs: Status of Indigenous Sector in India," *Economic and Political Weekly*, August 1984, p. 1342.

17. World production of bulk drugs was estimated in 1985 to be about 239 million kilograms, of which one-fourth was manufactured in the United States and 35 percent in Western Europe. M. D. Nair, "Indian Pharmaceutical Industry: A Global Perspective," *The Eastern Pharmacist*, 24, No. 347 (November 1986): 31.

18. HAL, *Open With the World Closer to Millions* (Pimpri: 1986).

19. Committee on Public Undertaking, *Eightieth Report on Hindustan Antibiotic Limited*, Ministry of Chemical and Fertilisers (New Delhi: Lok Sabha Secretariat, 1976), p.3.

20. Data presented in this section were obtained by the author while interviewing the senior managers of the company (general manager, R&D; general manager, Personnel and Management Services; materials manager, and corporate planning manager) on Oct. 20, 1986.

21. P. L. Narayana, "Indian Pharmaceutical Industry: Present Status and Problems," *Commerce*, March 12, 1985, p. 5.

22. Titer refers to the quantity of solution required to convert a compound into another form.

23. Committee on Public Undertaking, *Eightieth Report on Hindustan Antibiotic Limited (1975-76)*, Ministry of Chemical and Fertilizers (New Delhi: Lok Sabha Secretariat, 1976).

24. P. L. Narayana, *The Indian Pharmaceutical Industry: Problems and Prospects* (New Delhi: NCAER, 1984), p. 110.

25. Sulekha Sule's interview with Y. H. Gharpure, *The Economic Times*, January 28, 1982.

26. Rudolph and Rudolph, *In Pursuit of Lakshmi*, p. 27.

27. Y. H. Gharpure, "Drugs and Pharmaceuticals Industry," Paper presented at the National Seminar on Cost Competitiveness in Indian Chemical Industry, Feb. 4, 1983, ICMA, Calcutta, pp. 9-10.

28. Ibid. Gharpure, the former managing director of HAL, lists four other reasons: (1) high costs of raw materials, (2) high costs of utilities, (3) low productivity of labor, and (4) high cost of plants.

29. Committee on Public Undertaking, *Fifty-Sixth Report: Indian Drugs and Pharmaceuticals Limited, 1973-74*, Ministry of Petroleum and Chemicals (New Delhi: Lok Sabha Secretariat, 1974).

30. Santanu Saikia, "Who Will Cure IDPL," *Business India*, December 30-January 12, 1986, p. 63.

31. The only exception to this was Hindustan Machine Tool Company, which gave the Swiss firm Oerlikons 10 percent equity share in the company.

32. In an unpublished paper (R&D in IDPL—A Perspective, 1986), the IDPL Research Center, Hyderabad, gives details of the process improvements made in Soviet technology through in-house R&D effort.

33. Data presented in this section are based on personal interviews of the deputy manager, corporate planning; company secretary and the public relations officer, IDPL, Gurgaon on November 21 and 25, 1986.

34. Quoted in K. Jayaraman, "Drug Research and Development and Technology Status in India," *Chemsearch and Industry*, 1, No. 1 (July, 1986): 14.

35. B. K. Kaelya, former Manager, Corporate Planning, IDPL, in a personal interview on November 24, 1986.

36. Anil C. Ghosh, "Role of R&D in Choice of Technology for Drugs and Drug Intermediates—A Perspective View," *IDMA Bulletin*, 16, No. 35 (Sept. 21, 1985): 529.

37. See, for example, Samuel Paul, "Privatisation: A Review of International Experience," *Economic and Political Weekly*, February 6, 1988, pp. 273-276.

38. The Board for Industrial and Financial Reconstruction (BIFR) declared the state-owned IDPL "sick" on August 12, 1992. See *The Economic Times*, December 27, 1995.

39. N. N. Mehrotra et al., "R&D and Technological Development for Production of Essential Bulk Drugs," *IDMA Bulletin*, 16, No. 39 (1985): 5

40. *IDMA Bulletin*, 16, No. 18 (1985): 247.

41. A. V. Rama Rao and J. V. Rajan, "Transfer of Drug Technologies from Laboratory to Industry," *IDMA Bulletin*, 16, No. 6 (February 11, 1985): 6.

42. Y. K. Hamied, "Address to a Gathering in Pune on December 2, 1983," unpublished paper (Pune: 1983), p. 3.

43. Y. K. Hamied, the managing director, holds a Ph.D. in pharmacology from Cambridge University. Most industry managers I talked to, both in the public and private—national and multinational—sectors, admired his ability to identify the drugs for which there was a market in India. He is therefore seen by many industry insiders as one who has not only made his company grow in recent years but has also contributed significantly toward making India technologically self-reliant.

44. Expenditure of the CSIR's industrial laboratories in 1974 was Rs. 194 million.

45. The supporters of the CSIR, on the other hand, point to the list of its success records in many fields—from the Swaraj tractor to leather technology to raggi-based Amul milk for children. For details see Ashok Raj, "CSIR Review: Another Window Dressing," *Mainstream*, June 20, 1987, pp. 28-32; S. S. Gill "CSIR: Technology and Commitment," *Mainstream*, June 13, 1987, pp. 24-26; and Baldev Singh, "Reviewing the CSIR," *Economic and Political Weekly*, August 23, 1986, pp. 1511-1517.

46. *IDMA Bulletin*, 16, No. 6 (1985): 3.

47. This includes the following drugs: salbutamol (antiasthamatic), mebendazole (anthelmintic), naproxen (anti-inflammatory), Captopril (antihypertensive), cimetidine (antipeptic ulcerant), and ranitidine (antiulcer). *IDMA Bulletin*, 17, No. 7 (1986): 108.

48. Ghosh, "Role of R&D in Choice of Technology for Drugs," p. 532.

49. Narayana, *The Indian Pharmaceutical Industry: Problems and Prospects.*

50. Government of India, *Research and Development Statistics 1982-83* (New Delhi: Department of Science and Technology, n.d.).

51. A. V. Desai, "The Origin and Direction of Industrial R&D in India," *Research Policy*, 9, No. 1 (January 1980): 76-77.

52. While most developed countries devote 2 to 3 percent of their GNP on R&D, the figure for India in 1982-83 was 0.85 percent. See *Research and Development Statistics, 1982-83*, p. 29.

53. Government of India, *Research and Development Statistics 1982-83* (New Delhi: Department of Science and Technology, n.d.).

54. K. Jayaraman, "Drug Research & Development and Technology Status in India," *Chemsearch and Industry*, 1, No. 1 (July 1986): 12-14.

55. M. D. Nair, "R&D in Drug Industry," *Commerce*, March 2, 1985, p. 15.

56. Sanjaya Lall, *Learning to Industrialize: The Acquisition of Technological Capability by India* (London: MacMillan Press, 1987), p. 1.

57. Ibid., p. 3.

58. *Financial Express*, June 25, 1985.

59. "Drug Technology: The Neglected Factor," *Financial Express*, June 25, 1985.

7

Global Machine Tool Industry and Technological Development in the Indian Machine Tool Industry

The machine tool industry occupies a central place in the interrelations between the different branches of production. It provides the machines fundamental to the production of all the modern equipment needed for manufacturing, transportation, and agricultural sectors. Most of the developments in the field of production technology are epitomized in a machine tool and are made available to the engineering industries to increase the production of various commodities. The machine tool industry provides "mother machines" (machines that make machines) to stimulate downstream industrial activities, for it is in this industry that "the metalworking machinery of production that is used to fabricate all metal products and parts is itself made."[1] This chapter first examines the structure, growth, and technological development of the machine tool industry in the developed and developing countries and then looks at the development in the Indian machine tool industry in the last three decades.

IMPORTANCE OF THE MACHINE TOOL INDUSTRY

Historically, the machine tool sector was the precursor of substantial industrialization. The rate of industrialization and technical progress achieved in the industrialized countries has been explained partly by the way these countries have promoted their machine tool industries.[2] Without machine tools, everything would have to be made by hand. Machine tools thus form the backbone of a nation's industrial progress. "Machine tools are not just any industry," argues Harley Shaiken. "They are the very basis of an industrial economy. If you have a weakness there, it has an extraordinary multiplier effect."[3] It is, therefore, no exaggeration to say that modern industrial society could not exist without machine tools.[4]

        Machine tools were not only critical to an earlier era of industrialization, but they are equally important today because they are essential in what is more popularly thought of as the sunrise, high-tech industries. For the two "late-comers," Japan and the Soviet Union/Russia, the capital goods industries played a leading role, over the long run, in the industrialization process by stimulating capital formation and raising the productivity of individual investments.[5]

        In the industrialization of the Third World, however, consumer goods have led the manufacturing sector, and capital goods have been relegated in most cases to a minor place. Capital goods, for example, account for only 10 to 15 percent of total manufacturing production (in value added terms) in developing countries, compared with 30 to 35 percent in developed countries.[6] Developing countries have therefore been dependent, by and large, on the import of capital goods from the developed countries. But the salience of engineering and capital goods industries in general and the machine tool industry in particular in the development of technical progress and in increasing labor productivity has recently been emphasized by most Third World countries. In the 1950s and 1960s, however, only a few large developing countries with substantial natural endowments—Brazil, China, and India, for example—recognized the importance of the machine tool industry in the overall industrialization process and adopted policies that allowed the growth of this industry. A machine tool has been defined as

a power-driven tool, non-portable while in operation, used for carrying out, individually or in combination, the operations of machining, forming, and electro-chemical processing of metals, wood, glass, plastic and similar materials. Machine tools range from simple drilling machines and lathes to complex, fully automated and computerized machines, machining centres with tool changers, multi-station machines, transfer lines and flexible machining systems capable of automatically producing work that meets the required standard of quality and quantity.[7]

Machine tools may be divided into two basic groups: metal-cutting machines (turning, milling, planing, shaping, drilling, boring, gear-hobbing, tapping, broaching, and grinding, which, in 1980, accounted for about three-quarters of world machine tool production in terms of gross value) and metal-forming machines (presses, forge hammers, explosion-forming machines, welding units, and others).[8] Although industrial development of a country depends to a considerable extent on the number, age, quality, and types of machine tools it has, the machine tool production of a country depends largely on the needs of the user industries and the demands of its export sector.

        The UNIDO study has categorized machine tool manufacturing capability into four stages of industrial development: limited (bench drills, bench grinders, etc.), moderate (engine lathes, simple milling machines, small mechanical presses and brakes, etc.), substantial (turret lathes, precision grinding machines, horizontal boring machines, hydraulic or mechanical presses, etc.), and high (gear-grinding machines, special-purpose machines, NC drilling machines, NC lathes, etc.).[9] The study suggests that the decision to undertake the production of machine tools of a particular kind should correspond to the level of industrialization attained by a country.

STRUCTURE OF THE GLOBAL MACHINE TOOL INDUSTRY

Although the machine tool industry emerged simultaneously with industrialization and with the development of the engineering industry in the past 200 years, the share of machine tools in total manufacturing output is negligible. It is much less than 10 percent in most countries.[10] The machine tool industry is characterized by several peculiar features. First, it is a highly capital-intensive and technology-oriented industry with a gestation period longer than that of many other industries. Machine tools are technically complex and require a large initial overhead investment in design and testing. The rates of return on the capital in this industry are not attractive.

Second, the production and export of machine tools is highly concentrated in a few developed countries. Since these countries specialize in the production of certain kinds of machines—high-precision machine tools (in Switzerland), high-performance machines (in the United States), heavy-duty and high-production machines (in former centrally planned economies)—the leading machine tool manufacturing countries are themselves the principal importers of machine tools. In 1979, for example, 22 major machine tool producing countries—including China, India, and Brazil—accounted for 92 percent of the total production, "consumed about 75 percent of the total world machine-tool production and accounted for about 93 percent of world exports."[11] Thus, no country in the world is self-sufficient in machine tools.

Third, production and export of machine tools in the developing countries as a whole is negligible. Of the estimated $22.7 billion production of the world machine tool industry in 1979, the developing countries produced 6.37 percent of that total and exported only 3.5 percent of the world's machine tools. With the exception of the newly industrializing countries (NICs), the current levels of demand of machine tools in the Third World are insufficient for economic local production.

Fourth, there is a close technological collaboration between machine tool producers and users in product development and innovation to ensure that machine tools meet the technological requirements of user industries. In the United States, for example, the machine tool shops located in the Midwest region (Chicago, Cleveland, Rockford, Cincinnati, and Detroit) supply machines to the automobile industry, and those in California supply machine tools primarily to the aerospace industry. Finally, most of the machine tool firms, especially in the United States, are small manufacturers of special-purpose machinery or standard general-purpose machinery, although there are a few large firms in the industry, such as Cincinnati Milacron, Warner and Swasey, Kearney and Trecker, and Giddins and Lewis.[12]

The world output of machine tools in 1985 was $22 billion. Japan was the leading manufacturer of machine tools and accounted for 24 percent of the total world production, followed by West Germany and the former Soviet Union (see Table 7.1). Western Europe, led by Germany, is the dominant factor in the world machine tool scene; in 1985, 12 European countries accounted for 32 percent of world output. The leadership of the United States in the machine tool industry has been eroded in recent years, partly because of the technological advancements made by Japan and Germany in the production of highly automated machines. A notable feature of the Japanese machine tool industry is the high production ratio of numerically controlled (NC) machine tools to the total machine tools produced; it went up from 10 percent in 1971 to 42 percent in 1979 to 60.75 percent in 1983. This increasing ratio of high-technology machine tools in total production has been attributed as much to the rising demand from Japanese users for highly productive machine tools as to the rapid technological developments in the Japanese electronics industry.[13]

TECHNOLOGICAL DEVELOPMENT IN THE MACHINE TOOL INDUSTRY

Machine tools have played a crucial part in the history of technology. Beginning with the building of cylinder-boring machines by John Wilkinson in 1776, which made the manufacture of full-scale engines (based on the invention of James Watt) possible, machine tools have played an important role in the industrial revolution in the West. Without the machine tool industry, there would be no turbines, motor cars, bicycles, radios, airplanes, and washing machines—most of those industrial and domestic items on which "civilized" progress has come to depend. Great Britain dominated world markets in machine tools until the beginning of the twentieth century. The growth of the machine tool industry is intertwined with the increasing demand for machines in different industries. The First World War gave impetus to the growth of the industry, especially in Germany and the United States, and there was a dramatic expansion of world machine tool production. In the United States, for example, the output of machine tools increased from $49 million in 1914 to $212 million in 1919,[14] which was stimulated partly by the requirements of the user industries on account of the mass production of consumer durables, including automobiles.

Two major breakthroughs in machine tool technology in the first half of this century revolutionized the industry: the innovation of high-speed steel, which contained a substantial proportion of tungsten and chromium and replaced carbon steel, and the introduction of carbide cutting tools in Germany in the early 1930s. In the 1950s and 1960s the most significant innovation was NC machine tool technology, which was triggered by the revolution in the microelectronics industry. Numerical Control (NC) is a concept that provides for the automation of machining cycles on the basis of control information received in the form of numerical data.

Table 7.1
World Machine Tool Production and Trade, 1985
(Figures in $ Million)

Country		Total	Production		Trade	
			Metal-Cutting Machines	Metal-Forming Machines	Export	Import
1.	Japan	5269.7	4400.4	869.3	2098.9	222.5
2.	W.Germany	3123.1	2183.1	940.0	1899.8	591.4
3.	U.S.S.R.	3015.0	2409.0	606.1	193.7	1291.1
4.	U.S.A.	2575.0	1785.0	790.0	445.0	1725.0
5.	Italy	1056.4	742.6	313.8	611.9	193.5
6.	Switzerland	954.7	826.7	128.0	832.8	174.7
7.	E. Germany	789.3	626.2	163.1	750.2	118.7
8.	UK	722.9	593.8	129.1	335.6	342.1
9.	France	468.0	352.8	115.2	228.3	350.0
10.	China	453.3	340.0	113.3	34.2	136.7
11.	Czech.	334.4	293.9	40.5	267.1	71.4
12.	Romania	324.1	299.2	24.9	54.9	74.8
13.	India	282.7	226.2	56.5	20.2	161.6
14.	Taiwan	261.5	235.4	26.2	208.9	112.4
15.	Spain	242.6	179.2	63.5	146.9	58.2
16.	Yugoslavia	238.6	148.6	89.9	133.4	97.7
17.	Canada	216.6	175.3	41.3	106.9	320.6
18.	Sweden	197.3	116.1	81.2	150.9	174.1
19.	Bulgaria	192.5	175.0	17.5	140.0	160.0
20.	S. Korea	183.9	151.5	32.4	25.0	150.0
21.	Hungary	160.0	135.2	24.8	120.0	90.1
22.	Brazil	152.8	137.2	15.6	22.3	21.7
23.	Israel	130.0	130.0	0.0	116.0	89.4
24.	Poland	117.6	102.0	15.5	70.5	118.5
25.	Austria	116.8	65.2	51.6	127.3	87.3
26.	Belgium	95.9	17.3	78.5	129.5	153.8
27.	Denmark	49.5	28.3	21.2	25.0	17.4
28.	Netherlands	42.1	27.1	15.0	87.2	129.2
29.	Australia	39.6	26.4	13.3	4.2	60.9
30.	Singapore	34.1	30.9	3.2	83.6	143.1
31.	Finland	27.1	3.4	23.7	22.2	64.6
32.	Mexico	24.7	18.4	6.3	1.0	155.0
33.	Portugal	9.4	4.7	4.7	5.9	18.8
34.	Argentina	6.7	3.6	3.1	2.0	8.0
35.	S. Africa	5.9	4.1	1.8	0.5	75.2
36.	Hong Kong	4.2	3.6	0.6	0.9	5.2
	Total	21,918.1	16,997.7	4,920.7	9,502.4	7,764.7

Sources: American Machinist and Automated Manufacturing.

It is an "important improvement in the sequence control of machine tools because the travel of parts is no longer limited by steps that have to be adjusted with every change in the size of the workpiece, but by a feedback system to the NC unit itself, which counts the extent of the movements as they are performed and stops as soon as the desired dimension is reached."[15]

Technological developments in the machine tool industry in the last two decades reflect the structural changes taking place in many engineering fields. In order to reduce production costs through saving labor and increasing efficiency, demand for automated machine tools such as NC machines has increased considerably. The development of NC machines was further accelerated in the mid-1970s as microcircuits were developed in the field of electronics and applied increasingly in the control systems of machine tools. NC technology has recently been applied to many metal-working operations such as turning, milling, drilling, boring, grinding, gear cutting, electrodischarge machining (EDM), and laser cutting. Metal-forming machines such as press brakes, punch presses, shears, and pipe-bending machines are also appearing in their NC versions. Turning centers and machining centers are the modern equivalent of lathes and milling, drilling, and boring machines.

The NC technology itself has undergone revolutionary changes making possible simplified operations and higher degrees of flexibility and automation. Industrial robots, for example, have now been on the industrial scene for more than two decades. From applications initially limited to hazardous and strenuous functions, robots are applied in a wide range of tasks—from loading and unloading machine tools and presses and removing parts from die-casting machines to welding, painting, and simple assembly operations. In Japan and the United States, the two countries making maximum use of industrial robots, the advanced development of sensors has helped robots "attain human capabilities in final assembly sequences," and in the near future "almost 50 percent of the direct work in the final assembly of automobiles will be achieved by programmable automation and robots."[16] Lately, Japan has moved ahead of the United States in the computer numerical control (CNC) technology, which is more flexible than conventional NC systems. CNCs are electronic controls that serve as "the brains and nervous systems of such tools as lathes and milling machines. Under CNC direction they become . . . as nimble as a troupe of belly dancers, able to sculpture anything from aircraft wings to submarine propellers."[17] The advent of CNC made it possible to run machines safely at higher speeds and traverse rates to obtain rapid metal removal. Further development in machine tool technology has been made with the introduction of flexible manufacturing systems (FMS), computer-integrated manufacturing (CIM), EDM, electrochemical machining (ECM), and lasers.[18]

Japanese firms today are the leading exporters of NC and CNC machine tools. Recognizing the technological advantages enjoyed by the Japanese firms, a number of American firms have recently entered into joint ventures with the Japanese machine tool companies, for example, the 1987 fifty-fifty joint venture agreement between General Electric, the leading U.S. manufacturer of CNC machine tools, and Fanuc, the Japanese firm, which is the world leader in industrial robots technology.[19]

THE MACHINE TOOL INDUSTRY IN THE THIRD WORLD

The machine tool industry requires highly skilled labor because of the complexity and precision of its production. Since most Third World countries have a shortage of skilled labor, qualified engineers, and technicians, their possibility of their producing machine tools is seriously restricted. The development of the machine tool industry in developing countries has thus been slow. Until the 1970s, the engineering industries had not developed in most countries. The share of the Third World in total world consumption and production of machine tools has registered an upward trend only in the last decade. Whereas consumption increased from an average of 8 percent in 1970-71 to an average of 14 percent in 1979-80, the share of developing countries in world total gross output of machine tools increased from an average of 2.5 percent to 5.8 percent during the same period.[20] However, development of the machine tool industry has taken place only in a few Third World countries such as Singapore, Taiwan, the Republic of Korea, Brazil, Argentina, and India. While in the 1960s almost all the machine tool production of the developing world was concentrated in four countries—Argentina, Brazil, India, and the People's Republic of China—by the late 1970s, South Korea, Singapore, and Taiwan emerged as major machine tool manufacturers and exporters. Although the development of the machine tool industry—and industrialization in general—in Singapore, Taiwan, and the Republic of Korea was mostly export-led, its development in Brazil, Argentina, and India was due to import substitution policies of the governments.

The last decade-and-a-half has also witnessed a remarkable growth in machine tool exports from the Third World. The share of developing countries in world total exports of machine tools increased from 0.4 percent in 1966-67 to an average of 3 percent in 1979-80.[21] However, the aggregate export figures would be misleading because there are only a handful of machine tools exporters in the Third World. In 1966-67, for example, 71 percent of total exports from the Third World were accounted for by Brazil (33 percent), India (20 percent), and Argentina (18 percent). By 1979-80, approximately the same percentage was shared by Taiwan (47 percent), Singapore (11 percent), and Brazil (14 percent).[22] It is interesting to note that the export-led growth strategy of Taiwan and South Korea has led to an impressive rate of growth and development in their machine tool industry. By specializing in the manufacture of a few products—one or two types of general-purpose machine tools such as lathes, drilling machines, and milling machines—and keeping the number of employees low (100 to 800 personnel in small and medium-sized firms—a small number compared to public sector firms in many developing countries), the Taiwanese and Koreans have succeeded in achieving economy of scale and development of their export sector to a degree not found in other machine tool–producing Third World countries.

South Korea, in sharp contrast to Brazil and India, began exporting machine tools and other capital goods from the beginning. In order to compete in the international market, it had to keep up with the technological changes taking place in the machine tool industry in the developed countries. Government support in the form of subsidies and preferential access to credit have, however, been crucial to the expansion of exports in machine tools and other capital goods industries in South Korea.[23]

In the last three decades, the NICs—Brazil, Argentina, Singapore, Taiwan, Mexico, South Korea, and India—have acquired the technological capability to manufacture general-purpose machines and have become self-sufficient in their needs. The machine tool industry has been selected as a priority industry in the NICs. Most of these countries are now producing some advanced type of machines.[24] The real opportunity for the NICs, according to an industry analyst and a UNIDO consultant, is in the area of general-purpose machines:

As the industrially advanced countries give up manufacturing many types of general purpose machines in preference to the advance designs due to the relatively high labor content in the former type of machine tools, the developing countries are likely to expand their exports, provided they build high quality, modern machine tools needed in the markets of the industrialized countries and those of less developed countries of Asia and Africa.[25]

Further growth of machine tools in those NICs that have well-established machine tool industries will depend on their exports of universal machines as well as on the production of more advanced machines. According to a recent study, Taiwan is the leading producer of CNC machine tools among developing countries, followed by Brazil and South Korea. India and Argentina also produce CNC machine tools, but in small quantities.[26]

In the development of the machine tool industry in the Third World, the most remarkable case of import substitution occurred in India. The efforts made by the government had a positive effect on the growth of the industry and there has been a significant decrease in India's import dependence. According to a recent machine tool census, the percentage of Indian machine tools in the total machine tool population has increased from 63.8 percent in 1968 to 88.1 percent in 1986.[27] While in the early 1950s there were only three major units producing machine tools in the organized sector, by 1988 the number increased to 160 firms—in both the public and the private sector—with an installed capacity of Rs. 300 crores. Over the years, the machine tool industry has acquired the capability of producing a wide range of products for domestic use as well as for exports. The industry now produces a variety of machine tools, including lathe centers, turrets, radial drills, pillar drills, grinding machines, tool and cutter grinders, complicated designs like single-spindle automatics, vertical turret lathes, electric milling machines, gear hobbers, high-production copying lathes, multitool automatic lathes, multispindle automatics, drum turrets, horizontal boring machines, and others. Of late, India has entered the age of NC and CNC technology and ranks 18th in production among 35 machine-building countries and 16th in consumption among 25 leading machine tool–consuming countries.[28]

DEVELOPMENT OF THE MACHINE TOOL INDUSTRY IN INDIA

The production of machine tools in India started toward the end of the period of British rule. It is estimated that before the Second World War, Indian firms (P. N. Dutt and Co., India Machinery Co. Ltd., Cooper Engineering Ltd., and Kirlosker Ltd.) manufactured not more than 100 machine tools per annum. World War II gave impetus to the machine tool industry as it was called on to make greater efforts to supply the requirements of war. The government passed the Machine Tool Control Act in 1941 and appointed a machine tool controller to promote the industry in a systematic manner. The result was impressive: During the war years, India produced about 20,000 machine tools valued at Rs. 60 million.[29] However, after the Second World War, the Indian machine tool industry suffered a setback when the government withdrew assistance. The government decision to liberalize imports made it almost impossible for the Indian manufacturers to compete with the foreign machine tools, and by 1950 the industry had virtually collapsed. Production of machine tools in terms of their value dropped from more than Rs. 11 million in 1945 to Rs. 3 million in 1950 (see Table 7.2). Shortly after independence, the government recognized that the structural weaknesses of the machine tool industry—the absence of capital goods industry, and the limited engineering skills that the country possessed—were impeding its growth.

In order to help establish the machine tool industry, the government decided, in 1949, to set up a public sector company—Hindustan Machine Tool Limited (HMT)—in technical collaboration with a Swiss firm, Oerlikons-Buhrle Machine Tool Works. The government identified the machine tool industry as a priority area of investment. Thus, the model of development adopted in India's Second Five Year Plan (1955-56 to 1960-61) emphasized the development of heavy industry and the attainment of self-sufficiency in the machinery sector. The growth in productive capacity of the machine tool industry was the lynchpin to the Mahalanobis strategy,[30] which emphasized that the growth in national income is dependent on the capital stock that can be created only through investment of capital goods, which could be realized only through the development of investment goods industries. Mahalanobis argued:

In the long run the rate of industrialisation and the growth of the national economy would depend on the increasing production of coal, electricity, iron and steel, heavy machinery, heavy chemicals, and the heavy industries generally which would increase the capacity for capital formation. . . . The heavy industries must, therefore, be expanded with all possible speed.[31]

Accordingly, public sector companies were given the responsibility of initiating the indigenous manufacture of capital goods with the technological assistance of both socialist and market economy countries in at least two important sub-sectors: machine tool and electrical equipment. Three machine tool companies were established in the public sector. The government gave financial and fiscal assistance to the private sector companies, and they were allowed to import the required technology and know-how from abroad. More important, the import of machine tool types similar to those produced indigenously was totally banned. This resulted in an enormous increase in machine tool production after 1956—an 11-fold increase in two decades (see Tables 7.2 and 7.3).

By the late 1950s, both public and private sector companies were producing a variety of general-purpose machine tools. Moreover, there was a sudden growth of small-scale machine tool manufacturers in many states, especially in Punjab and Karnataka, yet the bulk of machine tool production was in the organized sector. In the late 1960s, for example, 66 firms in the organized sector accounted for 90 percent of the total output of machine tools.[32] Currently there are 160 firms in the organized sector, but only 10 major units—both public and private—account for about 80 percent of the value of output. In the organized sector, the government played a crucial role in the development of the industry, which is reflected in the share of HMT (the largest public sector company), which was more than 40 percent of the total production in the 1960s and has not changed much since.

Although the industry experienced a brief period of recession from 1966 to 1967, the 1960s was a decade of rapid growth in the machine tool industry, mainly because of the Second and Third Five Year Plans' priority investment in basic and heavy industry. The policy of import substitution industrialization (ISI) allowed the Indian machine tool manufacturers to enter into collaboration agreements with leading machine tool companies in Europe, Japan, and the United States and

Table 7.2
Machine Tool Production and Imports in India, 1942-1960
(Rs. million)

Year	Production	Import	Percentage of Production to Imports
1942	0.6	5.69	10.65
1943	6.36	5.37	118.48
1944	7.78	15.27	50.95
1945	11.16	18.19	61.35
1946	9.13	18.32	49.79
1947	4.59	36.79	12.47
1948	5.47	41.44	13.20
1949	4.73	41.96	11.27
1950	2.86	24.90	11.48
1951	4.73	25.00	18.82
1952	4.48	22.11	20.06
1953	4.40	31.27	14.09
1954	4.71	38.64	12.19
1955	6.78	52.89	12.88
1956	10.81	88.72	12.92
1957	23.47	146.43	16.03
1958	34.07	144.20	23.68
1959	41.63	163.27	25.49
1960	58.60	209.35	27.99

Source: IMTMA (Indian Machine Tools Manufacturers Association).

Table 7.3
Production and Consumption of Machine Tools in India, 1961-85
(Rs. Million)

Year	Production	Consumption	Share of Production in Consumption (%)
1961	73.3	315.3	23
1962	104.0	363.3	29
1963	167.8	481.8	35
1964	209.8	553.0	38
1965	254.8	602.7	42
1966	284.8	708.1	40
1967	254.7	642.0	40
1968	206.3	550.2	37
1969	266.8	427.2	62
1970	372.3	527.4	71
1971	502.5	689.0	73
1972	494.6	710.0	69
1973	622.6	872.4	71
1974	884.4	1107.8	80
1975	1040.3	1399.0	74
1976	1168.5	1444.2	81
1977	1095.7	1316.3	83
1978	1210.5	1405.5	86
1979	1558.2	2134.2	73
1980	1859.4	2699.6	69
1981	2342.1	3407.0	69
1982	2665.1	3823.2	70
1983	2846.9	3985.3	71
1984	3065.3	4547.4	67
1985	3031.6	5207.1	58

Source: IMTMA (Indian Machine Tool Manufacturers Association).

thereby import the required know-how and technology. The result was a rapid growth of the industry. In order to meet the growing needs of the metalworking industry, the Indian machine tool industry started producing all types of general-purpose machines including a number of new products such as combination turret lathes, single-spindle automatics, multispindle automatics, vertical turret lathes, gear shapers, precision copying lathes, multitool automatic lathes, drum turrets, horizontal boring machines, broaching machines, front-chucking machines, single- and special-purpose machines, transfer lines, and heavy-duty hydraulic and mechanical presses.[33] Indigenous production as a percentage of total consumption of machine tools improved considerably in the 1960s and 1970s, although in the 1980s and 1990s import dependence has increased. The percentage of production to total consumption went up from 23 percent in 1961 to 33 percent in 1968 to 71 percent in 1974 and down to 65 percent in 1980 (see Table 7.4).

Between 1978 and 1982, the growth rate of the industry was fairly high—10 to 29 percent per annum. Not only did the value of the machine tools produced double during this period, but the range of production widened to include all types of general-purpose machine tools, heavy-duty machine tools such as horizontal and vertical boring machines, jig mills, high-capacity mechanical and

Table 7.4
**Trade Dependence and Trade Balance in Machine
Tools in India, 1968-1980**

Year	Share of Imports in Consumption	Share of Exports in Gross Output	Share of Net Exports in the Sum of Exports and Imports (%)
1968	67	9	-91
1969	44	11	-73
1970	47	12	-73
1971	45	7	-84
1972	33	6	-75
1973	45	5	-88
1974	29	11	-52
1975	30	11	-56
1976	28	12	-50
1977	35	23	-29
1978	33	25	-20
1979	30	16	-39
1980	35	15	-50

Source: UNIDO, *World Non-Electrical Machinery* (New York: United Nations, 1984), p. 105.

hydraulic metal-forming presses, universal and cylindrical grinders, and special-purpose machines. India also manufactured a limited number of NC and CNC machines.[34] After 1982, however, growth rate in production tapered off because of recessionary conditions in the engineering industry and other machine tool user industries. The actual growth rate (after adjusting for inflation) for the years 1983 and 1984 was zero or negative. Thus, after more than two decades of strong growth, the industry was faced with a crisis by the mid-1980s. Although the industry recorded an annual growth rate of 13 percent during the Seventh Five Year Plan period (1985-86 to 1989-90), it fell to 1 percent in 1992 and to minus 18 percent in 1993. After a short period of recession, the industry started growing at a healthy rate (36 percent) in 1994.

The crisis has been due mainly to India's failure to modernize and keep pace with the latest developments in machine building technology. In recent years, user industries—especially the automotive and auto-ancillary industries—have considerably increased their requirements for high-technology machines, which the Indian machine tool industry does not yet manufacture on a large scale. The recent expansion and modernization of other user industries—electrical equipment manufacturers, railway workshops, defense production units, and heavy engineering industries—has further increased the demand for and consumption of machine tools.

There is a clear preference for high-technology and CNC machine tools. Although the consumption of machine tools has increased steeply in the 1980s and 1990s (it was around Rs. 500 crores in 1986), the growth in indigenous production has not kept pace with the rise in demand. As a result, there has been a substantial increase in the import of machine tools in the 1980s and 1990s. Machine tool imports increased four-fold between 1978 and 1984 (see Table 7.5), the bulk of

Table 7.5
Machine Tool Imports and Exports

Year	Imports	Percentage Change	Export	Percentage Change
1960	20.94	-	-	-
1961	24.22	15.7	-	-
1962	26.04	7.5	0.11	-
1963	31.50	21.0	0.10	-9.1
1964	34.44	9.3	0.12	20.0
1965	34.93	1.4	0.14	16.7
1966	42.99	23.1	0.66	371.4
1967	39.40	-8.4	0.67	1.5
1968	36.25	-8.0	1.86	177.6
1969	18.99	-47.6	2.95	58.6
1970	18.30	-3.6	2.79	-5.4
1971	21.70	18.6	3.05	9.3
1972	23.64	8.9	2.10	-31.1
1973	28.67	21.3	3.69	75.7
1974	29.46	2.8	7.12	93.0
1975	44.05	49.5	8.18	14.9
1976	44.49	1.0	16.92	106.8
1977	35.72	-19.7	13.66	-19.3
1978	40.00	12.0	20.50	50.1
1979	78.77	96.0	21.17	3.3
1980	104.86	33.1	20.85	-1.5
1981	129.70	23.7	23.25	11.5
1982	140.00	7.9	24.19	4.0
1983	150.00	7.1	26.66	10.2
1984	170.00	13.3	21.79	-18.3

Source: IMTMA (Indian Machine Tool Manufacturers Association).

which are sophisticated machines not produced in India—such as NC/CNC machines, electron-discharge machines (EDM), precision grinding machines, and special-purpose machines. In order to meet the user industries' growing demand for modern and sophisticated machine tools, the government liberalized imports in 1985.

Following the announcement of the Import Policy of 1985 to 88, 69 new items were included in the open general licence (OGL), bringing the total number of machine tool items on the OGL list to 142. In October 1985, a new scheme, an "import export pass book," was introduced for manufacturers/exporters to enable duty-free imports for export production. Furthermore, the process of simplifying the machine tool licensing procedure, which began in 1983 when the government decided to classify machine tool products into 15 broad categories for the purpose of industrial licensing, culminated in the delicensing of the industry in 1985. In order to encourage investment and production without resorting to licensing formalities, the government exempted large industrial houses falling within the purview of the MRTP Act and the FERA from seeking prior approval from the Company Law Board for establishing new projects or for expansion of existing capacity in the machine tool industry (and 26 other industries).[35] The industry was thus exposed to foreign competition before the Rao government adopted the policy of economic liberalization in 1991.

Recognizing that the development of India's entire industrial base is dependent on the machine tool industry, which was faced with the challenge of meeting the growing demand for high-technology machines of mass production in an increasingly competitive environment, the Ministry of Industry took a further measure to modernize and expand the industry. A ten-year perspective plan (1983-1993),[36] formulated by a committee set up by the Development Council for the Machine Tool Industry, was drawn up to serve as a corporate plan for the growth and development of the Indian machine tool industry. The plan envisaged an average growth rate for machine tool production of 15 percent per annum.[37] After assessing the requirements of various user industries, the perspective plan projected a growth of production of Rs. 1,160 crores per annum (at current prices) by 1992-93. In terms of the number of machine tools, it meant an increase from 14,700 machines manufactured in 1984 to 21,000 to be produced by 1992-93. Of this projected number, approximately 800 to 1,000 machines were expected to be CNC and other high-technology machines. For achieving this increase in production, the plan projected an investment of Rs. 300 crores at 1982 prices.

The plan emphasized that with the advent of the age of "mechatronics"—integration of machine functions with electronic systems and the computer—India had to forge ahead if it wanted to be self-reliant in machine tools and make a dent in the competitive market. In order to help the industry grow and modernize, the government has liberalized imports, simplified the procedure for transfer of technology, and rationalized duty structure for import of machine tools and components such as bearings, hydraulic systems, electronic controls, DC motors, servo systems, control of CNC machines, and ball screws. The policy of economic liberalization, however, has had a negative effect, at least in the short run, as it triggered a recession in the industry in the early 1990s.

The critics of the government policy, however, point out that the liberalized import policy will increase rather than reduce India's dependence on the machine tool multinationals, and hence on the West. Since, they argue, the international machine tool manufacturers enjoy tremendous technological advantage, the Indian companies will be unable to compete with them in either the domestic or international markets. In support of their argument, the critics cite the increase in India's imports (from Rs. 400 million in 1978 to Rs. 2,500 million in 1986), foreign collaboration agreements, and royalty and lump-sum payments to the international machine tool firms. The 1986 Machine Tool Census reveals that of a total of 1,182 NC machines purchased by Indian firms before 1985, almost 90 percent had been imported. Furthermore, the country was hit by cheap imports in the postliberalization period, which contributed to the recession in the industry in the early 1990s. Thus, the question whether India's liberalized import policy will increase its dependence or make it more self-reliant is an important one, which will be addressed in the Chapter 8, particularly in the context of our case study of the Hindustan Machine Tool Company.

TECHNOLOGY TRANSFER AND TECHNOLOGICAL DEVELOPMENT
IN THE INDIAN MACHINE TOOL INDUSTRY

In the engineering industry in general and the machine tool industry in particular, there are four forms of technology transfer: the outright sale of drawings, the know-how imparted through training programs and the loan of technicians, the establishing of local plants by sponsoring companies, and specialized joint venture operations.[38] In India, machine tool technology has been transferred through all these modes.

After independence, the Indian machine tool industry started with machine tools designed by collaborators from West Germany, Great Britain, Switzerland, the United States and, more recently, Japan. Both public and private sector firms entered into collaboration agreements with well-known multinational companies for the transfer of machine tool technology. Such collaboration agreements were viewed as most beneficial for the growth of the industry and industrialization of the country. HMT's tie-up with Oerlekons of Switzerland, for example, proved a great boon for the technological progress of the industry in subsequent years. The technology supplying firms not only transferred designs to the Indian firms but also provided training to Indian designers and technicians which was critical in the development of technological capability in the machine tool industry. Almost all machine tool manufacturers in the organized sector acquired technology through collaboration agreements with leading international firms. The government policy of import substitution facilitated such collaborative agreements with leading multinationals for the transfer of machine tool technology. Discussing the salience of foreign collaboration at this stage of development in the Indian machine tool industry, S. M. Patil, the former managing director of HMT and a doyen in Indian machine tool industry, comments:

Co-operation agreements with foreign machine-tool manufacturers were necessary in the beginning to speed up the process of growth of the domestic machine-tool industry and as an essential component for the training and development of engineers, technicians, designers, planners, managers and skilled operators. But the large-scale import of technology and know-how in such a vital field could not continue indefinitely, except on a selective basis, because foreign sources could not always be relied upon to respond positively where more modern and sophisticated export-oriented designs and production technologies were concerned.[39]

As a result, public and private sector firms entered into more than 100 foreign collaborations in the machine tool industry by the mid-1980s. Although, initially, European and North American companies provided drawings, designs, and technical training to the Indian machine tool industry, lately Japan has claimed more of the Indian market because of its competitive prices and its adoption of new technology. At present, Indian machine tool companies are looking toward industrially advanced countries for meaningful cooperation in their development of technology. They want to enter into more collaborations and joint ventures in high-technology areas such as CNC, EDM (electron-discharge machining), precision grinders, high-speed presses and press brakes, toolroom machines, and FMS (flexible manufacturing systems). In view of the large demand for CNC and other automated machine tools anticipated in the coming years, there has been a rush for setting up joint ventures in high-technology areas. But the costs of technology transfer (royalty payments, lump-sum fees, etc.), especially in the area of high-technology items, have gone up considerably in recent years.

It is important to emphasize that when India entered the field of machine tool production and showed interest in signing technical collaboration agreements with the leading multinational firms, the Western countries were moving toward the production of more sophisticated machine tools geared toward mass production of automobile parts and defense equipment. The leading international machine tool manufacturers were thus willing to give India what might soon have become obsolete technology in the West. There was thus a convergence of interest between the technological needs of India and the willingness on the part of the multinationals to transfer such technology. Since India did not want the latest machine tool technology, the multinationals were willing to give that for a "reasonable" royalty fee and lump-sum payment. At this stage in India's industrial development, what the country needed most was basic machine tool technology, not that which was required for producing sophisticated, advanced, special-purpose machines. Multinationals, on their part, found it profitable to sell drawings and designs of machines that had already become obsolete or were about to become obsolete, and to train technical personnel from the Indian machine tool companies to make those machines.

Although the indigenous machine tool industry in India did absorb imported technology, most machine tool manufacturers continued to use the collaborators' old drawings and designs without making much improvement. As a result, the Indian machine tool manufacturers had few innovations to offer to the user industries. The industry, however, made an effort to establish in-house research and development activities, and the government took the initiative in the matter of institutional research by establishing the Central Machine Tool Institute (CMTI) at Bangalore and the Central Metal Forming Research Institute (CMFRI) at Hyderabad as prime industry-oriented research and development organizations. These institutes have contributed significantly to the development of sophisticated, special-purpose machines.

The CMTI, which was established in 1962 with the technical assistance of Czechoslovakia and began its technical activities in 1965, has over the years designed and developed a number of machine tools, including NC systems and machines.[40] Machine tool manufacturers have taken advantage of the wide-ranging services offered by the CMTI, including development and testing of tools, tooling and production aids, newer methods of machining, and production advisory services. The institute is now going in a big way for computer-aided designs (CAD) and computer-aided manufacturing (CAM) applications in machine tool manufacturing.

The services offered by CMTI have contributed significantly to the development of technological capability in the Indian machine tool industry. The institute has maintained a close collaboration with the leading public and private sector machine tool manufacturers. HMT, for example, has employed the institute several times as the third party for product assessment. The institute's role in promoting import substitution has been widely recognized; in 1974 it won the National Award for Import Substitution for Flow Forming Lathes. The potentials of the Central Metal Forming Research Institute, which was set up recently, have, however, not been fully utilized because the Indian industry has yet to exploit metalforming as a production technology.[41]

An important indicator of technological development in an industry is its export potentials. Exports in the Indian machine tool industry increased steadily in the late 1960s. An organized export drive, undertaken by the industry in response to the recession in the domestic machine tool market between 1967 and 1970, pushed the exports from Rs. 0.7 crore in 1967 to Rs. 3 crores in 1969—representing approximately 5 percent of production capacity.[42] The ripples of another minor recession in the mid-1970s gave a second boost to export efforts; there was steady growth in India's machine tool exports after 1974-75, reaching a level of Rs. 23 crores (10 percent of production) in 1981 and Rs. 32 crores in 1985. India has been exporting machine tools not only to other developing countries such as Iran, Nigeria, Egypt, and Indonesia but also to the industrially advanced countries: Germany, the United States, United Kingdom, and the former Soviet Union. Until 1990, the Soviet Union was the leading importer of machine tools from India (see Table 7.6). Bharat Fritz Werner—a medium-sized machine tool company in the private sector—has exported drilling machines and machining centers to Russia in large quantities between 1983 and 1990. The export of machining centers to the former Soviet Union in 1986-87 alone represented 40 percent of the total turnover of the company. At the time I interviewed BFW managers in 1986, the company's agreement with the former Soviet Union for the export of machine tools was worth Rs. 80 million.[43] But the internal political changes in the former Soviet Union led to a sharp decline in exports to that country: Exports to the Soviet Union (Russia) fell from a high of Rs. 75.19 crores in 1990 to Rs. 12.43 crores in 1992.[44] The export of machine tools, which had grown significantly until 1978, remained stagnant after 1983 (around Rs. 24 crores). According to IMTMA—the representative organization of the machine tool industry since 1947—recessionary conditions in the major international markets, the high cost of Indian machine tools, and increasing competition from other developing countries such as Taiwan, South Korea, and China were the main reasons for the stagnation in India's machine tool exports in recent years.[45]

The decline in India's exports has been taken seriously by the government and the industry because exports are considered important not only to earn foreign exchange but also to keep abreast of the latest technological trends. Technological

Table 7.6
Ten Largest Importers of Indian Machine Tools,
1980-1984 (Rs. Million)

Country	1980	1981	1982	1983	1984
U.S.S.R.	6.14	14.50	90.50	137.40	45.90
Bulgaria	-	-	-	17.00	19.70
Iran	0.39	1.40	2.70	10.90	6.70
Nigeria	9.56	12.50	20.70	10.50	32.10
U.S.A	28.52	28.90	22.50	8.40	11.80
W. Germany	16.55	17.10	12.30	8.20	8.80
U.K.	16.82	11.50	7.60	7.70	5.20
Sweden	14.05	10.20	11.00	7.60	-
Egypt	0.84	0.80	1.10	6.00	-
Indonesia	6.83	4.60	1.20	3.90	6.60

Source: IMTMA (Original Source: Directorate General of Trade and Development).

development in the machine tool industries in South Korea and Taiwan, which was stimulated primarily by their export sectors, is a case in point. Although India's export of machine tools to the former Soviet Union grew in the 1970s and 1980s, it has not had the same effect on the technological development of the industry. Most machine tool experts agree that the growth in India's exports to the developed market economies would have contributed more to the technological development in the industry.[46] In sharp contrast to India, the rapid development of machine tool technology in Taiwan has taken place because of Taiwan's sustained effort to export its product to the industrially advanced market economies. The demand of being competitive in the international market has made the Taiwanese machine tool manufacturers keep up with the latest Western technology. Thus, in spite of the advent of the CNC machines in the developed countries, Taiwan has succeeded in maintaining and increasing its exports to the industrially advanced countries.

The technology gap that the Indian machine tool industry is facing is related, of course, to its inability to catch up with the technological advancements in machine tool technology. Although India followed the lead of the West and made use of the technology provided by the industrially advanced countries, there has always been a serious time lag. For example, NC technology was applied to the machine tool industry in the early 1960s, which revolutionized production in the West, but in India it was started on a very limited scale ten years later, and the production of NC/CNC machines was meager until the 1990s. Plagued by technological obsolescence, the industry has been unable to keep pace with a shift in demand toward the latest high-technology products. Thus, while Indian production and exports have stagnated, imports have been on the rise. The import of machine tools increased from Rs. 260 crores in 1988-89 to Rs. 470 crores in 1992-93.

The ability of the machine tool industry to modernize and boost production on a competitive basis will depend on its ability to develop advanced designs through domestic R&D efforts. The record of the industry in R&D so far has been poor, with the result that the Indian machine tool industry increasingly lagged behind the rest of the world. Instead of developing in-house R&D

capability and entering into collaborations, many machine tool manufacturers have opted for a shortcut of closing the technological gap by resorting to importing CKD (completely knocked down) and SKD (semi-knocked down) kits to assemble. With the exception of the public sector manufacturers such as HMT, there has been little initiative taken by private sector firms to establish in-house R&D activities. For example, the private sector machine tool manufacturers spent only Rs. 4.4 million on R&D in 1981-83, which is substantially below the perspective plan's expected R&D expenditure of 3 percent of total sales by the industry.[47] Furthermore, the common facilities available at CMTI have been used more by the machine tool users than by the manufacturers. It is important to note that the facilities of the NC research center at CMTI, Bangalore—set up in 1978 with a $2 million grant from the UNDP—have not been fully utilized by the machine tool manufacturers, nor did the manufacturers pursue, until the early 1990s, further development by applying NC technology to modern machine tools.[48] However, the expertise existing in the institute has been found to be "inadequate to focus on new technology machines and [it needs] to be augmented considerably."[49]

In order to alleviate the situation and to achieve the required level of technological development indigenously, the subgroup for the machine tool industry for the Seventh Five Year Plan recommended that the industry must spend on an average 3 to 4 percent of the value of total production each year on R&D activities[50]—an increase of 50 to 100 percent. The report emphasized the need for new investment for increasing volume of production on the one hand and product technology on the other. "Machine tool factories themselves need to replace their old plant and machinery and upgrade their own product technology with the acquisition of modern machine tools."[51]

The sluggish growth, technological obsolescence, and poor export performance of the industry are the results of policies related to the protection given to the industry, the import substitution, and the policy of stringent royalty payment pursued by the government for four decades. Although government protection of the machine tool industry was necessary in the beginning in order to save foreign exchange and to allow for the growth and development of indigenous industry, the continuation of such policies beyond the initial phase has resulted in inefficiency, lower productivity, and lack of competitiveness in the industry. The government regulations regarding royalty payment for collaborations have been such that the American and European firms are losing interest in technology transfer to India.[52] The perspective plan underlined the difficulty in obtaining collaborations in high-technology areas on the existing terms and conditions set down by the government, and recommended relaxation of conditions in specific areas.[53]

The fiscal policy of the government has until recently been backward-looking with its focus on revenue earning rather than on growth, which has thwarted all modernization impulses in the machine tool sector. Since 1980, the machine tool industry, through IMTMA, has been making representation to the government suggesting various measures that would provide impetus for the industry's speedier growth. The detailed representation in 1986 included, among other things, an exemption or nominal 5 percent excise duty on machine tools and a depreciation allowance of 50 percent to enable writing off up to 87.5 percent of the cost of machinery within a period of three years.[54] In 1994, IMTMA urged the government to correct the "anomalies" in tariff structure, which imposes high duty on raw material and components, and low duties on finished machines.[55] The government did respond to some of the demands, but the industry was not satisfied with the government policies.

Thus, despite the technological capability acquired by the industry in the last four decades, the technology gap between India and the developed machine tool manufacturing countries has widened. Some observers have commented that the industry has missed the electronics revolution that transformed machine tools manufacture in other countries, which caused its present technological backwardness.[56] In the period following the recent recession (1991-93) the machine tool industry reached a critical stage in its development. There are opportunities and challenges. The opportunity is to grow further because of the new demands—especially from the automobile and automobile components industry and defense equipment and railway—for CNC and other sophisticated machine tools, but it can do so only if it rises to the challenges of innovation and technological change.

CONCLUSION

The growth of the machine tool industry in India has been substantial in the 1960s and 1970s; the industry was able to maintain an average growth rate of 15 to 20 percent between 1960 and 1982. The share of indigenous production in the total consumption of machine tools kept improving until 1978. But in the 1980s and the early 1990s, the industry experienced stagnation, a decline in its exports, and a significant increase in imports of high-technology machine tools. Although NC machine tools were developed in India as early as 1972, the industry did not keep pace with the latest technology and lagged behind other countries in the production of more productive and sophisticated types of tools.

In the 1980s, the automobile industry—the biggest user of machine tools—underwent major changes, with new manufacturers entering the market and existing manufacturers diversifying and increasing production. The unprecedented growth in the production of cars, two-wheelers, three-wheelers, and light commercial vehicles created a new demand for high-precision and NC/CNC machines, which the industry was unable to meet. The requirements of high-technology transfer lines by Maruti Udyog Limited—discussed in Chapter 8—proved dramatically the inability of the machine tool industry to meet the growing demand of sophisticated machine tools indigenously. The government allowed the automobile and other industries to import machine tools not available indigenously, but at the same time it has taken several remedial measures to boost productivity by modernizing the machine tool industry.

Whether recent moves on the part of the government will enable India to catch up with the advanced machine tool manufacturing countries is hard to predict. But the study of the Hindustan Machine Tool Company in Chapter 8 suggests that the industry has a reasonably strong technological base on which it could build its strength further. In recent years, India's machine tool industry has had some positive effects of economic liberalization: increased competition resulting in cost and quality consciousness, financial sector reforms and credit policy changes resulting in lower cost of operation and investment, and reduction of custom duty lowering the cost of imported inputs. The industry overcame the global recession in 1994 when its production, especially of CNC machine tools, increased by 40 percent.[57] Furthermore, there has been an improvement in the level of technology in the quality and design capability of the machine tool industry despite the virtual absence of foreign collaboration—technology transfer or joint venture agreement—between 1988 and 1993. Such developments indicate that the degree of technological capability acquired by India in the last four decades is significant. There is a real possibility that the country can become more self-reliant in production of high-technology machine tools in the near future—if government and industry work together.

NOTES

1. David F. Noble, *Forces of Production: A Social History of Industrial Automation* (New York: Alfred A. Knopf, 1984), p. 8.

2. UNIDO, *The Machine Tool Industry* (New York: United Nations, 1974), p.1.

3. Harley Shaiken, *Work Transformed: Automation and Labor in the Computer Age* (New York: Holt, Rinehart and Winston, 1986).

4. See Robert S. Woodbury, *Studies in the History of Machine Tools* (Cambridge, Mass.: MIT Press, 1972).

5. See UNCTAD, *Case Studies in the Transfer of Technology: Policies for Transfer and Development of Technology in Pre-war Japan* (New York: UNCTAD Secretariat, TD/B/C.6/26); UNCTAD, *Experience of the USSR in Building Up Technological Capacity* (New York: UNCTAD Secretariat, TD/B/C.6/52).

6. UNCTAD, *The Capital Goods Sector in Developing Countries: Technology Issues and Policy Options* (New York: United Nations, 1985), p. 3; *American Machinist*, February 1982, p. 109.

7. UNIDO, *Technological Perspectives in the Machine-Tool Industry and Their Implications for Developing Countries* (New York: United Nations, 1985), p.3.

8. UNIDO, *Machine Tools in Asia and the Pacific* (New York: United Nations, 1975), p. 55.

9. UNIDO, *The Machine Tool Industry* (New York: United Nations, 1974), p. 21.

10. UNIDO, *World Non-Electrical Machinery* (New York: United Nations, 1984).

11. UNIDO, *Technological Perspectives in the Machine-Tool Industry*, p. 4.

12. In the last decade, however, there have been conglomerate mergers and acquisitions creating a new class of giants in an industry that has traditionally consisted of many small, medium-sized, and often family-owned, firms. In 1977, for example, there were 725 toolmakers in the United States, which dropped to around 525 in 1985. For details, see David Moberg, "The Cutting Edge," *Reader*, 14, No. 45 (August 9, 1985): 20.

13. For details, see HMT, "Machine Tool Link: Japan," Central Technical Information Center, Bangalore, pp. 13-15.

14. UNIDO, *World Non-Electrical Machinery*, p. 64.

15. UNIDO, *Machine Tools in Asia and the Pacific* (New York: United Nations, 1975), p. 43.

16. The robotics market has grown very fast in the last few years, from $164 million in 1983 to $700 million in 1989. See *Robotics World*, February 1985, pp. 19-21 and UNIDO, *Technological Perspectives in the Machine-Tool Industry*, p. 76.

17. Gene Bylinsky, "Japan's Robot King Wins Again," *Fortune*, May 25, 1987, p. 54.

18. For details see UNIDO, *World Non-Electrical Machinery*.

19. See Bylinsky, "Japan's Robot King Wins Again."

20. UNIDO, *World Non-Electric Machinery*, p. 104.

21. Ibid., p. 106.

22. Ibid.

23. See L. Westphal, "Empirical Justification for infant Industry Protection," World Bank Staff Working Paper No. 445 (Washington, D.C.: March 1981); and Charles Edquist et al., "Automation in Engineering Industries of India and Republic of Korea Against the Background of Experience in Some OECD Countries," *Economic and Political Weekly*, April 13, 1985, pp. 643-654.

24. See Martin Fransman, "International Competitiveness, Technical Change and the State: The Machine Tool Industry in Taiwan and Japan," *World Development*, 14, No. 12 (December 1986): 1376-1396.

25. S. M. Patil, "Technological Perspectives in the Machine-Tool Industry and Their Implications for Developing Countries," Summary of draft study commissioned by the Technology Program of UNIDO (Bangalore: May 1981), p. 47.

26. Daniel Chudnovsky, "The Diffusion and Production of Numerically Controlled Machine Tools with Special Reference to Argentina," *World Development*, July 1988, pp. 727-730.

27. CMTI, *Machine Tool Census India 1986* (Bangalore: Central Machine Tool Institute), p. 4.

28. *Financial Express*, November 29, 1985.

29. S. M. Patil, Technological Perspectives in the Machine Tool Industry and Their Implications for Developing Countries, Part I: Global Study of the Machine Tool Industry and a Case Study of the Indian Machine Tool Industry, Unpublished Paper (Bangalore: 1985), pp.160-161.

30. P. C. Mahalanobis, economic advisor to Nehru who later became a member of the Planning Commission, is believed to be the sole author of the "Draft Plan Frame," which, with minor changes, was adopted in the Second Five Year Plan. For a discussion of the Mahalanobis model, see Sunil K. Sahu, "The Politics of Industrial Planning in India: The Second Plan," *Indian Journal of Public Administration*, 30, No. 3 (July-September, 1984): 613-660.

31. P. C. Mahalanobis, *The Approach of Operational Research to Planning in India* (Bombay: Asia Publishing House, 1963), p. 92.

32. UNIDO, *Technological Perspectives in the Machine-Tool Industry*, p.31.

33. Patil, "Technological Perspectives in the Machine-Tool Industry," p. 167.

34. In 1984, India had a population of 1,000 NC/CNC machines, out of which only 42 were indigenously manufactured; the rest were imported mainly from West Germany, Britain, France, the United States, and Japan. See Machine Tool Census, India 1986.

35. IMTMA *Bulletin*, 3, No. 1 (April-June 1985): 1-2.

36. The committee, under the chairmanship of T. V. Mansukhani, Managing Director of HMT, consisted of some of the major manufacturers and users of machine tools, the concerned industry associations, and the DGTD and CMTI. See *The Indian Machine Tool Industry: A Perspective Plan, 1983-93* (Unpublished Report, November 1983).

37. Ibid., p. 190.

38. UNIDO, *The Machine Tool Industry*, pp. 16-17.

39. UNIDO, *Technological Perspectives in the Machine-Tool Industry*, p. 33. S. M. Patil is the author of this report. As a matter of policy, the UN reports do not publish the names of the authors.

40. The institute renders technical assistance to machine tool and other engineering industries in design and development of machine tools, attachments and accessories; research and investigation of machine tool problems, prototype and evaluation testing; standardization of machine tools; development of tools and tooling; production advisory services; design, development and selection of NC machines and systems; and training machine tool and production engineers. See *CMTI Services* (Bangalore: CMTI), pp. 1-3.

41. See *The Indian Machine Tool Industry: A Perspective Plan, 1983-93*, p. 187.

42. Ibid., p. 140.

43. Data obtained from the joint general manager (Adm.) and secretary of BFW during personal interview in Bangalore on November 10, 1986.

44. *Economic Times*, January 13, 1994.

45. Financial *Express*, November 29, 1985.

46. Dr. S. M. Patil in a personal interview in Bangalore on November 14, 1986.

47. *Economic Times*, April 18, 1985.

48. See S. M. Patil, "Machine Tool Industry: Need for Remedial Measures," *The Economic Times*, January 9, 1986.

49. Government of India, Ministry of Heavy Industry, *Report of the Sub-Group on Machine Tool Industry for the VII Plan Period 1985-90* (New Delhi: 1983), p. 9.

50. Ibid.

51. Ibid., pp.8-9.

52. In the 1980s, the government allowed royalty payment of up to 5 percent of the total sales. The royalty payment, however, has been subject to 40 percent income tax and was computed based on the net selling price arrived at by deducting the cost of imported components and components brought out in India. Thus, the royalty payment of 5 percent actually worked out to 1.5 to 2 percent for the collaborators. See "Machine Tool Industry: Gearing Up with a Little Help from Japan," *Business India*, September 23-October 6, 1985, p. 87.

53. The Perspective Plan recommended, among other things, waiving income tax on lump-sum fee and royalty; permitting fee and royalty up to 15 percent for a period of eight years; and permitting joint ventures with foreign equity exceeding 40 percent and reducing income tax on profits and dividends. See *The Indian Machine Tool Industry: A Perspective Plan 1983-93*, pp.137-138.

54. *IMTMA Bulletin*, 4, No. 1 (October 1986): 1-8.

55. *Economic Times*, January 3, 1994.

56. See the editorial in *The Economic Times*, April 18, 1985.

57. In 1992, not more than 30 to 35 percent of machine tools were numerically controlled machines, but two years later 80 percent of the machines produced were CNC machine tools. This shows that there has been high technological growth in the last three years, and since there have been no tie ups with any foreign firm, it shows that the effort has been in-house only.

8

Technological Self-Reliance in the Indian Machine Tool Industry: The Case of the Hindustan Machine Tool Company

A survey of the literature on technology transfer indicates that technology dependence has been either studied in a highly abstract manner, or empirical research on the subject has been skewed toward the technology supplier and recipient environment. The consequences of the behavior of the technology supplier for Third World development have also been examined in great detail. However, very little is known about the characteristics of the technology users, especially what is being done at the firm level to adopt and assimilate the acquired technology, to develop indigenous technological capability, to transfer vertically the technology to other firms, to improve the capability for managing the technology, and to promote the transfer of technology to other developing countries (South-South technology transfer). Although the literature on technology transfer is quite rich, certain aspects have remained neglected and unexplored. This chapter will focus on these unexplored aspects of technological self-reliance and technological dependence by studying the case of Hindustan Machine Tool Limited (HMT), a public sector company.

The chapter examines HMT's experience in acquisition, adoption, assimilation, and development, and attempts a cost-benefit analysis of this experience. This study addresses more precisely the specific nature of technological dependence and the conditions under which it may be overcome. The analysis suggests that a developing country can overcome, if not completely reverse, the initial situation of technological dependence if the country's policy choices are appropriate given its educational, organizational, and scientific infrastructure. But what happens at the firm level is equally important, for example, the commitment of the management to the idea of technological self-reliance.

It has been suggested by some scholars that Japan became a major economic power not by being an innovator but by being an imitator. The recent economic performance of the Taiwanese and South Korean economies has also been attributed to their ability to imitate Western technology.[1] India, a newly industrializing country (NIC), has, over the years, acquired the capability to transfer machine tool technology to less industrialized developing countries. It has done so not by being an innovator (like Great Britain between 1770 and 1840, or Germany and the United States in the second half of the nineteenth century) but by being an imitator. A number of developing Asian and African countries have benefited from the technological capability acquired by HMT through imitation and learning by doing. However, in modern technology, India is lagging behind the major machine tool manufacturers; hence, in this area, it does not enjoy the same degree of bargaining strength as it does with respect to general-purpose machine tools.

HINDUSTAN MACHINE TOOLS COMPANY (HMT)[2]

The machine tool industry is highly capital-intensive and technology-oriented. The gestation period is longer than that of many other industries, and its capital output ratio of 1:1 is comparatively low. In postindependent India, the private sector either lacked the capital or was reluctant to invest such large amounts in machine tool manufacturing. Given the importance of machine tools in India's drive toward rapid industrialization, the government undertook the venture and set up Hindustan Machine Tool Company in the public sector in 1953.

The company had a modest beginning. Initially, all its business was carried out from the dilapidated war barracks at Jallahali, a village eight kilometers to the north of Bangalore city in the Karnataka state. From this humble beginning, HMT has transformed itself into a multitechnology complex having 11 manufacturing units and 17 production divisions spread across 9 states. One of its two subsidiaries, HMT (International), is now selling the company's products internationally and has been engaged in offering projects and engineering services to other developing countries. The company employs today 30,000 workers, of which 4,000 are engineers. Its current annual turnover of $320 million indicates an increase of more than 160 times within a period of three decades.

Over the years, HMT has emerged as an important manufacturer of machine tools, producing 38 types of metal-forming machines, from simple lathes to the sophisticated computer numerically controlled (CNC) machine tools. The company produces the widest range of metal-cutting machine tools anywhere outside of the former Soviet bloc countries. The company's machine tool price range spans from the Rs. 5,000 drill to the Rs. 10 million transferline, especially designed for the automobile industry, or to the Rs. 20 million heavy-duty press, especially built for the aircraft industry.[3] HMT is rated as the sixth largest machine tool maker in the world, producing everything from simple hand-operated machines to computer-controlled machines. The activities of HMT have generated in India in the last three decades a healthy growth of machine tool manufacturers in the private sector and a vast number of industrial activities.

The company has recently been involved in updating its existing product range to fill the demand for high-technology, high-productivity machines. HMT has introduced and marketed a number of new products developed through in-house R&D, and it has played a crucial role in promoting machine tool technology in the country. It accounts for a production share of more than 50 percent in metal-cutting and metal-forming machine tools (see Table 8.1). In the diversified lines too, the company's production share is substantial: watches (85 percent), printing machines (80 percent), tractors (15 percent), and lamps (25 percent).[4] HMT has been a pioneer in establishing the horological industry in India. These accomplishments and others were recognized by the Harvard Business School Association of India and The Economic Times Research Bureau in 1985 when they ranked HMT as India's top public sector company.

A PROFILE OF THE GROWTH OF HINDUSTAN MACHINE TOOL (HMT)

Following the technical collaboration agreement that the government of India had made with the Swiss firm Oerlikons, in 1949, the construction of the factory began and Hindustan Machine Tool Limited was formally incorporated in 1953. The factory was inaugurated by Prime Minister Jawaharlal Nehru in October 1955, and production started in 1956, with an output of 135 machines. The plant was expected to produce 400 H-22 lathes per year by 1960. The lack of technical expertise in India necessitated the training of Indian engineers abroad. A team of four engineers was sent to Switzerland for training in machine tool building. (One of them, S. M. Patil, later became the company's chairman and managing director.) They returned with 84 Oerlikons engineers who were to "train the Indian engineers/technicians and workers to establish production of H-22 lathes."[5]

Table 8.1
Top Ten Machine Tool Manufacturers (1984)

Company	Production (Rs. Crores)
HMT Ltd.	115
The Mysore Kirloskar Ltd.	18
Walchandnagar Industries Ltd.	10.5
PMT Machine Tool	8
Praga Tools Limited	8
Bharat Fritz Werner Pvt. Limited	7.5
Godrej and Boyce Mfg. Co. Ltd.	7.5
Batliboi and Co. Ltd.	4.5
Ameteep Machine Tools	4.5
Beco Eng. Co. Ltd.	3

Source: Business India, Sept. 23-Oct. 6, 1985, p. 88.

In the beginning, the Swiss headed all the departments in the company. The newly established training center at HMT started training Indian engineers and technicians. The training imparted by the Swiss technicians was described by the senior managers I interviewed as crucial for the development and success of the company. According to the company's former managing director, it was "not only crucial for the future development of the company but also valuable for the acquisition of technological capability in the Indian machine-tool industry." Emphasizing the importance of practical training, Patil added, "We could really get our boys trained well though we were a bit harsh on them. We made our engineers dirty their hands because we required that they be trained for two years just like any other worker. This was the only way they could learn what is involved in the assembly of, for example, a lathe."[6] This commitment to technical learning by doing continued in the company after the departure of the Swiss technicians, and the company's managers today proudly refer to it as "HMT culture."

Although HMT started with the financial participation of a foreign company, the government decided to buy all the foreign shares to make HMT a wholly owned Indian company. Gradually, the management was taken over by Indian engineers. With the appointment of M. K. Mathulla as chairman of the company in 1956, HMT started a policy of diversification and expansion. By 1960-61, the company was producing 1,002 machines against a targeted estimate of 400. A second factory—HMT II, described as a "gift to the nation"—was built in 1961 out of the profits earned by the first unit over a period of five years. Carrying no financial aid from the government, it was planned, built, and commissioned without any foreign technical assistance. In 1961, HMT established an industrial estate consisting of 50 small-scale units spread across an area of 20 acres adjoining its plant in Bangalore to ensure a regular supply of special accessories and components. The expansion of HMT continued: HMT III at Pinjore (Punjab) began producing M2- and M3-type milling machines in 1963; HMT IV at Kalamassery (Kerala) began producing H-22 and LB lathes in 1966; and HMT V at Hyderabad (Andhra Pradesh) was set up for the production of special-purpose machines in 1967. When Machine Tool Corporation of India at Ajmer (Rajasthan) was absorbed in 1975, HMT VI was added to the company.

However, the period of serious recession in Indian industry during 1967-68, which lasted for three years when a "plan holiday" was declared, affected the growth of HMT. The sharp decline in public investment in 1966-67, and the severe recession that had gripped the engineering industry in India, caused a drastic change in HMT's fortune. To combat this, HMT diversified its production by enlarging its range and entering into the export market. Between 1965 and 1969, HMT added more sophisticated machine tools such as single spindle automatics, multispindle automatics, gear shapers, gear hobbers, horizontal surface grinders, die casting and plastic injection molding machines.[7] Even before the recession, and in recognition of the cyclical nature of the machine tool industry, the company undertook a program of aggressive diversification under the dynamic leadership of S. M. Patil, chairman and managing director of HMT from 1964 to 1978. The company decided to diversify *out* of machine tools into production of new but allied product lines, which were considered to have economic cycles that are different from those of machine tools such as watches (Bangalore, Srinagar), heavy-duty presses (Hyderabad), die-casting machinery (Bangalore), printing machinery (Kalamassery), lamps (Hyderabad), and tractors (Pinjore). Of all the diversified product lines, HMT owed its continued viability during the recessionary years to the profitability of a watch factory established in Bangalore in 1961 in collaboration with Citizen Watch Company of Japan.

The company's diversification drive, however, slowed down after the mid-1970s. Due to the technical difficulties experienced by the diversified product lines, such as the lamps division in the 1980s, the company has emphasized the idea of consolidation instead of expansion of its industrial activities. More important, there has been a substantial growth of services HMT could provide to other enterprises both in India and abroad: HMT's services range from "a techno-economic feasibility study of a proposed machine-tool accessories plant for the state government of Maharashtra to a complete turnkey project for the establishment of a machine-tool plant in the Philippines."[8] The technological capability that HMT has acquired over the years has allowed it to play an important role in the horizontal transfer of machine-tool technology to other manufacturing units in India and South-South transfer to other developing nations.

MODES OF ACQUIRING TECHNOLOGY

Four different modes of acquiring machine tool technology from abroad have been used by HMT: joint venture, licensing agreements, bulk purchase, and joint development and production.

Joint Venture Project

The first mode of acquiring technology was a broad-based joint venture project with the Swiss firm Oerlikons. The collaborator helped start the company by sending a team of 84 engineers who trained Indian engineers, supervisors, and craftsmen in the skills for producing quality machine tools. Oerlikons was given 10 percent equity share, and initially there was a period of joint management of the public sector company. The participation of the Swiss company in the initial phase in the development of HMT involved:

1. Transferring know-how for tool room lathe H-22;

2. Completing project planning;

3. Selecting, supply erection, and commissioning plant machinery and equipment;

4. Supplying jigs, fixtures, special tools, patterns, CKD parts, and castings;

5. Planning the organization and setting up of procedures and systems;

6. Training Indian personnel in Oerlikons (Zurich) and in HMT (Bangalore), and the deputation of Swiss experts in all areas;

7. Starting up and running production by Swiss experts with Indian understudies.[9]

It is obvious that HMT totally relied on the Swiss collaborators at this stage for the machine tool technology. According to S. M. Patil, this was the "full spoon-feeding" stage in the development of HMT because Oerlikons laid the foundations of the machine tool industry in India. Although the Swiss collaboration was crucial to the establishment and initial success of HMT, Indian engineers and managers soon became dissatisfied with the Swiss control over production and their insistence on the production of a single lathe in batches of 400. When M. K. Mathulla became the managing director of the Company in 1956, he took the initiative and terminated the 20-year collaboration agreement with Oerlikons. He succeeded in buying out their shareholdings in 1957, although the company retained the Swiss as technical consultants on an annual fee of Rs. 25,000. Managerial responsibility was taken over by the Indians and the foreign technicians—Swiss, German and Italian—were retained as employees of HMT.[10] By 1960, the company had built enough expertise that it decided to dispense with the services of the foreign experts altogether. Thereafter, except for the manufacture of watches, it did not enter into another "turnkey" type of collaboration agreement with a foreign machine tool technology supplier.[11] Because the collaborator in such a situation usually resists the idea of diversification of products or the development of local R&D, HMT preferred other modes of acquiring technology, such as selective purchase of know-how on payment after the termination of the agreement with the Swiss (see Table 8.2).

The United Nations Industrial Development Organization (UNIDO) recommends joint ventures and turnkey projects as appropriate forms of technology transfer for countries lacking technical knowledge in the field of machine tool production.[12] HMT's collaboration with Oerlikons seems to conform to this recommendation. Although in the 1950s, India had a few machine tool manufacturers in the private sector—Coopers, Kirloskars and the Tata's Investa Machine Tools, for example—these companies were generally reluctant to make large-scale investments in an industry with a long gestation lag. With the inception of the first in a series of the country's five-year plans, it soon became clear that India should build for itself sufficient machine-building capacity to sustain its march toward rapid industrialization. Following the priority given to the development of the capital industries in the Second Five Year Plan, the government's decision to set up a machine tool industry in the public sector was a logical one. At this early stage in India's industrial development, a joint venture with Oerlikons, which helped establish the first public sector machine-tool unit at Bangalore, was perhaps

Table 8.2
HMT's Foreign Collaborations in Machine Tools

No.	Year	Primary Product	Collaboration	Country
1	1949-53	Lathe	Oerlikons-I	Switzerland
2	1957	Milling	Fritz Werner-I	W. Germany
3	1958	Drilling	Kolb	W. Germany
4	1959	Lathe	LB	France
5	1959	Grinding	Olivetti	Italy
6	1961	Surface Grinding	Limex	GDR
7	1961	Spl.Purpose Mc.	Renault	France
8	1963	Gear Shaper	Drummond	UK
9	1963	Elec. Milling	Fritz Werner-II	W. Germany
10	1964	1 Sp. Auto Lathe	Manurhin-I	France
11	1964	Gear Hobber	Liebherr	W. Germany
12	1966	4-6 Sp. Auto Lathe	Gildemeister-I	W. Germany
13	1966	1 Sp. Chuck Auto	Manurhin-II	France
14	1966	Copying Lathe	Somua	France
15	1966	Multitool Auto	Jones & Lamson	USA
16	1966	Drum Turret Lathe	Gildemeister-II	W. Germany
17	1967	Horiz. Boring	Pagard-I	Belgium
18	1967	Broach	Forst-I	W. Germany
19	1968	Chucks	Berg	Switzerland
20	1969	Diecasting; Plastic Mldg.	Buhler-I	Switzerland
21	1969	Coord. Boring	GSP	France
22	1969	Press-Metal Forming	Verson-II	USA
23	1969	Spl.Lathe	Oerlikons-II	Switzerland
24	1970	Ram Milling	Fritz Werner-III	W. Germany
25	1970	NC Lathe	Am. Tool Works	USA
26	1971	Sliding Hd. Auto	Petermann	Switzerland
27	1971	Bed Milling	Fritz Werner-IV	W. Germany
28	1976	Spl. Purpose Mc.	Cross	USA
29	1979	Refractory Press	Laeis	W. Germany
30	1980	NC Boring	Pegard-II	Belgium
31	1982	Diecasting Tools	Buhler	Switzerland
32	1982	Press Low Cost	Verson-II	USA
33	1983	Electr. Instruments	Federal	USA
34	1983	Broach-Surface	Forst-II	W. Germany
35	1984	Gear Shaper-H.S.	Liebherr-II	W. Germany
36	1984	Gear Shaper-H.S.	Liebherr-III	W. Germany
37	1984	Machining Centre	KTM	UK
38	1984	Mini-Mcg. Centre	Wahli	Switzerland
39	1984	Mech. Instruments	Carl Zeiss	GDR
40	1984	Ball Screw	Carl Zeiss	GDR
41	1984	CNC-Systems	Siemens	W. Germany
42	1984	CNC-Multi Sp. Auto	Gildemeister-III	W. Germany
43	1984	Coining Press	Verson-III	USA

Source: HMT.

the best strategy suited for the country. By collaborating with India, the Swiss earned technical assistance fees but did not give the latest machine tool technology—in fact, they were not needed at this stage—but rather the technology that was near the end of the product life.

Licensing Agreements

In the debate on technology transfer, a distinction is made between "unpackaged" and "packaged" (including intermediate products, capital goods, spare parts, and training) transfer of industrial technology to the Third World. Among different institutional forms of technology transfer, licensing provides an opportunity to the recipient to buy technology in unpackaged form and to start production without delay. It has therefore been widely used by developing countries.[13] Although developing countries have shown a preference for licensing over direct foreign investment, this mode of acquiring technology has been criticized for leading to continued dependence on foreign technology, mainly because the technology recipient is reluctant to develop indigenous technology. HMT, in selective purchase of machine tool technology, has been able to enhance its technological capability and, as a result, it has moved toward a greater degree of technological self-reliance. This became possible because, over the years, HMT came to possess a sound knowledge of the alternative sources of technology, and it could bargain effectively with the technology suppliers.

Licensing agreement was HMT's dominant strategy for acquiring technology from 1957 until the early 1970s. When M. K. Mathulla, a chartered accountant by training who had served as a joint secretary in the Ministry of Production and earlier in Air India before its takeover by the Government, became the company's managing director, he took the decision to diversify production into milling, drilling, and grinding machines. He opted for acquiring technology through licensing instead of its in-house development. He believed that "when technology was available from abroad, why shouldn't India buy it? There was no point reinventing the wheel."[14]

Under Mathulla's leadership, HMT negotiated and acquired some of the basic and proven machine tool technologies from European firms by paying a "reasonable" technical fee and royalty. This included, among others, the milling machine technology from Fritz Werner of West Germany in 1957 (for a £50,000 lump-sum know-how payment and a 3½ percent royalty on the first 600 machines; the machine was under production for 20 years); the production lathe (LB) technology from Ernault-Samua of France in 1959 (for a £4,250 technical know-how fee and no royalty); the cylindrical grinding machine technology from Olivetti of Italy in 1959 (for a £4,000 fee and no royalty); and the gear hobber technology from Liebherr of West Germany in 1964 (for a DM 870,000 fee and no royalty)—the gear hobber machines are still manufactured.[15]

The buying of technology from leading European machine tool manufac-turers, however, did not result in HMT's continued dependence on foreign technology. In a study of 90 metal-working and chemical firms in Andean countries, Mytelka has found that licensing did not promote technological self-reliance. Licensing, he suggests, "creates a psychological environment of dependence. Managers become accustomed to relying on imported technology and incorporate assumptions of technology imports in future planning."[16] Contrary to the experience of Andean group countries, HMT has successfully adapted, assimilated, and further improved on the licensor's technology. The company has been successful in commercializing all the products for which it sought collaboration, with the possible exception of one or two. After setting up the first design office in 1960, the company made an earnest effort toward indigenization—for example, the company hired 300 designers between 1964 and 1966—and has succeeded in developing the capability to manufacture the machine indigenously within the collaboration period. The technical experience gained by the Indian engineers in the process further allowed them to design many machines indigenously. The cutter grinder, for example, was designed bottom-up at HMT and was commercialized in 1967. In order to further the development of the technology acquired from abroad and to introduce advanced models of the machines after the expiration of the initial collaboration agreement period, HMT established design teams in all the machine tool units by 1968, and a separate R&D center (metal cutting) was established in 1973 to strengthen the company's development efforts.

Technologically, HMT has attained enough maturity to design products on its own. At present, 50 percent of HMT's products are designed in-house. These products are equal in quality and sophistication to most of the machine tool manufacturers in the world. The company's effort to assimilate foreign technology has been so successful that during the 1970s the total number of collaborations in machine tool production dropped sharply. (The drop was also due to the com-pany's branching out and diversifying its product range into lamps, dairy ma-chines, and watches.) For example, the 1976 collaboration with Cross, USA, for the special-purpose machine cost India $250,000 in lump-sum fee and a royalty of 5 percent for seven years. The licensing agreement ended in 1983 and the technology had been fully absorbed. Whereas HMT manufactured 324 special-purpose machines using the Cross technology, the lump-sum fee it paid was equivalent to the price of one machine.[17]

In the 1980s, however, HMT found that it was lagging behind in CNC technology, and it realized that the in-house R&D effort for its development would take time. Therefore, it decided to enter into a number of licensing agreements for acquiring the latest high-precision technology in order to meet the Indian engineering industry's growing demand for CNC machine tools.

HMT acquired the following important technologies through licensing agreements in the 1980s:

1. The plastic extruder from Reifenhauser, West Germany, in 1981 by paying DM 1 million and a royalty of 5 percent for a period of eight years;

2. The one-time purchase of designs, standards, and process layouts of 40 presses from Verson International, USA, in 1982 against a lump-sum payment of $200,000;

3. The electronic instruments technology for a range of off-line and on-line machining systems from Federal, USA, in 1983 for a $412,000 technical fee and no royalty. By the end of 1986, HMT had already sold about 100 on-line gazing systems;

4. The CNC machining centers and flexible manufacturing systems from KTM, England, in 1984 by paying 5 percent royalty for a period of five years;

5. The machine tool control systems from Siemens, West Germany, in 1984 for a lump sum know-how fee of DM 4 million plus a royalty of 5 percent for ten years;

6. The multispindlle automatics from Gildermeister, West Germany, in 1984 for a lump sum fee of DM 1.5 million plus a royalty of 5 percent for eight years;

7. The ballscrew technology from Carl Zeiss, GDR, in 1984 for a Rs. 2.4 million fee. Because of this agreement, the ball screw is now being indigenously manufactured.

It is obvious from the list that HMT is acquiring modern technology from different sources in order to overcome the lag in CNC technology (to be discussed in the next section). Because of the high level of technical skill and organizational capability within the company, HMT engineers can easily identify the alternative sources of technology. Their thorough understanding of the trends in the machine tool development in the country vis-a-vis those in the world has allowed them to choose between different options available for bridging the product gaps, such as in-house development, joint development with CMTI, or acquisition of know-how through collaboration. Since high-technology CNC machines were identified as "market pull" products with good business opportunity and a high degree of profitability, HMT sought to overcome its weakness in this area by acquiring technology through licensing. At the same time, it targeted these machines as major thrust areas for in-house development.[18] Thus, the company's effort in negotiating technology transfer agreements with the major technology supplying firms and indigenizing them has been quite successful.[19]

Bulk Purchase

Bulk purchase is a variant of the licensing agreement. In this mode, the licensor provides know-how in return for bulk order of machines. The technology recipient pays no royalty or technical know-how fee; the advantage of this mode over licensing is one of cost. For the first time, HMT was able to acquire technology from a number of sources without paying either royalties or technical know-how fees because of special circumstances prevailing in the mid-1960s.

The Indo-Pakistani war of 1965 had led to an embargo on the shipment of certain kinds of machine tools to India from Western sources. As a result, the government was unable to purchase in the international market the machine tools needed by the ordinance factories. The Defense Ministry, therefore, approached HMT to negotiate and purchase on its behalf machine tools that it could not directly buy because of the embargo. The managing director of HMT, S. M. Patil, who under-stood the international machine tool market very well and had a keen business sense, proposed that HMT would like to acquire technology from the Western sources free of cost on the basis of placing bulk orders for the government. The government agreed to Patil's proposal and, in the winter of 1966, he went to West Germany, the United States, Belgium, France, and Britain to buy sophisticated machine tools worth $40 million and to acquire important machine tool technology free of cost for HMT.[20]

In 1966, HMT acquired the Fay multitool automatics technology from Jones and Lamson, USA, by placing a bulk order for Rs. 5 million; the Pilote copying lathe from Ernault-Somua, France, against a 4-million franc order; the single-spindle automatics from Manurhin, France, against a 3-million franc order; and the multispindle automatics from Gildermeister, West Germany, against a Rs. 10 million order (among others). HMT's success in acquiring these technologies free of cost depended as much on the negotiating skills of Patil as on the "recession experienced by machine-tool manufacturers in Europe [and the United States] at that time."[21] In the absence of technological competence on the part of the company, the acquisition of these technologies free of charge would not have been possible despite the recessionary condition in the industry.

The public sector company once again demonstrated its technological competence and negotiating skills in 1984 when it acquired the know-how for two machines—the microprecision gear hobber and the minimachining center—free of charge against the bulk order of 23 gear hobbers from Wahli of Switzerland.[22] Nevertheless, bulk order since that initial success following the Indo-Pakistani war of 1965 has not been a popular mode of acquiring technology.

Joint Development

Joint Development has been used by HMT, but the technology is expensive and no full-fledged collaboration can be undertaken. I will discuss three specific instances of joint development.

The first joint development was undertaken in 1967 with the Belgian company Pegard for the AZ9 horizontal boring machine (HBM). In this case, HMT provided the design of the horizontal boring machine and Pegard developed the prototype. HMT did not have to pay either a technical fee or royalty to the Belgian company. The joint project was highly successful and the horizontal boring machine was finally distributed as an HMT-Pegard product.[23] For more than two decades, the horizontal boring machine has been produced by HMT.

A less successful effort[24] at joint development was the collaboration with KTM to produce numerically controlled (NC) lathes. The idea of a joint, collaborative venture between HMT, Marwins (KTM after its merger with Kearneys), American Tool Works, and Yamazaki to produce an inexpensive NC machining (turning) center was initiated by Patil in 1967. During the course of negotiating the technical details of the project, which took more than two years, two companies—American Tool Works and Yamazaki—withdrew from it. In the HMT-KTM joint project, HMT was to manufacture the mechanical parts and KTM the control systems. The final product, according to the agreement, was to sell as HMT machines in India and as KTM machines abroad. KTM was designated as the marketing agent.

The design for the NC Mogul lathe was evolved by HMT and three prototypes were produced in Bangalore. After exhaustive testing of the prototypes at HMT, CMTI, and Brighton, and after meeting the accuracy standards of the NC machine tool as set by the collaborator, the prototype was approved by KTM, and HMT got an order for 75 NC Mogul lathes. Due to the lack of demand for NC machines in India, the first batch of 15 machines was sold by KTM in the United Kingdom.[25] In this joint project, the turning center in Bangalore and the turret and drilling centers in Pinjore were not profitable ventures. Still, according to the managers interviewed, the experience that the HMT engineers gained in the process was considered quite valuable. Since NC technology requires high accuracy standards—in order to enter into NC technology, a machine tool manufacturer has to step up at least two accuracy-standard steps—and since HMT is a multiproduct company, knowledge acquired by its engineers in one area can easily find application in different products. For example, the experience in the field of machine tool electronic-control systems can find application in printing machines or dairy machines.

A more successful and recent effort at joint development is the collaboration between HMT and Verson International, USA, to manufacture mint presses. The government of India wanted to buy several coin presses for the government mints, and it indicated preference for a particular source, Cincinnati Milacron, which was taken over by Verson International. Recognizing that a conventional collaboration would not be economical because of the exorbitant royalty demanded by the licensor for the transfer of current technology, HMT proposed to undertake jointly a Rs. 20 crore project and sought Verson International's collaboration in building presses. The initial order placed by the government was for 22 coin presses, with the prospect of buying more presses in the future; in fact, HMT was promised an order of 40 more presses.

Out of 24 coin presses sold by Verson, 15 came from the London subsidiary of the Verson Allsteel Press Company, and 9 were assembled at HMT from CKDs. HMT also provided after-sales service at its own factory. In the manufacture of 14 additional coining presses, for which orders came in late 1986, indigenous production was expected to reach 40 percent. Verson International gave full documentation—drawings and designs—free of charge for further manufacturing of more presses by HMT. In case of a repeat order, HMT expects that the ratio of indigenous production will reach 70 percent. Verson also stands to benefit from such an arrangement because parts would be imported from them.[26]

COST-BENEFIT ANALYSIS OF TECHNOLOGY TRANSFER

Dependency theory posits that technology transfer is usually costly to the buyer and involves considerable payment in foreign exchange because transactions in technology take place under imperfect market conditions. A UN study has calculated that in 1968, developing nations had spent $1.5 billion on direct costs (royalty and technical fees),[27] which was equal to 5 percent of their exports and 40 percent of their debt servicing costs.[28] The data on HMT, however, do not support the dependency hypothesis or the empirical findings of the UN study.

The government of India has a well-defined and strict policy on royalties, the length of the collaboration period, and financial compensation for transfer of technology. According to the established rules, the percentage of royalty will depend on the nature of technology but will not ordinarily exceed 5 percent. "Royalty is calculated on the basis of the ex-factory selling price of the product net of excise duties minus the cost of standard bought-out components and the landed cost of imported components."[29] The government allows the consideration of lump-sum payments in appropriate cases for the import of drawings, documentations, and other forms of know-how. In deciding on the reasonableness of such payments, the value of production is taken into account so that "the lump-sum and the recurring royalty, if any, is an acceptable proportion of the value of production."[30] Both royalty and lump-sum payments are subject to Indian taxes. The extension of collaboration agreements is usually difficult; these agreements are scrutinized carefully and granted only when the government is satisfied that there is a need for them. Even when extensions are considered and granted, the rate of royalty payment is usually reduced and the period of extension shortened.

Data on the lump-sum fees for technical assistance and the royalty payments made by HMT to foreign collaborators since 1955 are presented in Table 8.3. The company paid high technical-assistance fees during 1958-59 and 1959-60, mainly because the managing director, M. K. Mathulla, preferred paying lump-sum licensing fees to paying royalty, for reasons of accounting convenience. By contrast, his successor, S. M. Patil, favored paying royalty to paying lump-sum technical fees because he believed that it would maintain the interest of the collaborator during the entire term of the agreement. It is not surprising, therefore, that in the early 1960s the technical assistance fees dropped drastically. In the late 1960s and early 1970s, however, there was a sharp increase in the payment of technical assistance fees because of the diversification of HMT's product lines, and they dropped once again after 1972. The steady increase in the payment of technical assistance fees in the 1980s has been due mainly to the acquisition of the CNC and other high-precision technologies (see Table 8.4). It is important to emphasize that HMT has effectively mastered the technologies within the collaboration period and that the company never sought extension of an agreement.

HMT has successfully negotiated royalty payment for technology transfer agreements within the 5 percent limit set by the government. On only one occasion—while negotiating coordinate boring machine technology from GSP, France, in 1969—did it agree to pay a higher (7 percent for seven years) royalty fee, because of the unavailability of the technology from any other source.

Table 8.3
Technical Fees and Royalty Payments, 1955-86 (In Rs. Thousands)

Year	Technical Assistance Fee	Royalty	Total
1955-56	409		409
1956-57	321	109	431
1957-58	667	434	1,102
1958-59	2,180	476	2,656
1959-60	2,252	439	2,692
1960-61	739	143	883
1961-62	167	175	343
1962-63	593	217	811
1963-64	736	359	1,096
1964-65	1,316	303	1,620
1965-66	2,358	395	2,754
1966-67	2,308	700	3,009
1967-68	2,777	219	2,997
1968-69	2,978	244	3,223
1969-70	4,187	273	4,461
1970-71	3,574	280	3,875
1971-72	4,229	445	4,674
1972-73	6,479	261	6,740
1973-74	800	539	1,339
1974-75	464	670	1,135
1975-76		1,332	1,332
1976-77		1,940	1,940
1977-78		2,016	2,016
1978-79	1,883	5,666	7,549
1979-80	2,511	2,297	4,808
1980-81	3,387	2,157	5,544
1981-82	3,297	2,840	6,137
1982-83	2,810	3,193	6,003
1983-84	4,206	5,655	9,861
1984-85	6,751	1,701	8,452
1985-86	7,019	1,155	8,174

Sources: Masceranhas, *Technology Transfer and Development*, p. 76; and HMT's *Annual Report*.

An exercise in cost-benefit analysis of technology transfer shows more precisely the benefits from the collaborative agreements derived by HMT. In the first decade, HMT manufactured 11 types of machine tools based on the technology acquired from abroad. The company fully assimilated imported technology, not only producing machine tools during the collaboration period but also manufacturing machines after the collaboration ended. For example, HMT produced 2,209 high-precision lathes during the collaboration period, and after the expiration of the collaboration it produced 2,833 machines. These machines are still being produced by the company more than two decades after the collaboration agreement. The company's record indicates that while the agreements of the first decade during the collaboration period resulted in the manufacture of 10,771 machines, the number more than doubled (22,172) after the end of the collaboration period. Six out of eleven machines are still being manufactured (see Table 8.4). The number of machines produced after the expiration of the agreement, in most cases, was far more than during the collaboration period.

The collaborations of the third decade (see Table 8.5) are quite recent, and the data do not yield a comparative analysis; the manufacturing of most machines had, in fact, not commenced by the late 1980s. It should, however, be noted that although the company's decision to enter into technical collaboration is strategic and usually in response to the market demands, it considers the in-house development of technology equally important. The company has pursued foreign collaboration only if technology was available at a "reasonable" price from outside. Otherwise it has usually opted for in-house R&D. Even when the company did have a foreign collaboration, it always concentrated on in-house R&D and eventual indigenization of the product. Thus, while CNC technology has been imported in recent years, effort has also been made to develop the technology in-house at the Pinjore factory.[31] The company's record of product development through its own R&D is impressive indeed—more than 50 percent of its products are designed and developed in-house.[32] Whereas in the first decade, HMT produced 11 machines based on the technology acquired through collaborations and only one through its own R&D efforts, the numbers have increased, respectively, to 15 and 15 in the second decade and 18 and 22 in the third decade (see Table 8.6). The average cost of technology transfer in the third decade, however, is much higher (the going rate is DM 1 million or $1 million) than the technology acquired during the first and second decades, because the company has been trying to acquire the latest technology. The company's efforts to modernize machine tool production depend on successful assimilation of the newly acquired high-precision technology.

Table 8.4
Second Phase Collaborations

Collaboration Product No. Primary Line	Terms of Collaboration	During Collaboration Period	After Collaboration Period	Total
	Purchase/Jt. Marketing (No fee; no royalty) eq. No. Of machines			
MSA 12	17	108	172	280
SSA-PF 13	34	275	401	676
PIL 14	20	206	207	413
FAY 15	10	43	64	107
BM-RAM 16	30	52	54	106
BM-BED 17	36			
SHA 18	2	235	210	445
	Jt. Pdn. (No fee; no royalty)			
RTV 19		30	156	186
M-BOR 20		67	274	341
RISZ 21		139	87	226
A24 22		321	194	514
	Fee in terms of # of units purchasable	Royalty		
BERG 22	Rs.		(incl. among accessories)	
GSP 24	0.21	7%	26	
DIE C 25		5%	151+	80	231+
PRESS 26	13	5%	315	97	412
New lines				
WATCH 27	3,200	2%		
ADD 28	2,700	2%		30,369,022
Z-25 29	54	2.5%		90,763
POWER LIFTZ 30		2.5%		
Z-HYDR 31	Rs.	-among accs.		
PRINT 32	27	2.5%		
GLS 33		4%	3	-	3

Source: HMT Corporate Headquarters, Bangalore.

Table 8.5
Collaborations of the Third Decade

Collaboration Product		Terms of Collaboration		Production Numbers		
Primary Line		**Fee in terms of # of units purchasable**	**Royalty**	**During Collaboration Period**	**After Collaboration Period**	**Total**
CROSS	34	5	5%	324[b]		324
LAEIS	[a]35	Nil	5%	3[b]		3
H-BOR	36	Nil	5%	3[b]		3
DIE						
TOOL	37	Rs.	Nil			
PRESS	38	3	Nil			
S.						
BROACH	39	Nil	5%			
KTM	[a]40	Nil	5%			
GS	41	3	5%			
GH	42	3	3%			
WAHLI	[a]43	Nil	Nil[c]			
BALL-						
SCR	[a]44	(100)	Nil[c]			
CNC	[a]45	(100)	5%[c]			
MSA	46	DM	5%[c]			
IMMCO	[a]47	Rs.	[c]			
BUDER-						
US	48	2[b]	5%			
Diversified Lines						
HMSA	50	Rs.				
Z-59	51	Nil	2.5%	incl. in 29		
FTL	52	Nil	Nil			
FLM	[a]53	9	3%	310[b]		310
PL.						
EXTR	[a]54	2	5%			
ELECTR						
WATCH	[a]55	(42,000)				
KOBAU	56	2	5%[c]			
MABEG	57	9	Nil[c]			
MAXEL	[a]58		[c]			
FEDERAL	[a]59	26	[c]			
CZJ	[a]60	(160)	[c]			

[a] New technologies
[b] Under final negotiation in April 1984
[c] Under implementation (1984)
Source: HMT Corporate Headquarters, Bangalore.

Table 8.6
Number of New Products/Technologies Acquired

Decade	Principal Product Line		Diversified Product Line	
	Collaboration	R & D	Collaboration	R & D
1	11	1	1	-
2	15	15	6	1
3	18	22	9	5
Total	44	38	16	6

Source: HMT, Corporate Headquarters, Bangalore.

TECHNOLOGICAL LAG AND THE CASE OF MARUTI UDYOG LIMITED (MUL)

The foregoing discussion suggests that in the 1960s and 1970s, HMT was fairly successful in acquiring, adapting, and assimilating machine-tool technology. However, the technological capability of the company to manufacture high-precision machine tools was seriously questioned when it lost the Maruti Udyog Limited (MUL) bid to two Japanese companies, Sumitomo and Mitsubishi, in 1985.[33] The denial of the order worth Rs. 30 crores for the manufacture of machines for producing cylinder blocks for cars by Maruti Udyog to HMT evoked widespread concern in the company and the industry. Maruti Udyog's decision to import two machining lines from two Japanese companies dramatized the fact that HMT, formerly the industry leader, was incapable of manufacturing and meeting the growing demand for sophisticated, high-precision machine tools in India.

It is ironic that HMT, which had taken the lead in introducing the NC technology in the 1970s when there was hardly any demand for those machines, was found to be lagging behind the major machine tool manufacturers in the world in the 1980s. To understand why the company could not keep up, we must study the differences between the approaches to technology acquisition, management, and the style of running a public sector enterprise of M. S. Patil and his successors.

Hindustan Machine Tool had acquired its identity as a profit-making public sector company[34] committed to quality products under the leadership of Mathulla, who was the chairman from 1956 to 1964. Since the machine tool industry was one of the three basic industries given priority in the Second Five Year Plan, Prime Minister Nehru took personal interest in the success of HMT. As a result, Mathulla had direct contact with Nehru, who gave him full authority to run the company without government interference. Unlike most public sector undertakings, HMT had good management, and the company was run as a commercial undertaking from the beginning. Mathulla had groomed Patil, first as his factory manager and later as his general manager, to be his successor. During Patil's tenure as chairman and managing director from 1964 to 1978, his name became synonymous with HMT and the industry. Patil made HMT a household word in India and a well-recognized machine tool manufacturer in the world.

As mentioned earlier, it was Patil who took the initiative in collaborating with KTM for the production of NC Mogul lathes and vertical machining centers; the latter were successfully put into the market in 1978, the year of Patil's retirement. Thereafter, the company was faced with a leadership crisis; it had three managing directors in three years. From 1978 to 1982, when technological development, especially in electronic control systems, was taking place at a frenzied pitch everywhere in the world, HMT did not concentrate on the development of NC/CNC machine tools. When T. V. Mansukhani became chairman in 1982, he realized that the company was lagging behind in NC/CNC technology. Although Mansukhani emphasized the need to adapt the company's investment plans to meet the emerging demand for CNC machines,[35] the managers interviewed agreed that it was difficult to make up for lost time. Had the company continued with Patil's policy of developing NC machines, they argued, HMT would have been technologically much more competitive and perhaps the MUL deal would not have been lost.

Patil shared this view. He pointed out that HMT started manufacturing NC machines at a time when "the total population of such machines in the country was between 40 and 50; in 1986 its population was more than 1,000—most of which were imported because of their unavailability at home."[36] The time that the company has lost (four to five years) because of its inattention has definitely increased the technological gap between HMT and the leading machine tool manufacturers in the world, and it seems difficult to bridge the gap in the near future.[37] Although the company managers interviewed (including the newly appointed managing director, M. V. Naidu) expressed their disappointment with and resentment toward the government decision to import Japanese machining centers over a public sector's bid, objective observers and analysts of the industry expressed approval of the government decision.

Maruti Udyog, a public sector company, had entered into a technical collaboration agreement with Suzuki of Japan to manufacture fuel efficient small cars. The terms of the agreement included total indigenization of car manufacturing within ten years. Because of the provision of a phased indigenization program in the agreement, the collaborator and the company's managing director, Krishnamurti, wanted to acquire proven technology, and the firm floated a global tender. It was doubtful that high-technology equipment—machining lines for engine blocks—was domestically available. HMT[38] was one of the bidders for this tender along with a host of foreign companies, including the two from Japan, which finally bagged the order.

According to MUL, the technical evaluation of all the bids received showed that HMT did not meet the specifications stipulated by Maruti in the tenders. Discussions between HMT and MUL officials could not resolve the specifications issue.[39] Subsequently, MUL decided not to open the commercial offer to HMT, since the technical evaluation of its bid did not meet standards and specifications. However, on HMT's request, a team of its engineers was allowed to go to Japan and inspect the Suzuki works there—an unprecedented facility granted to HMT—to assess and understand the pattern followed by the Japanese for making the two machining lines. The HMT bid was revised thereafter. However, the revised bid indicated that to meet the order, HMT would import about 60 percent of the value of the total order. This meant that even the revised HMT offer was as good as imported to the extent of 60 percent of the machining lines in terms of value.[40] This factor is what influenced the MUL decision to go in for imports of the two machining lines.

According to MUL, the proposed combination of indigenous and imported components in the machining lines would not have been satisfactory, since, in such equipment, the total machining system was required for manufacturing engine blocks and cylinder heads. The consortium managers interviewed pointed out that HMT had the experience of manufacturing and supplying machining lines for cylinder heads and engine blocks for two-wheeler scooters but not for passenger car manufacturers. However, they argued that together they were capable of acquiring the technical know-how of manufacturing and supplying the machining lines to MUL. But the consortium's bid was rejected on the basis of tripartite discussions involving the managements of MUL and HMT and representatives of Directorate General of Trade and Development (DGTD) in the industry ministry.[41]

Not convinced that the consortium could supply the sophisticated machines, MUL insisted on acquiring proven technology from Japan. It emphasized the differences between the manufacturing process for engine blocks and cylinder heads for two-wheelers and those for four-wheel vehicles.[42] The MUL decision to import the Japanese machines raised considerable controversy in India. It was alleged that through such deals, the Indo-Japanese venture was ensuring imports of other Japanese equipment and components. Popular media, especially daily newspapers, took a nationalistic economic position, and several news commentaries argued that if this trend were to be encouraged, as much as Rs. 1,000 crores worth of machine tools would be imported into the country by the early 1990s.[43]

Although HMT managers—and those of four other companies in the consortium—felt bitter about losing the bid to the Japanese, they learned their technological backwardness the hard way. Therefore, it is not surprising that in the company's corporate plan in the post-1985 period, top priority has been given to the acquisition of high-precision machine tool technology from abroad and to increasing the share of CNC machines to 30 percent of total production. Since the sale of machine tools is largely dependent on the user industries, and the user industries—such as the automobile industry and its ancillary industries, tractors and other agricultural equipment manufacturers, industrial and mining machinery, power generation and electrical equipment manufacturers, railway workshops, defense production units and aircraft industry—need more and more high-productive, precision, and NC/CNC machine tools, HMT's strategy in the Third

Corporate Plan (1985-90) was to emphasize the introduction of high-technology state-of-the-art machines in all areas of metal cutting.

The thrust areas, according to the corporate plan, thus include the introduction of CNC machines of various types and sizes; the operation of a pilot flexible manufacturing system (FMS); the integration of computer-aided design and computer-aided machine (CAD/CAM) to the linked manufacturing system; the linking of machines with the automatic handling system; the tool transfer and other peripherals; and the preparation for the establishment of a computer-controlled, unitized micro factory for flexible production of a family of parts.[44] HMT was responding to the enormous expansion of the automotive sector in the early 1980s, which offered immense scope for an increase in the output of NC and computerized machine tools. The company finally recognized that its future lay in mastering high-precision machine tool technology. Toward meeting this goal, the company's corporate plan proposed to establish a computer systems division, an in-house R&D computer facility, which would provide the required CAD/CAM support for the machine tool and watch groups.[45] With R&D expenditure of about 3 to 4 percent of the sales turnover, and with the strength of 500 design engineers, HMT has the resources and infrastructure to close the technological gap that exists. By modernizing the industry, it hopes it can move quickly into the CNC age.

COLLECTIVE SELF-RELIANCE AND SOUTH-SOUTH TECHNOLOGY TRANSFER

In the development literature, considerable attention has been given in recent years to the concept of collective self-reliance through economic cooperation among developing countries. The development debate in the last decade has focused on an analysis of the Group of 77's emphasis on the need for promoting economic and technical cooperation among developing countries (TCDC).[46] At the 15-nation Third World economic summit held at Kuala Lumpur in June 1990, a number of steps were suggested that would lead to practical cooperation among developing nations, including the Malaysian proposal to set up a South Investment Trade and Technology Data Exchange Center (SITTDEC) to promote and disseminate information on investment and trade opportunities available among these countries. It has been proposed that the G-15 nations should make such cooperative deliberation an annual exercise. These ambitious self-help resolutions have yet to be translated into practice.[47]

The literature on South-South economic cooperation, however, is abstract and at a high level of generalization. Empirical studies on the subject are rare,[48] making it difficult to judge the merit of the concept. This discussion is a modest effort to bridge that gap by exploring the possibility of technical cooperation among developing countries through an examination of the experience of HMT in the export of technology to other developing countries. This analysis will show that India's ability to master machine tool technology and sell it internationally developed because of the country's desire to become technologically self-reliant and because of the specific policies followed by the government to expand domestic "know-why."[49]

The example of HMT is instructive in pointing to the possibility of technology transfer from an Asian NIC to less industrialized developing countries. HMT has exported, through its subsidiary HMT (I), not only its machines but also its technology and technical services to many African and Asian countries. The company's record looks impressive: By the late 1980s, more than 6,000 HMT machines were in operation in more than 70 countries, including many developed nations. HMT (I) offers services ranging from site selection, architecture, construction, machine design, and production planning to shop management, inspection, training, marketing, and finance. These services rendered by HMT have been recognized by UNIDO in a feasibility study for setting up a machine tool manufacturing complex in Nigeria and in a study of the capital goods industry in the Philippines and Indonesia. HMT has also helped set up new factories in India, Algeria, and Tanzania. The most successful of the company's overseas projects, in Indonesia and Nigeria, suggest the possibility of a meaningful South-South technology transfer.

Training Center-cum-Tool Room Project, Indonesia[50]

In 1983, HMT (I) entered into an agreement with Indonesia in 1983 to set up a Training Center-cum-Tool Room (TC-TR) for a contract value of Rs. 55.61 million ($5 million).[51] The government of Indonesia emphasized its development efforts, in the 1980s, of small-scale industries as part of its industrialization program. However, it lacked the capability to produce simple, standard machine tools, mainly because of the absence of a higher degree of skill and expertise in the metal-working field. The Ministry of Industry therefore decided to set up a TC-TR project on a turnkey basis.

In Surabaya, HMT offered to set up a TC-TR project, which was attractive to Indonesians for many reasons. First, the contract for this project had been awarded to HMT (I) on a competitive basis. The two parties had engaged in detailed negotiations extending over a period of two years during which time the Indonesians visited the company and found it to be technologically as good as the leading machine tool manufacturers in the world. Second, some of the terms offered by HMT were especially attractive to the Indonesians, for example, bringing experts to Indonesia to impart on-the-job training for a period of 1½ years (the cost of hiring Indian experts was considerably less than getting them from the developed West). Third, whereas the Western machine tool manufacturers had moved into high-precision technology, HMT was still manufacturing a range of simple machine tools designed to meet the needs of other developing countries. Finally, HMT had the kind of experience that most leading machine tool manufacturers lacked. The company, which was set up as a turnkey project itself, had the experience of executing turnkey projects in a variety of locations—HMT's third, fourth, and fifth units were located hundreds of miles from Bangalore. The company's personnel in the early 1980s had the majority of "first generation" people who had been involved in their respective units' operations right from the setting-up stage. They were quite familiar with, and used to working within, a "lack of infrastructure" environment—not only in setting up a unit but also running it. This "natural advantage" of HMT has been underscored by UNIDO and in the company's advertisements and trade literature.   It is therefore not surprising that shortly after the Indonesian team's visit to the HMT factory, the deal was finalized.

The project, which began in May 1983, was completed ahead of schedule in November 1985. During this period, 13 experts from HMT (I) were sent to Indonesia to teach tool designing and manufacturing. At the same time, eight diploma-holding Indonesian instructors and two tool designers underwent intensive training at the HMT training center in Bangalore for six to nine months. The training center also prepared about 19 special manuals on different topics for use by the Indonesian technicians. HMT managers (especially the center's director when interviewed) were very proud of this aspect of the service rendered by HMT to other Third World countries. They emphasized the possibility of a meaningful South-South technology transfer, especially if encouraged by international agencies.

The contribution of HMT to Indonesia's development, however, was not limited to erecting a factory or providing technology for a fee. Rather, the successful completion of the TC-TR project at the mini industrial estate in Surabaya (about 800 kms east of Jakarta) has given Indonesia the technological capability for the first time to impart basic and specialized production-oriented training in metal-working trades. The center, with 1,800 available training hours per year, will form the nucleus for setting up facilities under the industrial estate concept to manufacture simple, standard machine tools.   Furthermore, the government expects some of the TC-TR trainees to become successful entrepreneurs, thus contributing to the industrialization of Indonesia.

SONELGAZ (Société Nationale de l'Electricité et du Gaz) Meter Factory, Algeria[52]

SONELGAZ, a $2 billion Algerian Government undertaking engaged in the production and distribution of electricity and gas,[53] was totally dependent on imported meters for its consumers. In the late 1970s, it decided to set up a manufacturing unit at El Eulma (350 kms east of Algiers) so that it could become self-reliant in the production of meters. In March 1978, HMT (I) was awarded a $12 million contract, in face of stiff competition, for setting up the water meter division, gas meter division and toolroom of the meter complex.[54]   The confidence expressed by the Algerian government in the technological competence of HMT was partly due to their prior experience with the company. Even before the SONELGAZ project, HMT had earned a reputation for its technological capability when it had deputed 10 engineers for two years to Algeria to remedy some of the work German engineers had done there earlier.

The SONELGAZ meter factory was a turnkey project—a complex operation involving, among other things, supplying of machines, equipment, and sophisticated toolings; erecting and commissioning of machines and equipment; establishing trial production of gas meters and regulators to rated capacity; obtaining precision-oriented mass technology from the two licensors in the United States and Switzerland; training of Algerian personnel in India; and on-the-job training in Algeria. The project was completed in April 1983.[55] HMT (I) had sent a large number of supervisory and management staff—a total of 67—to Algeria, and 54 Algerian personnel were trained in HMT units in India. The transfer of know-how from HMT to SONELGAZ was thus quite similar to HMT's own experience in the 1950s as a recipient of machine tool technology from the Swiss firm Oerlikons. It differed, however, in one sense: Unlike HMT in the 1950s, Algeria could save substantially by hiring experts from India, where the average salary was one-third that of Germany or Great Britain—not to mention the American experts, who are the most expensive. India had not had this option in the 1950s. Algerians, on their part, preferred the training of their technicians in a developing country to a similar training in the West, because it involved the training of their first-generation technicians at the hands of the first-generation HMT engineers who could understand and appreciate the problems of the lack of basic infrastructure that engineers from developed countries would not be sensitive to.

Other Developing Nations

The HMT training center at Bangalore has provided technical training in basic trade and know-how to the Third World. A number of developing nations—including Kenya, Ethiopia, Zambia, Ghana, Iraq, Syria, Iran, Sri Lanka, Papua New Guinea, Nepal, Bangladesh, the Philippines, Nigeria, and Tanzania—have availed themselves of HMT's services.[56] The company's services and expertise have been recognized by world development organizations such as the United Nations Industrial Development Organization, the United Nations Development Program, the World Bank, the International Development Agency, the International Finance Corporation, the Asian Development Bank, the African Development Bank, and the Arab Fund for Economic Development in Africa.

UNIDO, which has taken a keen interest in technological cooperation among developing countries (TCDC), has identified HMT as a reliable source of machine tool and related technology for less developed Third World countries. A joint UNIDO-HMT workshop held in Bangalore in November 1975—organized by HMT on behalf of the Government of India and sponsored by UNIDO—made the Company quite visible in the Third World as a source of machine tool technology. The workshop participants from several Asian and African countries were favorably impressed by the advances made by the company in machine tool building. The result was a number of successful business deals with other developing countries. For example, the HMT-Nigeria collaboration, signed in June 1979, was a direct result of the participation of a Nigerian minister as a delegate of his country in the workshop. The benefit to Nigeria of such a collaborative project has been enormous. The setting up of the Nigerian Machine Tool Limited (NMTL) as a joint venture enterprise (valued at $80 million) has allowed the establishment of a much needed manufacturing facility for an engineering design and fabrication center in Oshogbo (230 kms north of Lagos). As a result of the collaboration, Nigerians have received training in India—by the end of 1986, 65 trainees had received 6 to 15 months of technical training in Bangalore.[57] The training of Nigerian personnel in Bangalore has been compared to the training the Swiss technicians had given HMT engineers in 1955.[58] The setting up in Nigeria of a training center equipped to train people in trades such as fitting, turning, milling, grinding, and so forth, has further reduced the dependence of Nigeria on the industrialized West.

A second UNIDO-HMT workshop on precision engineering techniques and horology, held at Bangalore in June 1986, further underscored India's ability to transfer technology and assist in setting up projects identified by UNIDO. The workshop emphasized that India was in a position to offer many of the "forgotten yet viable" technologies once used by the developed nations. A UNIDO consultant commented, "The expertise built over the years could best be put to use in countries less developed than India. This would save a considerable amount of money in repetitive imports and would also help groom an industrial infrastructure within the assisted country."[59] Furthermore, HMT's first-generation technicians were considered to be better prepared than, say, a third-generation German technician to train the first-generation Third World engineer mainly because they themselves went through a similar experience about 20 or 25 years ago.

Encouraged by the experience of HMT in technology transfer to other developing nations, India and UNIDO proposed to launch jointly an interregional project on technology identification in the engineering and capital goods industries and its transfer among the developing countries. The five-year program, covering 1986 to 1991, was designed to help identify the area of cooperation among different developing countries for a purposeful exchange of technologies.[60] It resulted in new business opportunities for HMT (I). For example, in 1993, the company secured a Rs. 12 crore contract to set up an Institute of Technical Education in Maldives, and it was participating in the setting up of a foundry in Dubai in a joint venture with Sri Ramakrishna Steel Industries Ltd. of Coimbatore and the Easa Saleh Al Gurg group of Dubai.[61]

The services of HMT (I) are thus wide-ranging and have been utilized by countries at different levels of development. In Tanzania, for example, HMT (I) has established eight common facility centers and has supplied machines, equipment, spare parts, raw materials, and tools valued at $3 million. In neighboring Kenya, the company conducted feasibility studies to set up a machine tool manufacturing complex. (After Jomo Kenyatta's death, however, the project was shelved.) At the request of several Third World governments—Ethiopia, Ghana, Zambia, Syria, Papua New Guinea, Bangladesh, St. Lucia, Nepal, Dubai, Maldives, and others—HMT (I) has conducted feasibility studies for setting up tractor plants, a spare parts manufacturing complex, a machine-tool manufacturing complex, central engineering workshops, engineering industries, maintenance workshops, and industrial estates. In Iraq, the company has provided technical assistance in setting up a toolroom and has supplied and installed the plant and equipment for a training project; it also conducted a market survey to determine machine tool demand. HMT (I) helped the Iranian Machine Saze Tabriz in establishing company standards and prepared for them a detailed project report in the area of machine tool design. It also provided technical assistance to Iran in setting up a toolroom. In short, HMT's technical services to other developing nations are numerous and valuable.

The technological capability of HMT thus allows it to make a two-fold contribution to South-South technology transfer. At the lower end of technology, it supplies technology to other Third World countries. At the higher end of technology, it interfaces with the developed countries, which will make the technology market more competitive and will enhance the bargaining power of the technology recipient countries.

CONCLUSION

The record of HMT in technology transfer is a mixed one. This analysis shows that the company has moved from the stage of "total spoon-feeding," when it acquired basic machine tool technology by entering into a turnkey agreement with Oerlikons in the 1950s, to a high degree of self-reliance when it acquired the capability of assimilating foreign technology and designing and producing a variety of machine tools, to that of technological maturity when it entered into joint production with leading international firms (KTM) for the manufacture of NC machine tools in the 1970s. By and large, it has set a pace in technological advancement of the Indian machine tool industry that has carried the whole industry to the present stage. The contribution of HMT is not limited to the production of machine tools: It has helped set up an industrial estate and has produced designers and entrepreneurs for the industry.[62] The company has successfully transferred technical know-how and provided consultancy services to many Asian and African countries, thus making a major contribution to the South-South technology transfer.

Yet, as events of the 1980s and early 1990s reveal, HMT is lagging far behind the major machine tool manufacturers in the area of modern, high-precision machine tool technology, especially NC/CNC. HMT managers are painfully aware of this fact, and in the last few years they have taken several steps to acquire or develop modern technology to narrow the technological gap.

This case study suggests that the appropriate mode of acquiring technology will vary depending on the level of a country's economic and industrial development and the nature of the technology market. Even within a company, the mode will vary over a period of time, depending on the technological capability of the firm. There cannot be a general prescription for all the developing countries. In the 1950s, when HMT had no experienced personnel and no operating procedures, the most appropriate and efficient mode of acquiring technology was the turnkey agreement. Once HMT acquired technological capability in the 1960s, it came to rely heavily on bulk purchase and licensing. When HMT was moving toward technological maturity in the 1970s, it resorted to joint development and production. The case study further suggests, contrary to the dependency hypothesis, that it is possible for a Third World country to move along a "dependence-independence-self-reliance continuum" for technological progress. In other words, a country may well start with a situation of technological dependence on Western multinationals and move slowly toward technological self-reliance by assimilating, adapting, improving, innovating, and diffusing the imported technology.

The strategy of imitation and learning by doing may seem appropriate for a Third World country. It is true that technical improvements made by HMT do not constitute major Schumpeterian "break-throughs"[63] and they are not even on the world frontiers of the machine tool technology, yet they do constitute technical progress. By developing indigenous technological capability, HMT has not only contributed to India's industrialization for three decades, it has contributed to the process of industrial development in many Third World countries. The case study shows that technology import can contribute to self-reliance if there is an environment for absorption, adaptation, and diffusion of technology at the firm level.

The unprecedented early success of HMT can also be attributed to the management and leadership of the company in its first 25 years. Mainly because of the initiative taken by Mathulla, the company in the late 1950s and early 1960s entered into the production of a wide range of general-purpose machine tools. The Second and Third Five-Year Plan priorities of increased investment in the public sector, which had resulted in a boom for the machine tool market, contributed significantly to the growth of the company at a critical stage in its life. However, under its most dynamic managing director, Patil, the company not only diversified its production and acquired technology through the most economical modes (licensing, joint development, and during the recessionary years, bulk purchase) but also developed the capacity to adapt, assimilate, innovate, and further improve on the imported technology. The company entered into the production of high-technology NC machine tools in the 1970s.

But Patil's retirement in 1978 brought a leadership crisis to HMT, which had an adverse effect on the company's technological development. Between 1978 and 1986, HMT had several managing directors, none of whom had the dynamism, dedication, and commitment of Patil or Mathulla, and it lost its earlier commitment to acquisition and development of modern technology during this period.

The leadership situation in the company became stable only in 1986 when, following Rajiv Gandhi's decision to increase the term of the chief executives of the public sector companies from two to five years, M. V. Naidu was appointed as managing director for a five-year term. Recognizing that the Indian machine tool industry was on the threshold of technology transition because of the trend to manufacture more and more advanced technology precision and NC/CNC machine tools, Naidu—like his immediate predecessor—emphasized technology transfer and technical collaborations from industrially advanced countries.

Although HMT continued to develop new technology machine tools through its own research and development efforts, it realized that such efforts would take a long time, necessitating large imports of machine tools in the interim. As a short-run strategy, it decided to pay high technical fees and royalties for obtaining the modern technology from leading machine tool multinationals. This would help the company expedite the process of modernization and catch up with the latest developments in machine-building technology.

In the context of technology import, it is important to emphasize that the technological capability acquired over the years by HMT allows it to identify alternative sources and different modes of acquiring technology. The company has bargained effectively and has often succeeded in negotiating the best technology transfer deals with the machine tool multinationals. If self-reliance means the maximization of choice through increased knowledge and capability and not self-sufficiency, HMT's increased dependence on foreign technology in recent years does not amount to technological dependence of the sort hypothesized by the dependency theorists. The HMT case could best be understood in terms of the dependence self-reliance continuum instead of a situation of dependency.

NOTES

1. See Peter F. Drucker, "Japan's Choices," *Foreign Affairs*, (Summer 1987): 923-24.

2. By the early 1970s, the company had diversified its product range into watches, tractors, printing machines, metal forming presses, die-casting machines, horological machinery, lamp-making machinery, and lamps. To reflect this change, the company's name was formally changed from Hindustan Machine Tools to HMT in September 1978.

3. HMT, *Annual Report*, 1977-78, p. 3.

4. HMT, *Annual Report*, 1985-86.

5. Dr. S. M. Patil, the former managing director of HMT, in a personal interview by the author on November 14, 1986.

6. Ibid.

7. HMT, "HMT I & II (MTB & DCB) Bangalore," unpublished paper, Bangalore, n.d.

8. In 1988, the project consultancy wing of the company was involved in the preparation of feasibility reports for Kenya, Nigeria, and Tanzania. See Ron Matthews, "Development of India's Machine Tool Industry," *Economic and Political Weekly*, Oct. 1, 1988, p. 2063.

9. R. C. Mascarenhas, Technology Transfer and Development: India's Hindustan Machine Tools Company (Boulder, Colo.: Westview Press, 1982), p. 66.

10. S. M. Patil, "25 Years in HMT," *Machine Tool Engineer*, April 1978, pp.4-5.

11. In watches, however, HMT entered into a collaboration agreement with the Japanese Citizen Watch Company in 1961, which was a turnkey project.

12. UNIDO, *The Machine Tool Industry: Perspectives for Industrial Development in the Second United Nations Development Decade* (New York: United Nations, 1974), pp. 16-17.

13. United Nations, *Guidelines for the Study of the Transfer of Technology to Developing Countries* (United Nations, 1973), Ch. 2.

14. A comment by S. M. Patil, in personal interview on November 14, 1986.

15. DGTD, "HMT Files," New Delhi: Directorate General of Trade and Development.

16. Lynn Krieger Mytelka, "Licensing and Technology Dependence in the Andean Group," *World Development*, 6, No. 4 (April 1978): 453. Also see her *Regional Development in a Global Economy: The Multinational Corporation, Technology, and Andean Integration* (New Haven: Yale University Press, 1979).

17. K. V. Ramchandra, personal interview, Bangalore, October 30, 1986.

18. "Comprehensive R&D Plan for Machine Tools: 1983-84 to 1992-93," R&D Center, HMT, Bangalore, Nov. 1983, p. 3.

19. The changes in tax rates announced by the government in 1985 on royalty and lump-sum fees seem to have helped HMT in negotiating licensing agreements with foreign firms. The tax rate was 40 percent on royalty and 20 percent on lump-sum know-how fees and was changed to a uniform 30 percent tax plus a 5 percent R&D cess.

20. S. M. Patil, personal interview, November 15, 1986.

21. Mascarenhas, *Technology Transfer and Development,* p. 63.

22. M. V. Ramchandra, personal interview, Nov. 14, 1986.

23. M. V. Ramchandra, General Manager Projects, Corporate Office, HMT, Bangalore, in a personal interview on October 30, 1986.

24. For many years, HMT has been negotiating with the former Soviet Union for a joint project for the development of electro-discharge machines. HMT has the basic machine but not the control system (pulse generators); it has therefore proposed that the two could be joined, that HMT's basic machines could be interfaced with the Russian control system. Russia was especially attractive to HMT because it would have given an easy and assured access to the huge Russian market. Due to the disintegration of the former Soviet Union, however, the success of a joint project between HMT and Russia seems less likely.

25. In 1973 HMT had shown its NC Mogul lathe at the Hanover fair. Personal interview, M. S. Patil, Bangalore, November 16, 1986.

26. M. V. Ramchandra, personal interview, October 30, 1986.

27. It is difficult to calculate indirect costs of technology transfer such as the overpricing of goods purchased from the technology supplier, the restrictive practices, notably export restrictions and the transfer of inappropriate technology. For these reasons I will consider only the direct cost of technology transfer.

28. United Nations, *Guidelines for the Study of the Transfer of Technology to Developing Countries* (New York: United Nations, 1973), p. 7.

29. Government of India, *Guidelines for Industries, Part I: Policy and Procedures* (New Delhi Ministry of Industry, Department of Industrial Development, 1982), pp. I-14.

30. Ibid.

31. A. K. Gangopadhyay, R&D manager, personal interview, Bangalore, November 12, 1986.

32. Ibid.

33. *Financial Express*, November 18, 1985.

34. The company went into the red for the first time in the early 1990s because of the recession in the industry.

35. HMT, *32nd Annual Report*, 1984-85, p. 3.

36. The production of CNC machine tools has accelerated in the 1990s. In 1995, its number stood at 800 and by the year 2000 it is expected to reach 3,000 units worth over Rs. 1,100 crores.

37. S. M. Patil, personal interview, November 15, 1986.

38. After missing initially an order of Rs. 7 crores, five leading Indian machine tool manufacturing units led by HMT formed a consortium under the guidance of the Indian Machine Tool Manufacturing Association. The other members of the consortium were Bharat Fritz Werner, which has a German collaboration; Kirloskar, which has collaboration with an American company; FORMAC; and XLO, which also has American collaboration.

39. *Financial Express*, November 18, 1985.

40. *Financial Express*, November 17, 1985.

41. DGTD's assessment of the technical feasibility of the bid was quite favorable. A. K. Gangopadhyay, personal interview, November 12, 1986.

42. The differences between the two are quite significant. For instance, passenger cars need three or four cylinders compared to only one cylinder for scooters. Similarly, a scooter engine is air-cooled, while a car engine is water-cooled and as such should have water-cooling provision. More than 29 machines are required in the machining line for cylinder heads and 44 machines for engine blocks for passenger cars. On the other hand, no more than 10 machines are needed for a machining line for scooters' cylinder heads and engine blocks.

43. In 1985, the annual production of machine tools in the country was of the order of Rs. 250 crores. These stories therefore implied that the import would be equal to that of four or five years of national production. This, however, has not happened. See the *Indian Express*, August 27, 1985.

44. HMT, *Third Corporate Plan (Extended) 1986-87 to 1989-90* (Bangalore: HMT, May 1986), pp. 10-11.

45. Ibid., p. 11.

46. The Group of 77 articulated these ideas in 1979 and 1981. See the two documents "Group of 77, Arusha Program for Collective Self-Reliance and Framework for Negotiations," Manila: UNCTAD V, Doc. TD/236/1979 and "Group of 77, Final Report of the High-Level Conference on Economic Cooperation among the Developing Countries,"

Caracas: G/77/FR.

47. G-15 includes a broad spectrum of nations from each continent (Mexico, Jamaica, Yugoslavia, Venezuela, Algeria, Senegal, Peru, Brazil, Nigeria, Egypt, Zimbabwe, Argentina, India, Malaysia, and Indonesia) with a "respectable" standing in international affairs and among Third World nations. These countries were selected to represent the Third World at the 1989 Nonaligned Summit in Belgrade. See *India Abroad*, June 15, 1990.

48. One exception to this is a recent volume by Jerker Carlsson and Timothy M. Shaw (eds.), *Newly Industrializing Countries and the Political Economy of South-South Relations* (New York: St. Martin's Press, 1988).

49. Lall makes a distinction between technological know-how—production technology—and technological "know-why"—"the assimilation of basic design technology and the ability to engineer all the components of a complete new plant." See Sanjaya Lall, "Technological Learning in the Third World: Some Implications of Technology Exports," in Frances Stewart and Jeffrey James (eds.), *The Economics of New Technology in Developing Countries* (Boulder, Colo.: Westview Press, 1982), pp. 168-169.

50. Data presented in this section were gathered during personal interviews of HMT (I) officials, especially the group manager, projects, at its headquarters in Bangalore in November 1986.

51. HMT, "Training Center-Cum-Tool Room Indonesia: An HMT (International) Turnkey Project," unpublished Paper, n.d.

52. Data presented in this section were obtained from the HMT (I) headquarters in Bangalore through personal interviews. I interviewed, among others, N. G. Kudva, chief engineer, projects, on November 7, 1986.

53. SONELGAZ has recently been split into small companies.

54. *Deccan Herald*, March 21, 1978.

55. "SONELGAZ Meter Factory, Algeria: An HMT (International) Turnkey Project," Unpublished Paper, HMT (I), Bangalore, n.d.

56. *Deccan Herald*, July 25, 1978.

57. HMT's services to Nigeria include project formulation, technical documentation, technical assistance, training of Nigerian personnel, erection and commissioning, supply of SKDs and CKDs, deputation of management and professional engineering personnel, technicians and skilled craftsmen, and formulations of systems. However, due to economic problems in Nigeria associated with the falling oil revenue in the post-1982 period, the joint venture could not be completed as scheduled. The project should have been finished by 1984-85, but had not gone into production even in 1987. Personal interview with M. S. Parthiv, senior manager, projects, Bangalore, November 8, 1986.

58. Bernard Martyris, chief of training and OD, personal interview, November 6, 1986.

59. *The Economic Times*, August 9, 1986.

60. *The Economic Times*, June 19, 1986.

61. *The Economic Times*, December 11, 1993.

62. A large number of HMT designers and engineers have taken better paying jobs in the private sector or have become entrepreneurs by resigning their positions in the company or after retirement.

63. Contrary to Joseph Schumpeter's theory of the uniqueness of inventor-entrepreneurs, Katz and other economists have argued that "inventive activities lie in the process of technical apprenticeship"—the assimilation and adaptation of known techniques of production rather than the development of new productive techniques. See Lynn K.

Mytelka, "Technological Dependence in the Andean Group," *International Organization*, 32, No. 1 (Winter 1978): 105.

Conclusion

In this study I have made an effort to test empirically on technology transfer some of the main propositions of dependency theory and the bargaining school using industry-level data from India, a newly industrializing country. The study was motivated by the claim of dependency theorists to the universality of their propositions—despite the regional context in which the propositions were developed (to explain the phenomena in Latin America)—and by the claim of the advocates of the bargaining model to analytical superiority and a better alternative to dependency theory. Empirical research testing the hypotheses of the two theories has focused mainly on the extractive industries in Latin America. Although a few studies in recent years have sought to verify these claims by analyzing the data from Asian and African countries, there is a limited base of empirical research testing the hypotheses of the two theories. By empirically examining the technology transfer experience of two manufacturing industries in India—pharmaceuticals and machine tools—this study contributes to the understanding of the processes and determinants of the bargaining power of the technology user and the technology supplier.

This study has tested the main propositions of the two theories on technology transfer in order to understand technological dependence and self-reliance in the manufacturing industry in the Third World. It has focused on understanding the shifting bargaining power of the multinationals, the state, and private national capital; the process of acquisition, assimilation, adaptation, and generation of technology at the firm level; the role of the public sector and state regulations and control in the development of technological capability; the relationship between technological capability and self-reliant development in the Third World; the domestic and international conditions that allow a developing nation to move from dependency to self-reliance; and the reverse flow of technology from the Third World.

This study of the complex cases of two industries in India finds dependency theory to be inadequate because of its structural mode of analysis, which portrays dependency as a "determinant international structure rather than as a set of shifting constraints within which states seek to maneuver."[1] Although its single-cause explanation of technological dependency in the Third World is helpful in explaining the phenomenon of the technological gap between India and its technology suppliers, and consequently India's technological dependence in the early postindependence period (especially in the 1950s and early 1960s), it does not explain the growing bargaining power of the state and the national capital vis-a-vis the multinationals in the last two decades. But the more sophisticated and dynamic bargaining framework, which considers dependency to be one of the many possible outcomes of technology transfer, creates a better understanding of the Indian situation—especially in explaining what has happened since the early 1970s. This study confirms some of the propositions of the bargaining school. The product cycle model is helpful in explaining the lag in India's modern drug technology, but it does not adequately explain HMT's lag in the latest machine tool technology because of the difference in the nature of the technology market. While the technology market in the modern pharmaceutical industry is monopolistic, in the machine tool industry it is oligopolistic, which accounts for the difference in the experience of the two industries in the transfer of modern technology.

Nevertheless, the bargaining theory is limited, because it does not take into account the politicoeconomic constraints within which firms operate, constraints which make the process of assimilation, adaptation, and generation of technology more or less successful at the firm level. The concept of "organizational involution" helps explain how a technological lag in both industries is due in part to government policies as well as inefficiencies at the firm level. Therefore, although the bargaining theory is more useful than the dependency theory in explaining the Indian situation, both theories fail to take into account factors at the firm level, which contribute to the development of technological capability. Since technological capability is an important determinant of relative bargaining power, and makes a country technologically self-reliant, this study has carefully analyzed what happens to technology at the firm level once it has been transferred. The findings will now be synthesized.

THE STATE, MULTINATIONALS, AND PRIVATE NATIONAL CAPITAL

In empirical and theoretical studies on technology transfer, drug multinationals have been criticized for making huge profits, "dumping" worthless or "irrational" combination drugs, avoiding taxes in the host country through transfer pricing methods, underspending on R&D in the host country, not producing bulk drugs from the basic stages, and hindering the development of indigenous technological capability. Empirical studies on the Indian pharmaceutical industry have confirmed a pattern of technological dependency, overpricing, and exploitation found in many Third World countries,[2] but the Indian pharmaceutical and machine tool industries are moving forward along a dependence/self-reliance continuum. There has been a significant increase in the bargaining power of the state; the multinationals no longer constitute the dominant sector of the industry. Thus, the Indian situation could be better explained through the use of bargaining framework than dependency theory.

India started with a dependence on a handful of transnational firms, which had a monopoly on drug technology. The national sector was almost nonexistent—a common characteristic of most Third World countries. But the objective of achieving technological self-reliance soon led to the establishment of two public sector companies—HAL and IDPL—for the manufacture of antibiotics and synthetic bulk drugs. These companies have contributed to the development of technological capability in the manufacture of basic drugs in India. Once India unbundled technology from foreign capital, the government took legal and administrative measures—the Patent Law (1970), FERA (1973), the New Drug Policy (1978), and the DPCO (1979)—to increase its bargaining power. Government control and regulation of the industry through compulsory licensing, stringent rules regarding royalty and lump-sum fees, weak patent protection, canalization of bulk drugs, and the reservation of a large number of drugs for the national sector resulted in unprecedented growth of the private sector and a decline of the foreign sector. In other NICs—notably Brazil and Mexico—multinationals continue to dominate the pharmaceutical industry, but in India they had by the early 1980s been dislodged from their preeminent position to the position of junior partner. India's signing in 1994 of the Uruguay Round, which will strengthen patent protection in the pharmaceutical industry, is unlikely to reverse the position of the national sector in the industry in the near future.

Dependency theorists often cite the example of pharmaceuticals to support their claim that multinationals dominate the most profitable industries in the Third World because of their monopoly over modern process and product technology. But this study shows a striking contrast between India and other NICs: Whereas India succeeded in unbundling technology from foreign equity in the 1970s, Brazil has continued to rely on foreign investment both as a source of technology and capital. Brazil has allowed foreign multinationals to increase their equity investment in joint ventures and subsidiaries when India controlled DFI.[3]

This study has shown that India's drug prices are among the lowest in the Third World,[4] that the profitability of the multinationals is substantially below the level in other countries; that transfer pricing practices have been checked, that foreign firms have increased their R&D expenditure and have manufactured the required ratio of bulk drugs to formulations, and that the multinationals have diluted their equity share to 40 percent (with the exception of a handful of companies) making them the minority equity holders. These findings support the bargaining hypothesis that, since the parties involved in the technology transfer negotiating process are usually the multinationals and the Third World governments, the latter have the advantage because they not only make the laws and lay down the conditions under which technology transfer takes place, but they can change the rules of the game unilaterally to increase their bargaining power.

That there has been an increase in the bargaining power of the state vis-a-vis the multinationals is beyond question. Contrary to the assertion of the dependency theorists, the bourgeoisie in the Third World are not subordinate to foreign capital and the bargaining strength of the private national sector has grown mainly because of the protection given by the state under the Patent Law and the policy of reservation under the New Drug Policy (1978). The rapidly growing national sector has acquired the characteristics of a sophisticated interest group within the industry. Its industry association (IDMA) has effectively lobbied against the multinationals' interests with the government bureaucrats, citizen health groups, health professionals, intellectuals, and—most important—a vocal group of MPs in both Lok Sabha and Rajya Sabha. Through its lobbying efforts, the national sector created an environment in which the national government found it difficult (until 1994, when India signed the Uruguay Round) to accept the demand of the multinationals that India should join the Paris Convention on patent protection of intellectual property.

The bargaining power of the state and the private national sector must, however, be qualified. This study shows that the foreign sector (FERA and ex-FERA companies) is an indispensable component of the pharmaceutical industry in India. Because the subsidiaries of multinationals have access to modern drug technology from the parent company, which India needs, the government has never considered the option of nationalizing this sector—even in the 1970s when nationalist sentiment was at its peak. (The Hathi Committee Report had categorically rejected the idea of nationalization.) The private national sector has not seriously advocated the idea of nationalization, either. Thus, there is a definite limit to the state's bargaining power because of the technological advantage enjoyed by the multinationals, especially in high-technology modern drugs.

The multinationals "subverted" some of the objectives of the New Drug Policy by shifting production from less profitable essential drugs in categories I and II to more profitable nonessential drugs in categories III and IV, resulting in a shortfall of essential drugs and a ten-fold increase in their import in 14 years. Many multinationals evaded the implementation of drug price controls under the DPCO (1979) by resorting to legal recourse. By filing an injunction in the Delhi high court, they obtained a stay that allowed them to continue charging higher prices. Furthermore, they successfully bargained to persuade the government to accept their demand that the equity dilution be accomplished "through a wider distribution of shares, rather than their merger with local enterprises."[5] Thus, by diluting their equity holdings to 40 percent, most multinationals became legally Indian companies, avoiding the restrictions imposed on the foreign firms under the Foreign Equity Regulation Act but maintaining managerial control.

Through the sophisticated lobbying efforts of its industry association (OPPI), the foreign sector has neutralized some of the negative perceptions of the multinationals on the part of the public. The foreign sector has succeeded in convincing government bureaucrats, politicians, and the public that its contribution has made the Indian pharmaceutical industry technologically one of the more developed in the Third World (UNIDO's category V).

The multinationals also battled with the national sector over the revision of the New Drug Policy (1978) in the early 1980s. While the citizen groups and the private national sector wanted the continuation of the policy of sectoral reservation, the multinationals were opposed to it. Concerned with the decline in production and an increase in imports in the early 1980s, the government first delicensed 94 bulk drugs in 1985 and then announced the revised drug policy in 1986, which raised the profit margin allowed in the category of essential drugs, followed by the 1994 policy to abolish industrial licensing for most drugs, which freed about 70 bulk drugs from price control. These instances indicate the limits of the state's and the private national sector's bargaining power in an industry that is research-intensive with a high rate of technological innovation and obsolescence. However, the technological capability acquired by the national sector makes it almost impossible for a return to the dependency of the 1950s and 1960s.

This study suggests an "uneasy triangle"[6] in the Indian case and not a "triple alliance" as suggested by the new wave of revisionist dependency writers such as Peter Evans[7] and Gary Gereffi. [8] Unlike the "dependent development" model of Brazil as articulated by Evans, where the process of industrialization has involved an alliance of multinationals, national private capital, and the state, in India the three actors continue to bargain over access to technology, pricing, production, and markets. Therefore, the thesis of Evans, that India (like Brazil) provides the institutional and contextual conditions that "make dependent development possible,"[9] must be rejected on empirical grounds. The Indian case suggests that states respond differently to the constraints associated with the phenomenon of technological dependence. Whereas India responded to its technological dependence by creating its indigenous technological capability, Brazil and Mexico concentrated on increasing production by importing sophisticated technology. Over the years, India has increased its technological capability to the extent that, among the NICs, it is least dependent on the multinationals.

PUBLIC SECTOR AND TECHNOLOGY TRANSFER

Some dependency theorists have argued that public sector firms pursue policies that lead to an increase in the technological capability of the firm and hence greater technological self-reliance. For the bargaining theorists, the mode of ownership of a firm is not important. Instead, they emphasize the complex factors that influence managers in their technology decisions at the firm level. By studying the three large public sector firms—HMT in machine tools, IDPL and HAL in pharmaceuticals—we find that public ownership is not in itself an automatic road to strengthening technological capability. Bargaining in the public sector is the same process as anywhere else. The study suggests that while all three public sector companies have contributed to India's technological capability, HMT has been more successful in technology transfer because of certain characteristics at the firm level.

I have noted the technological difficulties experienced by HAL, with the one-time transfer of Western technology, and by IDPL, with the second-rate technology it got from the former Soviet Union. Both companies had difficulties making imported technology more efficient through their own R&D efforts. They could not buy the latest technology off the shelf because multinationals are reluctant to share their modern technology without financial participation in a company. The drug multinationals are willing to sell only second-generation technology. HAL and IDPL have therefore fallen behind the international pharmaceutical firms in antibiotic technology and are now trying to overcome this by entering into joint venture partnership with private companies. By contrast, HMT has been successful in acquiring general-purpose and modern machine tool technology in various ways, assimilating and adapting imported technology to its own needs, and further developing new designs through in-house R&D.

The early success of HMT was due to internal firm characteristics and the domestic and international environment. The Nehru-Mahalanobis model of industrialization gave priority to the development of the machine tool industry in India, which made HMT a more important public sector company than either HAL or IDPL. HMT's first technical collaboration with Oerlikons brought the company not only basic machine-building technology but also experience with quality and precision, which has since become a part of what is known as HMT culture. The rigorous training of first-generation HMT engineers and designers by a team of Swiss technicians in India and Switzerland was critical to the development of HMT's technological capability.

But HAL and IDPL have lacked similar experience. HAL, which was set up with the assistance of WHO and UNICEF, has experienced technological obsolescence from its beginning. In IDPL, the government opted for second-rate Soviet technology because the multinationals were not willing to share their technology without equity participation. Nehru had hoped that Indian scientists and techno-logists would be able to make the Soviet technology more efficient, but the training of the Indian technologists in the Soviet plant—unlike the training of the HMT engineers by their Swiss collaborators—did not prepare them to undertake such a modernization plan.

The management of HMT had a lot to do with its success in technology transfer. Whereas all the HMT managing directors except one have been insiders, and all of them except Mathulla and Naidu were professional engineers, both HAL and IDPL have been headed by professional Indian Administrative Service (IAS) bureaucrats who came to the company for a short term (two years until 1985) with no background in the industry. By the time an IAS chief executive acquires the technical understanding of the functioning of a pharmaceutical firm, his term is over, and the company acquires another IAS managing director who starts the learning process all over again. The seriousness of this problem was emphasized by the senior managers I interviewed in both the public sector companies.

One important reason why the two public sector companies have performed poorly is political intervention from the central government, especially govern-ment appointment. The degree of political intervention can be observed in the financially troubled IDPL, where the government appointed five managing directors in three years in the early 1980s. HMT, by contrast, had only two managing directors between 1956 and 1978. The long tenure of Mathulla and Patil was crucial to HMT's growth, diversification, and development of technological capability. Their respective management styles shaped the future of the company. While Mathulla protected the company from bureaucratic interventions from New Delhi, because of his personal access to Nehru, and favored the purchase of technology at a "reasonable" price, Patil's approach was more that of an "engineering man" who wanted HMT to be on the cutting edge of technology.

Patil acquired NC technology in the early 1970s by collaborating with KTM, and HMT produced a few NC Mogul lathes at a time in the late 1970s when there was not much demand for these machines in India. But the chief executives of HMT, since Patil's retirement, have acted more like "economic men" more interested in short-term profits than in the latest NC/CNC machine tool technology. Since there was not much domestic demand for these sophisticated machines until the early 1980s, when there was an enormous expansion of the automotive sector, it was rational for economic men not to acquire them. Had HMT managers continued to behave like engineering men after Patil's retirement, HMT would not have fallen behind international manufacturers in NC/CNC technology, nor would it have lost the MUL bid or undergone a recession between 1991 and 1993.

The structure of the Indian machine tool industry, which is different from the pharmaceutical industry, is partly responsible for the success of HMT. In the machine tool industry, production has been undertaken mainly by the public sector or private locally owned companies; multinationals in this field have been the major source of technology. In the pharmaceutical industry, on the other hand, the multinationals are both the suppliers of technology and competitors in the domestic market through their subsidiaries. Thus, the absence of foreign subsidiaries as actors in the machine tool industry has increased HMT's bargaining power vis-a-vis the technology-supplying multinationals. HMT has acquired modern technology with arm's-length licensing agreement in the 1980s, which was not possible in the pharmaceutical industry.

Finally, the nature of technology and the international technology market, which is industry-specific, have further contributed to the success of HMT. Unlike the automobile industry and to some extent the machine tool industry, global integration of the operation of the multinationals has not taken place in the pharmaceutical industry. In the research-intensive pharmaceutical industry, where the average cost of the discovery of a new drug is about $200 million, drug multinationals are reluctant to share their latest technology for a fee, at least for a few years after the discovery of a new drug. Since the drug multinationals have subsidiaries in more Third World countries than any other industry, it is a disincentive for them to license their new technology. Therefore, they prefer not to introduce new drugs in the Third World immediately after discovery because they want to earn large returns on their R&D investments. Since most pharmaceutical innovations are commercially not very successful, multinationals depend for positive cash flows on a small number of successful innovations. Glaxo's salbutamol case is a typical example of the drug multinationals' strategy in the Third World.[10] Because of the monopolistic nature of the modern drug technology market, multinationals delay introducing new drugs into India until a local firm develops the technology through some other process. Consequently, there is a time lag of four to five years between the discovery of a new drug and its introduction in India.

In the machine tool industry, however, mature technology is easily available, and competition among rivals—American, German, French, British, and Japanese suppliers—accelerates the product life cycle. HMT's experience in the acquisition of modern technology shows, contrary to the prediction of the product cycle model, that machine tool multinationals are prepared to transfer high technology under terms that assure rapid and efficient implantation of the latest automated manufacturing systems into a developing country. The market for modern machine tool technology, unlike that for modern drug technology, is less monopolistic and, perhaps, more oligopolistic in nature.

There is also a difference in the patterns of demand and technical changes between the two industries. Since there is not much demand for high-technology machine tools in the Third World, and since the rate of technological change has been very rapid in the industry in the last two decades, it is rational for machine tool multinationals to license their latest technology selectively. By transferring drawings and designs to Third World firms and by training their designers and technicians, multinationals earn handsome fees for technology that will soon become obsolete. Thus, the international technology market in machine tools, although expensive in recent years, is very different from that of pharmaceuticals. The availability of technology from many sources and the competence and sophistication of the HMT negotiators have allowed HMT to bargain effectively with technology suppliers and, in most cases, to get the best deal. Because of its technological capability, HMT has succeeded in acquiring technology through those modes (bulk purchase and joint development), which are more advantageous to the recipient firms.

This study of the machine tool industry does not fully support the product cycle hypothesis that the costs of high technology are so great that Third World countries would not be able to stay abreast or that these circumstances may create inseparable obstacles to the development cycle of poor countries. Although multinationals usually sell technologies that are late in the life of a product's cycle, machine tool multinationals have transferred high technology to India. HMT decided to buy modern technology at a high cost from the international market, instead of developing it indigenously through in-house R&D because it wanted to save time and narrow the technology gap quickly. The international technology market in modern drugs, however, shows a pattern that supports the bargaining hypothesis that it is more difficult for the NICs to bargain for, and master, high technology that is undergoing continuous change in production processes or in products. This study shows that the international technology market is industry-specific and is imperfect on both the supply and the demand side, regardless of the transfer mechanism. Therefore, any generalization that is based on the study of technology transfer in one industry would be misleading.

TECHNOLOGICAL CAPABILITY AND SELF-RELIANCE

Technology is not absolute and static, but relative and dynamic. To the developing nations, what matters most in a global economy that is highly interdependent is not the ability to invent but the capacity to exploit new technological opportunities. Therefore, the growth in a country's technological capability has become central to the Third World's drive to achieve technological self-reliance. This study suggests that there has been a tremendous growth, unparalleled in the Third World, in India's technological capability in the machine tool and pharmaceutical industries in the last four decades.

A number of recent studies have focused on India's weak export performance resulting from its inward-looking industrial policy and the government control and regulation of the industrial sector, at least until the beginning of economic liberalization in 1991; however, not enough attention has been given to the technological capability that India has acquired over the years because of its policies of import substitution, regulation and control of technology import, and other restrictive policies of the 1960s and 1970s.

India has emphasized self-reliance from the beginning of its planned development. In policy terms, this has meant an emphasis on creation of a substantial infrastructure in science and technology, which has had impressive results: By the early 1980s, India had 1,300 R&D institutions employing over a million people. In the drug and pharmaceutical industry, a superstructure of institutions for indigenous research (two research institutes of the CSIR—CDRI and IIEM, NCL and RRLs) was created, and R&D laboratories were set up in both public sector companies. Similarly, in the machine tool industry, the government established two industry-oriented R&D organizations (CMTI and CMFRI) and an R&D center in HMT. A design department was also set up in all HMT machine tool units.

The success rate of up-scaling of technology from the laboratory to the industry has been very small, and there has been a lack of coordination between national laboratories and public sector R&D centers in the two industries. However, the most valuable contribution of the public-funded R&D institutions has been the generation of a high degree of scientific and technological capability rather than economic returns. HMT engineers and technologists acquired the capability of designing and producing general-purpose machine tools by the early 1970s and undertook the design of more sophisticated NC/CNC machine tools in the late 1970s, 1980s, and 1990s. In the pharmaceutical industry, many private sector national firms have acquired, through in-house R&D, the capability of developing processes for newly invented drugs.

With their technological capability thus enhanced, the two industries have acquired technology competitively from the technology-supplying multinationals, adopted acquired technology to suit their firms' requirements, developed skills at firm level to assimilate imported technology, developed indigenous science and technology for more effective R&D programs, and transferred technology and know-how horizontally to other Indian firms and to developing countries.

Recognizing the importance of R&D at the firm level for the absorption, assimilation, and generation of technology, the government has given fiscal and other incentives to the private sector to increase in-house R&D. These incentives have resulted in a significant increase in R&D expenditure (a concrete measure of technological self-reliance) in the private sector in recent years, especially in the pharmaceutical industry. Although the public sector pharmaceutical companies have experienced difficulties in improving imported technology and developing efficient processes for production of synthetic drugs, especially in antibiotics technology, the industry has acquired technical know-how to handle the most sophisticated process technology in bulk drug production. India is self-sufficient in the production of a wide range of formulations and most bulk drugs. Its private sector companies have acquired the capability to develop indigenous processes for new drugs within five years of their introduction in the international market, which used to take 10 to 15 years. With the recent increase in R&D expenditure of the leading Indian companies, the gap between the discovery of a new drug abroad and its introduction in the Indian market should be narrowed further.

India's pharmaceutical industry has reached a level of technological maturity from which it no longer fears multinational domination. India's pharmaceutical export to developed and developing countries has grown sharply in recent years; between 1985-86 and 1994-95, exports grew 14 times from Rs. 140 crores to more than Rs. 2,000 crores. The machine tool industry has developed enough for no further collaborations to be needed for general-purpose ma-chines—although there is a need for continued collaboration, for more sophisti-cated products like CNC machine tools. Public sector firms in both industries have transferred technology horizontally to other firms within India and to less industrialized countries—HMT has been particularly successful in transferring machine tool technology to a number of Asian and African countries, especially Algeria and Nigeria.

If technological self-reliance means the capability to identify national technological needs and select and apply both foreign and domestic technology under conditions that enhance the growth of indigenous technological capability, then India is more self-reliant than other NICs. India has developed its own learning capacity and creating capacity in the pharmaceutical and machine tool industries. However, it has paid a price for this independence: Its inward-looking industrial policy has resulted in technological obsolescence. Unlike the products of other NICs, India's products are not yet internationally competitive.

CONCLUDING REMARKS

These case studies suggest that India is behind only in the area of high technology. The liberalization of the Indian economy in the 1990s has, however, brought competition to the industrial sector. Indian industries realize that they can become competitive only by increasing production, lowering costs, and improving the quality of products—and these steps require modernization. The inefficiencies resulting from what the Rudolphs call "organizational involution"—the government policy of protecting the small-scale sector, resulting in the horizontal growth of the industry and suboptimal plant size—continue to be a major problem in Indian firms in both the public and private sectors. The horizontal growth of firms in the pharmaceutical industry has had a negative effect on the growth of R&D. Inefficiencies are most pronounced in public sector firms, which have incurred huge losses. But recent developments suggest that Indian industries, especially the machine tool industry, have exhibited their dynamism in meeting the challenge of the global competition in the postliberalization period by introducing necessary reforms. In particular, the public sector companies are offering equity participation to private companies and are forging strategic joint venture partnership with them in an effort to become more competitive.

India's growing technological capability has resulted in the increased bargaining power of the state and the national private sector vis-a-vis the multinationals. However, there are definite constraints on India's bargaining power because of the imperfect nature of the international technology market, the multinationals' domination of high technology, the inefficiencies in public sector companies, and the lack of political will, until recently, on the part of policymakers to bring about necessary reforms in the public sector. The simultaneous presence of these two tendencies leads to the cautious conclusion that the technological situation in India's manufacturing industries should be conceptualized as a dependence self-reliance continuum instead of an either-or situation.

India has moved up the dependence/self-reliance continuum, and its record of progress is better than other NICs. It has overcome the technological depen-dency found in most Third World countries and enjoys a high degree of bargaining power vis-a-vis the multinationals. Its substantial technological capability, with the largest pool of technically qualified manpower in the Third World, has made India mature enough to attempt to absorb the technological developments of what Walt W. Rostow has called the third and the fourth industrial revolution. (India has emerged as a major player in the computer software industry.) Whether it will further increase its bargaining power and self-reliance will depend on its ability to narrow the gap with the industrialized countries in the high-technology area. Given the high level of India's technological capability, its bargaining power should increase in the present global economy.

NOTES

1. Stephen Haggard, "Newly Industrializing Countries in the International System," *World Politics*, 38 (Jan. 1986): 345.

2. Sanjaya Lall, "The International Pharmaceutical Industry and Less-Developed Countries, with Special Reference to India," *Oxford Bulletin of Economics and Statistics*, 56, No. 3 (August 1974): 143-172; UNCTAD, *Case Studies in the Transfer of Technology: The Pharmaceutical Industry in India* (United Nations: 1977, TD/B/C.6/20); P. L. Badami, "The Pharmaceutical Industry: A Survey," *Commerce*, No. 116 (1968): 12-13; P. S. Agarwal et al., "Anomalies in Drug Prices and Quality Control," *Economic and Political Weekly*, Nov. 18, 1972; Nagesh Kumar and Kamal Mitra Chenoy, "Multinationals and Self-Reliance: A Case Study of the Drugs and Pharmaceutical Industry," *Social Scientist*, No. 107 (April 1982): 13-35.

3. For a comparison between India and Brazil, see Dennis Encarnation, *Dislodging Multinationals: India's Strategy in Comparative Perspective* (Ithaca: Cornell University Press, 1989), Ch. 5. Also see Carl J. Dahlman, "Foreign Technology and Indigenous Technological Capability in Brazil," in Martin Fransman and Kenneth King (eds.), *Technological Capability in the Third World* (New York: St. Martin's Press, 1984).

4. The prices have shown an upward trend in the post-GATT period.

5. Encarnation, *Dislodging Multinationals*.

6. The concept "uneasy triangle" was used by Michael Kidron more than 25 years ago in his study *Foreign Investment in India* (London: Oxford University Press, 1965). In a recent study, *Dislodging Multinationals: India's Strategy in Comparative Perspective*, Dennis Encarnation found the concept to be useful in explaining the interplay of finance, technology, and markets in India's political economy in the 1980s.

7. Peter Evans, *Dependent Development: The Alliance of Multinational, State, and Local Capital in Brazil* (Princeton, N.J.: Princeton University Press, 1979).

8. Gary Gereffi, *The Pharmaceutical Industry and Dependency in the Third World* (Princeton, N.J.: Princeton Univerity Press).

9. Evans, *Dependent Development*, p. 51.

10. Glaxo applied for an industrial license to produce salbutamol in India. The government issued a letter of intent, but Glaxo waited for three years before it decided to convert the letter of intent into an industrial license. Meanwhile, an Indian company (CIPLA) developed the technology through in-house R&D and applied for an industrial license to manufacture salbutamol. The government granted the license to CIPLA and not to Glaxo on the technical ground that Glaxo had failed to convert its letter of intent into an industrial license within the specified period of one year.

Bibliography

ARTICLES

Adikibi, Owen T. "The Multinational Corporation and Monopoly of Patents in Nigeria." *World Development* 16 (1988): 511-526.

Agarwal, Anil. "U.N. Takes a Stand on Drugs." *New Scientist*, November 9, 1978, pp. 442-443.

Agarwal, P. S. et al. "Anomalies in Drug Prices and Quality Control." *Economic and Political Weekly*, November 18, 1972, pp. 2285-2292.

Agmon, Tamir and Seev Hirsch. "Multinational Corporations and the Developing Economics: Potential Gains in a World of Imperfect Markets and Uncertainty." *Oxford Bulletin of Economics and Statistics* 41 (1979): 333-344.

Alam, Ghayur. "India's Technology Policy and Its Influence on Technology Imports and Technology Development." *Economic and Political Weekly*, Special Number, 1985, pp. 2073-2080.

Asante, S. K. B. "Restructuring Transnational Mineral Agreements." *American Journal of International Law* 73 (1979): 335-371.

Ayivor, Eddies C. K. "The Economics of Pharmaceutical Policy in Ghana." *International Journal of Health Services* 10 (1980): 479-99.

Badami, P. L. "The Pharmaceutical Industry: A Survey." *Commerce* 116 (1968): 12-13.

Bagchi, Amiya Kumar et al. "Indian Patents Act and Its Relation to Technological Development in India." *Economic and Political Weekly*, February 18, 1984, pp. 287-302.

Baranson, Jack. "Technology Exports Can Hurt Us." *Foreign Policy* 25 (1976-1977): 180-194.

Barnett, Andrew, Andrew Lacey Creese, and Eddie C. K. Ayivor. "The Economics of Pharmaceutical Policy in Ghana." *International Journal of Health Services* 10, No. 3 (1980): 479-499.

Bhagavan, M. R. "Technological Implications of Structural Adjustment: Case of India," *Economic and Political Weekly*, 30, Nos. 7 and 8 (1995).

Bhatt, V. V. "Development Problem, Strategy and Technology Choice: Sarvodaya and Socialist Approaches in India." In V. V. Bhatt (ed.), *Development Perspectives: Problem Strategy and Policies*. New York: Pergamon Press, 1980.

Bylinsky, Gene. "Japan's Robot King Wins Again." *Fortune*, May 25, 1987, pp. 53-58.

Carney, David. "Conditions and Perils of Nonalignment: an Interpretation of Events Since Bandung." *The Nonaligned World* 2 (1984): 609-617.

Chaudhuri, Sudip. "Manufacturing Drugs without TNCs: Status of the Indigenous Sector in India." *Economic and Political Weekly*, August 1984, pp. 1341-1383.

Chetley, Andrew. "Drug Production with a Social Conscience: The Experience of Ganoshasthaya Pharmaceuticals." *Development Dialogue* 2 (1985): 94-96.

Chudnovsky, Daniel. "The Challenge by Domestic Enterprises to the Transnational Corporations' Domination: A Case Study of the Argentine Pharmaceutical Industry." *World Development* 7 (1979): 45-58.

———. "The Diffusion and Production of Numerically Controlled Machine Tools with Special Reference to Argentina." *World Development* 16 (1988): 723-732.

"Comprehensive R&D Plan for Machine Tools: 1983-84 to 1992-93." (Unpublished Paper), HMT, Bangalore, Nov. 1983.

Cooper, Charles "The Transfer of Industrial Technology to the Underdeveloped Countries." *Bulletin of the Institute of Development Studies* 3 (1970): 3-23.

Dahlman, Carl J. "Foreign Technology and Indigenous Technological Capability in Brazil." In Martin Fransman and Kenneth King (eds.), *Technological Capability in the Third World*. New York: St. Martin's Press, 1984.

Dahlman, Carl J. and Larry E. Westphal. "The Meaning of Technological Mastery in Relation to Transfer of Technology." *Annals of the American Academy of Political and Social Science* 458 (November 1981): 12-25.

Desai, A. V. "The Origin and Direction of Industrial R&D in India." *Research Policy* 9 (1980): 75-96.

———. "Indigenous and Foreign Determinants of Technological Change in Indian Industry." *Economic and Political Weekly*, Special Number, November, 1985, pp. 2081-2094.

Dore, Ronald. "Technological Self-Reliance: Sturdy Ideal or Self-Serving Rhetoric." In Martin Fransman and Kenneth King (eds.), *Technological Capability in the Third World*. New York: St. Martin's Press, 1984.

Dos Santos, Theotoni. "The Structure of Dependence." In K. T. Fann and Donald C. Hodges (eds.), *Readings in U.S. Imperialism*. Boston: Peter Sargent Publisher, 1971.

Drucker, Peter F. "Japan's Choices." *Foreign Affairs*, Summer 1989, pp. 923-924.

Edquist, Charles et al. "Automation in Engineering Industries of India and Republic of Korea Against the Background of Experience in Some OECD Countries." *Economic and Political Weekly*, April 13, 1985, pp. 643-654.

Enos, J. L. "The Transfer of Technology." *Journal of Asia-Pacific Economic Literature*, 3, No. 1 (March 1989).

Fagre, N. and Louis T. Wells, Jr. "Bargaining Power of Multinationals and the Host Government." *Journal of International Business Studies* 13 (1982): 9-21.

"Farce of Drug Policy." *Economic and Political Weekly*, March 8-15, 1986, p. 409.

Fransman, Martin. "International Competitiveness, Technical Change and the State: The Machine Tool Industry in Taiwan and Japan." *World Development* 14 (1986): 1376-1396.

Furtado, Celso. "The Concept of External Dependence in the Study of Under-development." In Charles K. Wilber (ed.), *The Political Economy of Development and Underdevelopment*. New York: Random House, 1970.

Ghosh, Anil C. "The Role of R&D in Choice of Technology for Drugs and Drug Intermediates—A Perspective View." *IDMA Bulletin* 16 (1985): 527-530.

Gill, S.S. "CSIR: Technology and Commitment." *Mainstream*, June 13, 1987, pp. 24-26.

Glucksberg, Harold and Jack Singer. "The Multinational Drug Companies in Zaire: Their Adverse Effect on Cost and Availability of Essential Drugs." *International Journal of Health Services* 12 (1982): 381-387.

Govindarajulu, V. "India's S&T Capability: SWOT Analysis." *Economic and Political Weekly*, February 17-24, 1990, pp. M35-M40.

Grabowski, Henry G. and M. Vernon. "The Pharmaceutical Industry." In Richard R. Nelson (ed.), *Government and Technical Progress: A Cross-Industry Analysis*. New York: Pergamon Press, 1982.

Grieco, Joseph. "Between Dependency and Autonomy: India's Experience with the International Computer Industry." *International Organization* 36 (1982): 609-632.

Grynspan, Devora. "Technology Transfer Patterns and Industrialization in LDCs: A Study of Licensing in Costa Rica." *International Organization* 36 (1982): 795-806.

Gwin, Catherine and Lawrence A. Veit. "The Indian Miracle." *Foreign Policy* 58 (1985): 79-98.

Haas, Ernst B. "Technological Self-Reliance for Latin America: The OAS Contribution." *International Organization* 34 (1980): 541-570.

Haggard, Stephan. "The Newly Industrializing Countries in the International System." *World Politics* 38 (1986): 345.

Hart, Jeffrey. "Three Approaches to the Measurement of Power in International Relations." *International Organization* 30 (1976): 289-305.

Helleiner, G.K. "International Technology Issues: Southern Needs and Northern Responses." In Jagdish N. Bhagwati (ed.), *The New International Economic Order: The North- South Debate*. Cambridge, Mass.: MIT Press, 1977.

Herriot, Peter J. "Development Alternatives: Problems Strategies, Values." In Charles K. Wilber (ed.), *The Political Economy of Development and Underdevelopment*. New York: Random House, 1979.

"Industrial Policy: Opening New Doors." *India Today*, June 30, 1990, pp. 9-15.

Jayaraman, K. "Drug Research and Development and Technology Status in India." *Chemsearch and Industry* 1 (1986): 9-15.

———. "Drug Policy: Playing Down Main Issues." *Economic and Political Weekly*, June 21-28, 1986, pp. 1129-1132.

———. "Drug Policy: Reinterpreting Issues." *Economic and Political Weekly*, May 3, 1986, pp. 798-800.

Katrak, Homi. "Imported Technology, Enterprise Size and R&D in a Newly Industrializing Country: The Indian Experience." *Oxford Bulletin of Statistics and Economics* 47 (1985): 213-229.

Kobrin, Stepen J. "Testing the Bargaining Hypothesis in the Manufacturing Sector in Developing Countries." *International Organization* 41 (1987): 609-638.

Kumar, Nagesh and Kamal Mitra Chenoy. "Multinationals and Self-Reliance: A Case Study of the Drugs and Pharmaceutical Industry." *Social Scientist*, April 1982, pp. 13-35.

Lall, Sanjaya. "The International Pharmaceutical Industry and Less-Developed Countries, with Special Reference to India." *Oxford Bulletin of Economics and Statistics* 56 (1974): 143-172.

―――. "Multinational Companies and Concentration: The Case of the Pharmaceutical Industry." *Social Scientist*, March-April, 1979, pp. 3-29.

―――. "Transfer Pricing and Developing Countries: Some Problems of Investigation." *World Development* 7 (1979): 59-71.

―――. "Technological Learning in the Third World: Some Implications of Technology Exports." In Frances Stewart and Jeffrey James (eds.), *The Economics of New Technology in Developing Countries*. London: Westview Press, 1982.

―――. "Exports of Technology by Newly-Industrializing Countries: An Overview." *World Development* 12 (1984): 471-480.

―――. "Trade in Technology by a Slowly Industrializing Country: India." In Nathan Rosenberg and Claudio Frischtak (eds.), *International Technology Transfer: Concepts Measures, and Comparisons*. New York: Praeger, 1985.

Lall, Sanjaya and Seneka Bibile. "The Political Economy of Controlling Transnationals: The Pharmaceutical Industry in Sri Lanka (1972-76)." *World Development* 5 (1977): 677-697.

Lecraw, Donald J. "Bargaining Power, Ownership, and Profitability of Transnational Corporations in Developing Countries." *Journal of International Business Studies* 15 (1984): 27-43.

Long, F. A. "Science, Technology and Industrial Development in India." *Technology in Society* 10 (1988): 395-416.

―――. "Science and Technology in India: Their Role in National Development." In John W. Mellor (ed.), *India: A Rising Middle Power*. Boulder, Colo.: Westview Press, 1979.

"Machine Tool Industry: Gearing Up with a Little Help from Japan." *Business India*, Sept. 23-Oct. 6, 1985, p. 87.

Matthews, Ron. "Development of India's Machine Tool Industry." *Economic and Political Weekly*, October 1, 1988, p. 2061-2068.

Mazrui, Ali. "The Non-Aligned Movement: Changing Focus from Detente to Development." *The Nonaligned World* 1 (1983): 255-257.

McClloch, Rachel. "Technology Transfer to Developing Countries: Implications of International Regulation." *Annals, American Academy of Political and Social Science* 458 (1981): 110-122.

Mehrotra, N. N. et al. "R&D and Technological Development for Production of Essential Bulk Drugs." *IDMA Bulletin* 16 (1985): 1-16.

Mikesell, R. F. "Conflict in Foreign Investor-Host Country Relations: A Preliminary Analysis." In R. F. Mikesell (ed.), *Foreign Investment in the Petroleum and Mineral Industries*. Baltimore: Johns Hopkins Press, 1971.

Moberg, David. "The Cutting Edge." *Reader* (Chicago), August 9, 1985, p. 20.

Moran, Theodore H. "Multinational Corporations and the Developing Countries: An Analytical View." In Theodore H. Moran (ed.), *Multinational Corporations: The Political Economy of Foreign Direct Investment*. Lexington, Mass: Lexington Books, 1985.

Morris, Sebastian. "Foreign Direct Investment from India: Ownership and Control of 'Joint Ventures' Abroad." *Economic and Political Weekly*, February 17-24, 1990, pp. M23- M34.

Mytelka, Lynn Krieger. "Licensing and Technology Dependence in the Andean Group."
     World Development 6 (1978): 447-459.
————. "Technological Dependence in Andean Group." *International Organization* 32
     (1978): 105.
Nair, Arvind. "Drug Industry: Prospects for the Seventh Plan." *Chemsearch and Industry*
     1 (1986): 30.
Nair, M. D. "The Indian Pharmaceutical Industry: A Global Perspective." *The Eastern
     Pharmacist* 24 (1986): 29-34.
————. "R&D in Drug Industry." *Commerce*, March 2 (1985): 9-15.
————. "Recent Advances in Pharmaceutical Technology." *IDMA Bulletin* 16, No. 37
     (1985): 561-562.
Narayana, P. L. "The Indian Pharmaceutical Industry: Present Status and Problems."
     Commerce (March 12, 1985): 3-8.
Parker, John E. S. "Pharmaceuticals and Third World Concerns: The Lall Report and the
     Otaga Study." In Robert B. Helm (ed.), *The International Supply of Medicines:
     Implications of U.S. Regulatory Reform*. Washington, D.C.: American Enterprise
     Institute for Public Policy Research, 1980.
Parthasarthi, Ashok. "India's Efforts in Building an Autonomous Capacity in Science and
     Technology for Development." *Development Dialogue* 1 (1979): 46-59.
————. "Technological Bridgeheads for Self-Reliant Development." *Development
     Dialogue* 1 (1979): 33-38.
Patel Surendra J. "The Cost of Technological Dependence." *Cerces* 6, No. 2 (March-April
     1973): 16-19.
————. "The Technological Dependence of Developing Countries." *The Journal of
     Modern African Studies* 12 (1974): 1-18.
————. "Editorial to the Special Issue on 'Integrated Technology Transfer'." *Impact of
     Science on Society* 28 (1978).
————. "Plugging into the System." *Development Forum*, October 1978, pp. 12-13.
————. "Editor's Introduction." *World Development* 11 (March 1983): 165-167.
————. "Main Elements in Shaping Future Technology Policy for India." *Economic and
     Political Weekly*, March 4, 1989, pp. 463-466.
Patil, S. M. "25 Years in HMT." *Machine Tool Engineers*, April 1978, pp. 4-5.
————. "Machine Tool Industry: Need for Remedial Measures." *Economic Times*
     (Bombay), April 18, 1985.
Paul, Samuel. "Privatisation: A Review of International Experience." *Economic and
     Political Weekly*, Feb. 6, 1988, pp. 273-276.
Pillai, P. Mohanan. "Technology Transfer, Adaptation and Assimilation." *Economic and
     Political Weekly*, Nov. 24, 1979, pp. M121-M126.
Plasschaert, Sylvain. "Transfer Pricing Problems in Developing Countries." In Alan M.
     Rugman and Lorraine Eden (eds.), *Multinationals and Transfer Pricing*. New
     York: St. Martin's Press, 1985.
Rahman, A. "Evolution of Science Policy in India after Independence." In A. Rahman and
     P. N. Chowdhury (eds.), *Science and Society*. New Delhi: Center of R&D
     Management, CSIR, 1980.
Rahman, A. et al. "Research and Development in the Indian Drug and Pharmaceutical
     Industry." *Lok Udyog* 4, No. 5 (1970): 635-640.
Raj, Ashok. "CSIR Review: Another Window Dressing." *Mainstream*, June 13 (1987), pp.
     28-32.

Rama Rao, A.V. and J.V. Rajan. "Transfer of Drug Technologies from Laboratory to
    Industry." *IDMA Bulletin* 16 (1985): 6.
Rama Rao, A. V. and J. V. Rajan. "Transfer of Drug Technologies from Laboratory to
    Industry." *IDMA Bulletin* 16 (1985): 6.
Raman, Anand P. "Strong Medicine." *Business World*, December 7-20, 1987, pp. 37-47.
"Review of Pharmaceutical Industry in India." *Industrial Research* 12 (1985): 199-201.
Rosenberg, N. "The International Transfer of Industrial Technology: Past and Present." In
    North/South Technology Transfer: The Adjustment Ahead, Paris: OECD, 1982.
Sahu, Sunil K. "The Politics of Industrial Planning in India: The Second Plan." *Indian
    Journal of Public Administration* 30 (1984): 613-660.
————. "Changing Regime in Technology Transfer and Intellectual Property." In C. Steven
    La Rue (ed.), *The India Handbook*. Chicago: Fitzroy Dearborn, 1997.
————. "Technology Transfer and the Indian Experience," *Asian Profile*, 22, No.3 (1994):
    239-255.
Saikai, Santanu. "Who Will Cure IDPL." *Business India*, December 30-Jan. 12, 1986, pp.
    62- 68.
Schnee, Jerome E. "R&D Strategy in the U.S. Pharmaceutical Industry." *Research Policy*
    8 (1979): 364-382.
Shiva, Mira. "Towards a Healthy Use of Pharmaceuticals: An Indian Perspective."
    Development Dialogue 2 (1985): 69-93.
Silverman, Milton, Philip R. Lee, and Mia Lydecker. "The Drugging of the Third World."
    International Journal of Health Services 12 (1982): 585-596.
Singh, Baldev. "Technology and Import-Export Policy." *Mainstream*, May 1984, pp. 43-46.
————. "Reviewing the CSIR." *Economic and Political Weekly*, August 23, 1986, pp.
    1511-1517.
Subrahmanian, K. K. "Technology Import: Regulation Reduces Cost." *Economic and
    Political Weekly*, August 9, 1986, pp. 1412-1416.
————. "Towards Technological Self-Reliance: An Assessment of Indian Strategy and
    Achievement in Industry." In P. R. Brahmananda and V. R. Panchamukhi (eds.),
    The Development Process of the Indian Economy. Bombay: Himalaya, 1987.
————. "Technological Capability under Economic Liberalization: Experience of Indian
    Industry in the 80s." In Yoginder K. Alagh et al. (eds.), *Sectoral Growth and
    Change*. New Delhi: Har-Anand Publications, 1993.
Sunkel, Osvaldo. "National Development Policy and External Dependence in Latin
    America." *Journal of Development Studies* 6 (1969): 23-48.
————. "Underdevelopment, the Transfer of Science and Technology, and the Latin
    American University." *Human Relations* 24, No. 1 (1971): 1-18.
Tharp, Paul A., Jr. "Transnational Enterprises and International Regulation: A Survey of
    Various Approaches in International Organizations." *International Organization*
    30 (1976): 47-73.
Thrupp, Lori Ann. "Technology Policy and Planning in the Third World Pharmaceutical
    Sector: The Cuban and Caribbean Community Approach." *International Journal
    of Health Services* 14 (1984): 189-216.
Thurow, Lester C. "Maintaining Technological Leadership in a World Economy." *MRS
    Bulletin* 14 (1989): 43-48.
Vaitsos, C. "Government Policies for Bargaining with TNE in the Acquisition of
    Technology." In Jairam Ramesh and Charles Weiss (eds.), *Mobilizing
    Technology for World Development*. New York: Praeger, 1979.
Vedaraman, S. "The New Indian Patent Law." *IDMA Bulletin* 15 (1984): 115-124.

Wadhva, Charan. "Import and Export Policy 1988-91: A Provisional Appraisal." *Economic and Political Weekly*, June 25, 1988, pp. 1331-1337.
————. "Economic Advisory Council's Report on the Economy: An Appraisal." *Economic and Political Weekly*, March 3, 1990, pp. 447-456.
Wartensleben, Aurelie Von. "Major Issues Concerning Pharmaceutical Policies in the Third World." *World Development* 11 (1983): 169-175.
Wells, Louis T., Jr. "Economic Man and the Engineering Man." In Robert Stobaugh and Louis Wells (eds.), *Technology Crossing Borders: The Choice, Transfer, and Management of International Technology Flows*. Boston: Harvard Business School Press, 1984.
Westphal, L. "Empirical Justification for Infant Industry Protection." World Bank Staff Working Paper No. 445. Washington, D.C., March 1981.
Yudkin, John S. "The Economics of Pharmaceutical Supply in Tanzania." *International Journal of Health Services* 10 (1980): 455-477.

BOOKS

Agarwal, Anil. *Drugs and the Third World*. London: Earthscan, 1978.
Ahluwalia, Isher Judge. *Industrial Growth in India: Stagnation Since the Mid-Sixties*. Delhi: Oxford University Press, 1985.
Ayyangar, Rajagopala. *Report on the Patent Law*. New Delhi, 1959.
Balasubramanyam, V. N. *International Transfer of Technology to India*. New York: Praeger, 1973.
Bardhan, Pranab. *The Political Economy of Development in India*. Oxford: Basil Blackwell, 1984.
Barnet, Richard and Ronald Muller. *Global Reach: the Power of the Multinational Corporations*. New York: Simon and Schuster, 1974.
Bennett, Douglas C. and Kenneth E. Sharpe. *Transnational Corporation versus the State: The Political Economy of the Mexican Auto Industry*. Princeton, N.J.: Princeton University Press, 1985.
Bosson, Rex and Bension Varon. *The Mining Industry and Developing Countries*. New York: Oxford University Press, 1977.
Braithwaite, John. *Corporate Crime in the Pharmaceutical Industry*. London: Routledge and Kegan Paul, 1984.
Cardoso, Fernando Henrique and Enzo Faletto. *Dependency and Development in Latin America*. Berkeley, Calif.: University of California Press, 1979.
Clark, Norman. *The Political Economy of Science and Technology*. Oxford and New York: Basil Blackwell, 1985
Clarke, Robin. *Science and Technology in World Development*. Oxford: Oxford University Press, 1985.
CMTI. *Machine Tool Census India 1986*. Bangalore: Central Machine Tool Institute, 1986.
Cortes, Mariluz and Peter Bocock. *North-South Technology Transfer: A Case Study of Petrochemicals in Latin America*. Baltimore: Johns Hopkins University Press, 1984.
Desai, Vasant. *Indian Industry: Profile and Related Issues*. Bombay: Himalaya Publishing House, 1987.
Emmanuel, Arghiri. *Appropriate or Underdeveloped Technology?* New York: John Wiley and Sons, 1982.

Encarnation, Dennis J. *Dislodging Multinationals: India's Strategy in Comparative Perspective.* Ithaca: Cornell University Press, 1989.

Evans, Peter B. *Dependent Development: The Alliance of Multinational, State, and Local Capital in Brazil.* Princeton, N.J.: Princeton University Press, 1979.

Gereffi, Gary. *The Pharmaceutical Industry and Dependency in the Third World.* Princeton, N.J.: Princeton University Press, 1983.

Gilpin, Robert. *U.S. Power and the Multinational Corporation: The Political Economy of Foreign Direct Investment.* New York: Basic Books, 1975.

Goulart, Dennis. *The Uncertain Promise: Value Conflicts in Technology Transfer.* Washington, D.C.: Overseas Development Council, 1977.

HMT. *Third Corporate Plan (Extended) 1986-87 to 1989-90.* Bangalore: HMT, 1986.

Hymer, Stephen. *The International Operation of National Firms: A Study of Direct Foreign Investment.* Cambridge: Mass.: MIT Press, 1976.

India Investment Center. *Changing Forms of Foreign Investment in India.* New Delhi: India Investment Center, 1982.

India Offers Technology. New Delhi: India Investment Center, 1983.

Ingerson, Earl and Wayne C. Bragg, eds. *Science, Government and Industry for Development.* Austin: University of Texas Press, 1976.

Jain, S. K. *The Drug Policy 1987-88.* Delhi: India Investment Publication, 1987.

Jayasuriya, D. C. *The Public Health and Economic Dimension of the New Drug Policy of Bangladesh,* Pharmaceutical Manufacturers Association. n.d.

Keayla, B. K. *New Patent Regime: Implications for Domestic Industry, Research and Development and Consumers.* New Delhi: National Working Group on Patent Laws, 1996.

Kidron, Michael. *Foreign Investment in India.* London: Oxford University Press, 1965.

Kindleberger, Charles P. *American Business Abroad: Six Lectures on Direct Investment.* New Haven: Yale University Press, 1969.

Kindleberger, Charles P. and Bruce Herrick. *Economic Development,* 3rd ed. New York: McGraw Hill, 1977.

Lall, Sanjaya. *The New Multinationals: The Spread of Third World Enterprises.* Chichester and New York: John Wiley and Sons, 1983.

———. *Learning to Industrialize: The Acquisition of Technological Capability by India.* London: Macmillan Press, 1987.

Lang, Ronald W. *The Politics of Drugs.* England: Saxon House, 1974.

Mahalanobis, P. C. *The Approach of Operational Research to Planning in India.* Bombay: Asia Publishing House, 1963.

Mascarenhas, R. C. *Technology Transfer and Development: India's Hindustan Machine Tools Company.* Boulder, Colo.: Westview Press, 1982.

Mazumdar, Badiul Alam. *Innovations, Product Developments, and Technology Transfers: An Empirical Study of Dynamic Competitive Advantage, the Case of Electronic Calculator.* Washington, D.C.: University Press of America, 1982.

Mikesell, Raymond. *Foreign Investment in Copper Mining: Case Studies in Mines in Peru and Papua New Guinea.* Washington, D.C.: Resources for the Future, 1975.

Montgomery, John. *Technology and Civic Life. Making and Implementing Development Decisions.* Cambridge, Mass.: MIT Press, 1974.

Moran, Theodore H. *Multinational Corporations and the Politics of Dependence: Copper in Chile.* Princeton, N.J.: Princeton University Press, 1974.

Mytelka, Lynn Krieger. *Regional Development in a Global Economy: The Multinational Corporation, Technology, and Andean Integration*. New Haven: Yale University Press, 1979.

Narayana, P. L. *The Indian Pharmaceutical Industry: Problems and Prospects*. New Delhi: NCAER, 1984.

Nayar, Baldev Raj. *India's Quest For Technological Independence: The Results of Policy*. 2 vols. New Delhi: Lancers Publishers, 1983.

NCAER. *Foreign Technology and Investment: A Study of Their Role in India's Industrialization*. New Delhi: National Council of Applied Economic Research, 1971.

Newfarmer, Richard, ed. *Profits, Progress and Poverty: Case Studies of International Industries in Latin America*. Notre Dame: University of Notre Dame Press, 1985.

Noble, David F. *Forces of Production: A Social History of Industrial Automation*. New York: Alfred A. Knopf, 1984.

Pinelo, Adalberto S. *The Multinational Corporation as a Force in Latin American Politics: A Case Study of the International Petroleum Corporation in Peru*. New York: Praeger, 1973.

Rahman, A. *Science and Technology in India*. New Delhi: National Institute of Science, Technology and Development Studies, 1984.

Ramesh, Jairam and Charles Weiss, eds. *Mobilizing Technology for World Development*. New York: Praeger, 1979.

Rosenberg, Nathan. *Perspectives on Technology*. London: Cambridge University Press, 1976.

Rudolph, Lloyd I. and Susanne H. Rudolph. *In Pursuit of Laxmi: The Political Economy of the Indian State*. Chicago: University of Chicago Press, 1987.

Sideri, S. and S. Johns, eds. *Mining for Development in the Third World: Multinational Corporations, State Enterprise and the International Economy*. New York: Pergamon, 1980.

————. *Structure and Strategy in the International Copper Industry*. New York: U.N. Center on Transnational Corporations, 1981.

Shaiken, Harley. *Work Transformed: Automation and Labor in the Computer Age*. New York: Holt, Rinehart and Winston, 1986.

Sklar, Richard S. *Corporate Power in an African State: The Political Impact of Multinational Mining Companies in Zambia*. Berkeley: University of California Press, 1975.

Stepan, Alfred. *The State and Society: Peru in Comparative Perspective*. Princeton, N.J.: Princeton University Press, 1978.

Stewart, Frances. *Technology and Underdevelopment*, Boulder, Colo.: Westview Press, 1977.

Tsurumi, Yoshihiro. "Technology Transfer and Foreign Trade: The Case of Japan, 1950-1966." Unpublished DBA Thesis, Harvard Business School, 1968.

Tugwell, Franklin. *The Politics of Oil in Venezuela*. Stanford: Stanford University Press, 1975.

United Nations. *Guidelines for the Study of the Transfer of Technology to Developing Countries*. New York: United Nations, 1973.

————. *The Acquisition of Technology from Multinational Corporations by Developing Countries*. New York: United Nations, 1974.

United Nations Center for Transnational Corporations. *Transnational Corporations and Pharmaceutical Industry*. New York: United Nations, 1979.

UNCTAD. *Case Studies in the Transfer of Technology: The Pharmaceutical Industry in India.* New York: U.N., 1977.

———. *Technology Policies and Planning for the Pharmaceutical Sector in the Developing Countries.* UNCTAD, Trade and Development Board: Committee on Transfer of Technology, 1980.

———. *The Capital Goods Sector in Developing Countries: Technology Issues and Policy Options.* New York: United Nations, 1985.

———. *Case Studies in the Transfer of Technology: Policies for Transfer and Development of Technology in Pre-war Japan.* UNCTAD Secretariat, n.d.

———. *Experience of the USSR in Building Up Technological Capability.* UNCTAD Secretariat, n.d.

UNIDO. *The Machine Tool Industry: Perspectives for Industrial Development in the Second United Nations Development Decade.* New York: United Nations, 1974.

———. *Machine Tools in Asia and the Pacific.* New York: United Nations, 1975.

———. *Technological Self-Reliance of the Developing Countries: Towards Operational Strategies (Development and Transfer of Technology Series No. 15).* Vienna: United Nations, 1981.

———. *World Non-Electronic Machinery: An Empirical Study of the Machine-Tool Industry.* New York: United Nations, 1984.

———. *Technological Perspectives in the Machine-Tool Industry and Their Implications for Developing Countries.* New York: United Nations, 1985.

———. *Appropriate Industrial Technology for Drugs and Pharmaceuticals.* UNIDO Monograph on Appropriate Industrial Technology, No. 10, n.d.

Vaitsos, Constantine V. *Transfer of Resources and Preservation of Monopoly Rents.* Harvard Center for International Affairs Economic Development Report No. 168, 1970.

Vernon, Raymond. *Storm Over the Multinationals: the Real Issue.* Cambridge, Mass.: Harvard University Press, 1977.

Wallender, Harvey W. *Technology Transfer and Management in the Developing Countries: Company Cases and Policy Analyses in Brazil, Kenya, Korea, Peru, and Tanzania.* Cambridge, Mass.: Bellinger, 1979.

Wells, Louis T., Jr., ed. *The Product Life Cycle and International Trade.* Cambridge, Mass.: Harvard University Press, 1972.

———. *Negotiating Third World Mineral Agreements.* Cambridge, Mass.: Bellinger, 1975.

———. *Third World Multinationals: The Rise of Foreign Investment from Developing Countries.* Cambridge, Mass.: MIT Press, 1983.

Woodbury, Robert. *Studies in the History of Machine Tools.* Cambridge, Mass.: MIT Press, 1972.

REPORTS AND GOVERNMENT DOCUMENTS

HAL. *Open with the World Closer to Millions.* Pimpri, 1986.

IDMA. *A Report on the Indian Drug Industry, 1980-2000 A.D.* Bombay: IDMA, n.d.

India, Committee on Public Undertaking. *Fifty-Sixth Report: Indian Drugs and Pharmaceuticals Limited (1973-74).* New Delhi: Ministry of Petroleum and Chemicals, 1974.

———. *Eightieth Report on Hindustan Antibiotic Limited (1975-76).* New Delhi: Ministry of Chemicals and Fertilizers, 1976.

————. *Report of the Sub-Group on Machine Tool Industry for the VII Plan Period 1985-90.* New Delhi: Ministry of Heavy Industry, 1983.

————. *Guidelines for Industries.* New Delhi: Ministry of Industry, Department of Industrial Development, 1982.

India. National Committee on Science and Technology. *Report on the Science and Technology Plan of the Chemical Industry,* 1973.

————. National Drugs and Pharmaceuticals Development Council. *Report of the Steering Committee.* Delhi: Ministry of Chemicals and Fertilizers, August 1984.

India. Planning Commission. *The First Five Year Plan.* New Delhi, 1952.

————. *Draft Fifth Five Year Plan—1974-79.* New Delhi, 1974.

————. *Sixth Five Year Plan 1980-85.* New Delhi: Planning Commission, n.d.

————. *Seventh Five Year Plan,* 2 Vols. New Delhi: Planning Commission, n.d.

India. *Report of the Committee on Drugs and Pharmaceutical Industry.* New Delhi: Ministry of Petroleum and Chemicals, 1975.

————. *Research and Development Statistics 1982-83.* New Delhi: Department of Science and Technology, n.d.

————. *Technology Policy Statement.* New Delhi: Department of Science and Technology, 1983.

Indian Drug Manufacturers Association. *Voice of the National Sector Annual.* Bombay: IDMA, 1986.

The Indian Machine Tool Industry: A Perspective Plan, 1983-93 (Unpublished Report), Delhi, November 1983.

Organization of Pharmaceutical Producers of India (OPPI), *Annual Report.* Bombay: OPPI, 1985.

OPPI Bulletin, May-June 1985.

Reserve Bank of India. *Foreign Collaboration in Indian Industry: Fourth Survey Report, 1985.* Bombay: RBI, 1985.

NEWSPAPERS

The Economic Times (Bombay), January 28, 1982; September 20, 21, 1982; April 18, 1985; February 16, 1987; August 21, 1987.

Financial Express, December 3, 1983; June 25, 1985; November 29, 1985.

India Abroad (New York), June 2, 1989.

New York Times, April 17, 1989.

Index

ABOUT THE AUTHOR

SUNIL K. SAHU is associate professor of Political Science at DePauw University, Greencastle, Indiana. He specializes in the areas of Third World development; international political economy; and African, Chinese, and South Asian politics. He holds a B.A. (Honours) and an M.A. in Political Science from Bihar University in India, and an M.A. and a Ph.D. in Political Science from the University of Chicago.

ISBN 0-275-95961-9

90000>

HARDCOVER BAR CODE